Closing the Shop

This book is printed on recycled paper.

Closing the Shop

Conversion from Sheltered to Integrated Work

by

Stephen T. Murphy, Ph.D.
Associate Professor of Counselor Education
University of Southern Maine
Gorham

and

Patricia M. Rogan, Ph.D.
Associate Professor
Indiana University School of Education
Indianapolis
and
Research Associate
Institute for the Study of Developmental Disabilities
Bloomington

·P A U L·H·
BROOKES
PUBLISHING Cº **Baltimore • London • Toronto • Sydney**

Paul H. Brookes Publishing Co.
Post Office Box 10624
Baltimore, Maryland 21285-0624

Typeset by Brushwood Graphics, Inc., Baltimore, Maryland.
Manufactured in the United States of America by
The Maple Press Company, York, Pennsylvania.

Unless otherwise noted, the people and situations described in this book
represent multiple, composite case studies from throughout the United
States. The names of individuals are pseudonyms. Any similarity to actual
individuals or circumstances is coincidental, and no implications should
be inferred.

Library of Congress Cataloging-in-Publication Data
Murphy, Stephen T.
    Closing the shop : conversion from sheltered to integrated work /
by Stephen T. Murphy and Patricia M. Rogan.
       p.   cm.
    Includes bibliographical references (p.) and index.
    ISBN 1-55766-153-7
    1. Sheltered workshops—United States—Case studies.
    2. Handicapped—Employment—United States—Case studies.
    3. Vocational rehabilitation—United States—Case studies.
    I. Rogan, Patricia M., 1956–   . II. Title.
HD7256.U5M868   1995
362'.0425—dc20   95-7795
                                         CIP

British Library Cataloguing-in-Publication data are available from the
British Library.

Contents

About the Authors

Stephen T. Murphy, Ph.D., has written extensively on issues such as assessment practices, consumer views of human services, integrated employment, agency change, and natural supports. He has published books titled *On Being LD: Perspectives and Strategies of Young Adults* and *Developing Natural Supports in the Workplace: A Practitioner's Manual* with Patricia Rogan, Marjorie Olney, Bryan Dague, and Nancy Kalina.

Before coming to the University of Southern Maine, Dr. Murphy was on the faculty of Syracuse University's Divisions of Counseling and Human Services and Special Education. He received his doctorate from the State University of New York at Buffalo.

Patricia M. Rogan, Ph.D., trains teachers and other rehabilitation professionals to work with youth and adults with disabilities in inclusive settings. She is involved in statewide systems change efforts and personnel preparation in the areas of transition, employment, and community living. Dr. Rogan coauthored the book *Developing Natural Supports in the Workplace: A Practitioner's Manual* with Stephen Murphy, Marjorie Olney, Bryan Dague, and Nancy Kalina.

Prior to her present position, Dr. Rogan was on the faculty at Syracuse University and taught in the areas of rehabilitation and special education. She received her doctorate from the University of Wisconsin–Madison in Rehabilitation Psychology and Special Education.

Foreword

There is probably no group in the United States more in need of the provision of timely, well-planned, and effective rehabilitation and employment services than the 69% of unemployed people with disabilities who are of working age. By contrast, only 19.7% of people without disabilities are unemployed. Discrimination is often a significant part of the lives of people with disabilities, and physical, psychological, social, and attitudinal barriers abound. All of these factors can effectively stifle equal opportunities and preclude the ability to strive for independence for many people with disabilities in the United States.

To help lower the historically high unemployment rate for people with disabilities, various strategies for achieving successful employment outcomes have been developed: 1) the state–federal vocational rehabilitation (VR) program, which is aimed at achieving integrated employment through a variety of rehabilitation strategies; 2) sheltered employment; and 3) supported employment with its various models. Sheltered employment was developed when there were no laws prohibiting discrimination against individuals with disabilities in the employment market and when adults with disabilities who wanted to enter the employment arena were excluded. Sheltered workshops, like most segregated education programs, were a way to prove that people with disabilities could indeed work and learn. Sheltered programs were not envisioned to develop into industries that precluded people with disabilities from being integrated into society and all facets of community life. If we had believed in the past what we believe today—that people with severe disabilities can work in integrated settings with appropriate supports—sheltered workshops might never have evolved. Now we are in the position of having to convert sheltered programs to reflect more modern thinking.

Options in this regard have met with varying degrees of success over time, and no one option is right for everyone. There has long been a debate in the rehabilitation community regarding the value of sheltered employment versus that of integrated employment. Some people believe that sheltered employment perpetuates "institutionalized behavior" on the part of people with disabilities, but others believe that a positive sheltered work experience is better than no work experience at all. In terms of integrated employment, many proponents believe that individuals who have been mainstreamed improve their occupational success rates because they have typical citizens as their role models.

This leads purportedly to more "normalized" work behaviors and fuller integration into the community. Additionally, professionals in the rehabilitation community have stated that because more and more individuals with severe disabilities have been mainstreamed during their years in school, they are consequently much better prepared for integrated employment.

Given the imperfections that exist in our society, there may be truth in both points of view. *Closing the Shop*, then, adds yet another chapter to this complex and important inquiry, examining all aspects of the issues involving agency conversion from sheltered to integrated employment models.

This book accepts the premise that with the right tools and the right knowledge, many sheltered settings can undergo a process of conversion that will allow them to offer the same level of support in a more integrated environment. The concept of conversion involves restructuring a rehabilitation agency's program and changing its focus from segregated, sheltered employment to mainstream, integrated employment—a complex and difficult process.

Among the issues involved for a nonprofit agency to convert or restructure the way in which its programs operate are 1) retraining staff regarding a new way of providing services for individuals with disabilities in work settings, and 2) recognizing the accompanying need to be sensitive to a business's needs. Also, funding issues are significant to nonprofit agencies as they undertake conversion, in that funding sources are often different or nonexistent for integrated employment programs. In addition, the work in integrated settings is more labor intensive and individualized and is likely to be more costly. Furthermore, the management aspects of dealing with staff who are based in a multitude of locations with a myriad of competing problems is a challenge to nonprofit agency managers and supervisors.

This book addresses actual examples of agency conversion and documents the experiences of people with disabilities and other stakeholders during the conversion process. Certainly, in applying the material contained in this book to the variety of specific settings that now exist, its precepts and methods will be useful to some and breakthrough experiences for others.

Judith E. Heumann
Assistant Secretary
Office of Special Education and Rehabilitative Services
U.S. Department of Education

Preface

Sheltered workshops are one of the last bastions of therapeutic paternalism facing people with disabilities. Under the rubric of "needs," "treatment," and/or "rehabilitation," people assigned to workshops become what Glasser (1978) termed "prisoners of benevolence" because they are deprived of the right to pursue meaningful work opportunities of their choice. They are said to need permanent or temporary shelter and separation from their communities for their own good. Increasingly, however, people with disabilities are becoming more organized and vocal, insisting on having the right to define for themselves what is in their best interests. In the state of New York, for example, the Association for Independent Living Centers has been joined by other self-advocacy groups in opposing sheltered workshops, calling for a new definition of what constitutes meaningful work opportunities and insisting on the right of individuals with disabilities to make their own vocational decisions. We support the efforts of these groups, and in this book we attempt to point out the inherent and ongoing inadequacies of workshops as vocational training and employment settings for people with disabilities.

This book describes in detail the conversion of Pioneer, a sheltered workshop in Syracuse, New York, which has merged with an agency called Enable. Pioneer's conversion began in 1987 when Steve Murphy took a partial leave from his university duties to become the director of Pioneer. For the next 2½ years, a collaborative, qualitative research project was conducted with Pat Rogan to document the conversion from a totally segregated program to an exclusively integrated employment service. Changes were carefully documented and the perspectives of all involved parties before, during, and after the agency's conversion were recorded. Data were collected over a 6½-year period by observing workshop participants, utilizing an in-depth, open-ended interviewing process, and by examining documents. We were personally committed to success in order to offer people a distinct alternative to segregated employment and also to prove to ourselves and the surrounding community that workshops could be closed and the people assigned to them could prosper as a result. Although the conversion of Pioneer may not be seen as remarkable given its small size, we believe it offers valuable insights into common workshop issues and the perspectives of those involved in the conversion process.

In writing this book we tried to provide readers with as much depth and breadth of information about the nature of workshops and the process of conversion as possible. The book moves from an examination of the historical roots of sheltered workshops in Chapter 1 to an analysis in Chapters 2 and 3 of one workshop's underlying assumptions, functions, and organizational changes.

In an effort to present in-depth examples of agency conversion and the related perspectives of those who experienced it, we examine in Chapters 4 and 5 the process and outcomes of conversion as it occurred within Pioneer as described by workshop participants, agency staff, board representatives, family members, and community professionals.

We also try to go beyond a single example of agency conversion and broaden our inquiry by including detailed descriptions of agencies from other parts of the United States that also reported successful conversion efforts. In Chapters 6–8, we present the reports of directors from three organizations: Kaposia, New Horizons, and Avatrac. In Chapter 9, the data gathered from each of the four agencies are synthesized and translated into specific strategies for pursuing organizational conversion to integrated employment.

Finally, Chapter 10 provides recommendations for a national agenda aimed at revitalizing the supported employment movement and promoting full citizenship for all people with disabilities.

Segregated adult day programs continue to exist nationwide and are supported actively at every governmental level. Even though effective, viable alternatives to workshops and day activity programs have been identified; federal and state laws have been passed to increase competitive employment opportunities and reduce discrimination against people with disabilities; and a growing number of people with disabilities and their families are objecting vigorously to segregation, relatively few people are asking why workshops and day activity programs remain so pervasive. Although we hope this book is a valuable resource to those who commit to eliminate such programs, we will be satisfied if, after reading it, more people ask, "Why?"

Acknowledgments

There are many people who participated in the development of this book. Marjorie Olney, Dave Hagner, Anita Yuskauskas, Michelle Sures, Ellen Fisher, and Dimity Peter, graduate students at Syracuse University, participated in our research. We would particularly like to thank Marj for her work on Chapter 5.

We are indebted to all those associated with Pioneer who shared their perspectives with us, especially those who had been in the workshop. Gratitude is extended to the fine Pioneer staff who worked tirelessly throughout the conversion process.

We would like to thank Mary Jo Snell of Avatrac, Diana Strzok of New Horizons, and Jackie Mlynarczyk of Kaposia for sharing their stories and for paving the way for others to follow. We truly appreciate Judith Heumann's interest in writing the Foreword for this book and for her work in Washington on behalf of all Americans with disabilities.

Many thanks to those who willingly reviewed versions of this text and offered valuable comments, including David Hagner, Dale DiLeo, and the project staff of the Indiana Employment Initiative: Kathy Osborn, Steve Savage, Susan Rinne, Connie Ferrell, and Michelle Carie.

To all who remain in segregated settings against their wishes

Closing the Shop

I

KNOWING THE PAST, CHANGING THE FUTURE

1

Looking Back, Looking Ahead

From Workhouses to the Community

In November of 1989, The Association for Persons with Severe Handicaps (TASH), a national advocacy organization comprising professionals, parents, advocates, and people with disabilities, called for "rapid and immediate development of individualized and integrated employment for all people with severe disabilities, and the rapid and permanent replacement of segregated activity centers and sheltered workshops" (The Association for Persons with Severe Handicaps, 1989). Four years later, the Association of Independent Living Centers in New York (AILCNY), a statewide advocacy group composed primarily of people with disabilities, called for "an immediate end to referrals to sheltered workshops and an immediate, permanent moratorium on new workshops, including any in the 'pipeline.' Beyond this we urge phased closure of all sheltered workshops in New York State, with careful planning to minimize disruption for people with disabilities" (Association of Independent Living Centers in New York, 1993, p. 3). Both organizations advocate replacing workshops with community-based supports, competitive employment outcomes, and consumer-controlled organizations that, the AILCNY asserted, should be "free from conflicts of interest inherent in the concurrent operation of segregated programs" (Association of Independent Living Centers in New York, 1993, p. 3).

These statements reflect some important developments in the evolution of employment initiatives for people with disabilities.

They indicate an increasing insistence that people with disabilities control their own vocational destinies. In addition, they equate successful vocational rehabilitation with successful community employment. Finally, they affirm the need for consonance between policy rhetoric and practice regarding integrated employment for people with disabilities.

Although the fight for individual choice and control is one that is relatively new, the call for integrated employment is a very old war that has been waged with varying levels of intensity in the United States since the 19th century. Ironically, during its earliest phases, the fight for integrated employment was spearheaded by an administrator from a large institution and sheltered workshop, Samuel Griddley Howe. Howe, director of the Perkins School for the Blind in Massachusetts and the believed-to-be head of the first sheltered workshop in the United States, wrote the following in 1849:

> It should be a cardinal principle of the education of the blind to keep ever in view the fact that they are to become members of general society and not a society of blind people. . . . The blind youth needs, as much as any other . . . to wrestle with difficulties; and to get strength and courage by long and varied exercise of his faculties. . . . I do earnestly hope that in enlarging our work department and putting it on a permanent basis, that we may adopt the system which will give them the greatest possible personal independence consistent with their true interests. (Nelson, 1971, p. 182)

Although Howe was advocating for community living for people who are blind, he was not rejecting sheltered workshops. Using logic similar to that employed today to justify the existence of workshops, Howe believed that such facilities could serve as avenues for community entry. Now, despite the success of supported employment programs across the United States in finding competitive jobs for people with disabilities, the heightened vocational expectations held by people with disabilities and their families, and the increased calls by groups like TASH and the AILCNY to abolish sheltered workshops, a majority of people still believe that workshops are legitimate avenues for community entry and/or sources of long-term sheltered employment for people with disabilities. Wehman and Kregel (1994) observed that all one has to do to verify the continuing success of workshops is to visit "almost any city or town in any state and there will be an adult day activity center, developmental center, or sheltered workshop" (p. 14).

Although workshops have become an integral part of the vocational landscape for people with disabilities, especially those classified as having severe developmental, psychiatric, and/or multiple disabilities, this book presents the argument that workshops should be abolished as both places of employment and means of preparing people for community jobs. A necessary prerequisite for changing the vocational opportunities and services available to people with disabilities is reaching some consensus regarding the segregated workshop as an untenable service alternative. As the introduction to a book on workshop conversion, this chapter focuses on a long-neglected area of inquiry: the historical antecedents of the workshop. Although the debate regarding workshops has raged for decades, relatively little attention has been paid to the origins of workshops and to how their history might reveal a great deal about their nature and current relevance.

Sheltered workshops have an evolutionary history based on particular social, political, and cultural assumptions that reflect specific societal conditions, interests, beliefs, traditions, and methods. By examining the antecedents of modern workshops and comparing their missions and achievements to those of contemporary workshop programs, this book argues that workshops are anachronistic institutions whose cultural roots and current methods are inherently inconsistent with the present social expectations, vocational demands, and political realities of people with disabilities.

Before delving into a historical analysis, the authors offer an overview and definitions of the sheltered workshop concept and summarize some of the arguments that have been given for and against workshop programs. It is hoped that this chapter will encourage people with disabilities, practitioners, administrators, educators, and policy makers to examine carefully the assumptions and methods underlying modern workshops and to decide if the fight to retain, reform, and reinforce workshops for future generations of people with disabilities should continue.

SHELTERED WORKSHOPS: DEFINITIONS, FUNCTIONS, AND PARTICIPANTS

Workshop Definitions

According to the National Association of Sheltered Workshops and Homebound Programs (1968), sheltered workshops are "nonprofit rehabilitation facilities utilizing individual goals, wages, supportive services and a controlled environment to help handicapped persons achieve or maintain their maximum potential as workers" (p. 2). Conte (1983) pointed out that in the past, the terms *sheltered employment* and *sheltered workshop* have been used synonymously.

However, the expansion of sheltered services to community employment settings has afforded the sheltered concept a broader application. Thus, sheltered employment has also come to include work crews or enclaves. These are groups of workers with disabilities located in community work settings who typically earn subminimum wages and receive significant agency supervision (Conte, 1983; Rhodes & Valenta, 1985; Vash, 1980). This chapter utilizes a narrow definition of sheltered workshops, although most comments could also be applied to enclaves and work crews that have been classified erroneously as supported competitive employment.

Workshop Functions

Central to the sheltered workshop concept is the centuries-old belief that some people are incapable of community employment because of physical or cognitive disabilities or a lack of moral will to work. These people have been separated from typical workers and settings either to learn the skills and discipline required to work in an integrated setting or to function permanently in protective environments where they can achieve some level of vocational productivity and proficiency.

In order to meet the identified vocational needs of people classified as having severe disabilities, workshops have been divided by function into two distinct types: transitional and extended. Transitional employment workshops attempt to find competitive community employment for individuals who, after periods of workshop evaluation, work adjustment training, and/or vocational instruction, are deemed vocationally ready for community work. Extended employment workshops provide sheltered, remunerative work for an indefinite period of time to those considered "unable to compete in the open labor market" (Flexer & Martin, 1978, p. 416).

There are also programs designed for people who cannot gain admission to sheltered workshops. Such programs have been classified as nonvocational and, depending upon how they are funded, have been variously termed *adult day activities centers, day treatment centers,* and/or *work activities centers.* People assigned to these facilities are viewed as "unemployable" even in sheltered settings. They are enrolled to learn adaptive and social skills and to perform nonremunerative work activities until they are deemed ready to progress to the next program level.

In some cases, yet another readiness step has been developed. *Day training centers* 1) are described as work oriented, and 2) serve as bridges of advancement between day treatment centers and sheltered workshops for people who are considered to have potential for workshop entry (Bellamy, Rhodes, Mank, & Albin, 1988). The practice of starting a person at one program level and slowly graduating him or her to advanced levels has been termed a *continuum* or *readiness* approach to rehabilitation (Durand & Neufelt, 1980; Taylor, 1988). This approach, its logic, and its purported strengths and weaknesses are discussed later in this section.

Adult day activity centers, day treatment centers, work activity centers, and sheltered workshops all evolved from the same historical model. Thus, the analysis in this chapter applies to any such segregated day program.

Workshop Participants

Workshops may be classified not only by the types of employment programs they provide (i.e., transitional or extended), but also by the kinds of people they serve. Nelson (1971) indicated that most workshops serve, either exclusively, primarily, or occasionally, people labeled as having mental retardation. Additionally, workshops serve as primary sources of training and/or employment for those with developmental disabilities such as cerebral palsy, seizure disorders, and autism. Workshops also serve individuals with psychiatric disorders and sensory impairments, veterans with disabilities, and/or people who are older. In short, there are sheltered workshops that serve almost any group of people with devalued vocational potential.

Updated figures regarding the total number of participants in workshop programs are difficult to obtain. However, based on available statistics, the proliferation of sheltered workshops in the latter half of the 20th century has been astounding. Nelson (1971) estimated that in 1970, there were 1,500 sheltered workshops in the United States serving about 160,000 people with disabilities. By 1987, the number of people served in sheltered workshops had swelled to over 650,000 (Menz, 1987). Citing numerous sources, Albin and Rhodes (1993) concluded that "the vast majority of adults with severe mental retardation or other severe disabilities continue to be served in segregated sheltered work or nonwork settings" (p. 1).

The figures for people with mental retardation or developmental disabilities illustrate well the proliferation of sheltered workshops since the early 1960s. In 1968, the U.S. Department of Labor certified 468 sheltered workshops serving about 13,722 people diagnosed with mental retardation. This figure did not include private workshops, state institutions, and schools (Nelson, 1971). Including facilities and individuals not previously discussed, Nelson (1971) estimated that in 1969, sheltered workshops served approximately 18,000 individuals. Between 1968 and 1976, there was reportedly a fivefold increase nationally in the number of people with developmental disabilities served in sheltered workshops and day activity centers (Albin, 1992; Bellamy, Rhodes, Bourbeau, & Mank, 1986; Bellamy, Sheehan, Horner, & Boles, 1980). In a national survey of state mental retardation/developmental disabilities (MR/DD) agencies, McGaughey, Kiernan, McNally, and Gilmore (1993) found that a total of 228,325 people were served in segregated workshops and day activity centers, representing 82% of those enrolled in vocational services. In New York alone, more than 20,000 people with developmental disabilities were enrolled in 149 state and private sheltered workshops by 1993, according to the New York State Office of Mental Retardation and Developmental Disabilities. According to the AILCNY, the figures for New York are even worse if day programs are included. According to its 1994 *Disability Rights Agenda* report, AILCNY estimates that approximately 70,000 New York residents with disabilities are currently receiving services in segregated day programs rather than in integrated work programs (Association of Independent Living Centers in New York, 1994).

Clearly, sheltered workshops are a prevalent form of employment for many people with disabilities (Albin, 1992; Lam & Chan, 1988). As Flexer and Martin (1978) indicated, regardless of whether a person with severe disabilities is deemed competitively employable, it is likely that he or she will be considered in need of sheltered employment services for at least part of his or her working life.

WORKSHOP RATIONALE

Sheltered workshops are most frequently characterized as commendable programs that provide needed vocational training and employment opportunities to those who face societal prejudice and exclusion. According to Nelson (1971), the earliest workshops were founded to counteract the exclusionary practices of schools, churches, social services organizations, and businesses as well as to develop and demonstrate the vocational potential of people with disabilities. Nelson (1971) equated the concept of sheltered workshops with the Judeo-Christian beliefs regarding the importance of the individual, the importance of personal choice, the value and dignity of work, and the obligation of society to help those in need. Affirming this sentiment, Flexer and Martin (1978) related that "central to all workshops then and now has been the goal of providing work programs and the benefits which come from work to the handicapped" (p. 416).

It is beyond the scope of this chapter to review all the specific reasons that have been given to justify the existence of sheltered workshops. However, because workshops represent a significant source of vocational services and a major alternative to direct community entry for people with disabilities, they are analyzed carefully in terms of their purported benefits. In the following sections, the three major needs that workshops claim to address—shelter, vocational readiness, and vocational choices—are discussed briefly.

Shelter

Shelter refers to a protective setting—as Gellman and Friedman (1965) termed it, "a special place"—where people with disabilities who are "unacceptable or unready for competitive employment, but capable of some productivity, enter work activity" (p. 34). Some people purportedly need shelter because their disabilities are simply too severe for them to work in the community. Lam (1986) concluded that many people require the extensive structure of and the hours offered by sheltered work. Contending that intelligence quotient (IQ) and community employability are related, Lam (1986) argued that supported work in the community may be most appropriate and cost effective for people with mild mental retardation and least desirable for those classified as having moderate or severe retardation.[1] Bolton (1982) believed that the only feasible alternative for people with severe disabilities is to de-emphasize the economic rationale for employment and, through sheltered and homebound programs, to stress the personal and psychological benefits of work.

Nelson (1971) felt that shelter has therapeutic as well as practical value in its ability to effect a delicate balance between promoting individual competence by exposing people to the demands of the world of work and allowing individual inadequacy and inability by providing a protective environment and flexible performance standards. According to Nelson (1971), the workshop process is a continuous synthesis between a demand for adequate functioning and an acceptance of inefficiency at varying levels. To maximize the continuing achievement of adequate performance, he recom-

---

[1]New terminology adopted in 1992 by the American Association on Mental Retardation (AAMR) (Luckasson, Coulter, Polloway, Reiss, Schalock, Snell, Spitalnik, & Stark, 1992) does not utilize the classification scheme of mild, moderate, severe, and profound retardation. Because the utility of this new definition is under debate, and the forthcoming edition of the psychiatric classification system continues to diagnose levels of mental retardation (American Psychiatric Association, 1994), AAMR's earlier terminology (Grossman, 1983) has been used here.

mended that workshops measure objectively participants' production performance against the industrial criteria toward which they should strive in a series of graduated, achievable steps. In this way, workshop participants would be exposed to an important individual and societal need, namely, vocational productivity, and assisted in achieving socially relevant performance goals. At the same time, they would be protected against failure because an inability to achieve industrial goals would lead to a reduction of performance expectations to a level more consistent with their abilities.

Another primary reason given for providing shelter for people is the pervasive prejudice of the general public and the unwillingness of employers and co-workers to hire and accept people with disabilities as part of the primary workforce. In an address to the New York Association of Retarded Citizens, Nitzberg (1989) argued that

> For most retarded adults . . . [the] outside world is indifferent and hostile. . . . Normal workers are hardly likely to treat retarded persons working in the same place as equals—to discuss last night's TV program, the morning paper, the weekend game on the same level, or to drink with them, to elect them as union stewards. . . . At best a retarded person may make it as the company mascot. (p. 2)

Most advocates of shelter are not as pessimistic or devaluing as Nitzberg. However, to bolster their defense for sheltered environments, they point to the inordinately high unemployment rate (Harris & Associates, 1986) and the many reported occurrences of job discrimination among people with disabilities, both of which disability rights groups and proponents of integration acknowledge as serious problems.

The argument for sheltered employment seems to revolve around the widely held belief that sheltered settings serve people better than do their surrounding communities. This view was succinctly summarized by Turner (1983) when he noted that

> Everything we have learned in our research is consistent with the assertion that the workshop does provide a more normal way of life for most members of a workshop society. . . . Due partially to their disability and limitations inherent in the larger society, many . . . human concerns, which are well provided for in the workshop setting, are unlikely to be met in the world "outside." (p. 170)

Vocational Readiness

Workshop proponents operate on the *readiness principle*. Operationalized, this principle holds that people with disabilities need to be taught sufficient work and/or social skills before they are ready to enter the competitive work world. To facilitate this, rehabilitation professionals have constructed a services continuum that comprises various steps. It begins with the most restrictive situations, the most intensive instruction, and the least challenging tasks, and it extends to the least restrictive situations, the least intensive instruction, and the most challenging tasks (Durand & Neufelt, 1980; Taylor, 1988).

Within this continuum, a person is assigned to do specific work tasks based upon his or her measured vocational proficiency, interests, and potential. When it is determined that he or she has acquired more skills, the person is promoted to higher-level tasks that have more challenging requirements. Over time, the person is expected to move through various skill levels until he or she is deemed ready for the highest and least restrictive level—competitive work. With this continuum approach, the most funding is allocated for the most segregated, restrictive levels with the assumption that once people enter the community, they will require little if any assistance.

Vocational Choices

Because criticisms of workshops have increased and integrated employment approaches have emerged, workshop proponents have cited the fact that people with disabilities need to be able to decide in which vocational programs they will participate. Many practitioners, parents, and people with disabilities argue that people with disabilities and their families should be able to choose between sheltered and integrated employment options. Concluding not only that people with mental retardation live in a hostile and indifferent community, but that they also have severely deficient skills and attributes, Nitzberg (1989) contended that "there is nothing *inherently* and *universally* [authors' emphasis] habilitating, uplifting, or happy about pressing retarded people into jobs along with the rest of us" (pp. 1–2). Nitzberg (1989) further stated that he is not opposed to nonsheltered employment, but that he believes that if people "cannot or should not manage 'on the outside'" (p. 1), they should have the option of selecting a sheltered workshop.

Likewise, Rosen, Bussone, Dakunchak, and Cramp (1993) argued that many people with mental or physical disabilities require special services that are not available in many community work settings. They contended that

> No program or approach has provided all the solutions to all the people involved. . . . Indeed, the promise of such options provided by supported work, work enclaves within industry, and job coaches has

proven effective and offers new hope. Yet such options do not work equally well for everyone; nor are they generally available. (p. 33)

Workshop proponents have also asserted that workshops should remain a viable employment and training option for people with disabilities, especially for those who have formed valuable social relationships as a result of their workshop participation. Turner (1983) implied that leaving people without the workshop option would sever an important source of contacts and provide no guarantee that the larger community would or could fill the social void.

ANTECEDENTS OF MODERN SHELTERED WORKSHOPS

Historically, workshops have been described as places designed to segregate troublesome people, ostensibly for their own good. Despite the rhetoric of community integration that has been used to describe workshops and their predecessors (i.e., community workhouses) since the mid-1800s, workshops have established a remarkably consistent record of community exclusion and professional dominance of people with disabilities. In the following section, some of the relevant historical information regarding workshop development and expansion is reviewed and related to contemporary workshop functions.

Responses to People with Disabilities

Rothman (1971, 1978) and Stone (1984) described comprehensively the perceptions of and policies regarding people with disabilities who were poor in the United States in the 19th century. This section relies heavily on their analyses.

At the beginning of the 19th century, U.S. public policy regarding people with disabilities mirrored that of England and reflected a preoccupation with eliminating vagrancy. People of the period became disenchanted with a public relief policy that either provided *outdoor relief* (i.e., support for people in their homes) or offered the services of people who were poor to local farmers or the highest bidder. The latter activities were viewed as unnecessarily cruel; the former were characterized as overly permissive.

The Yates Report of 1824 (Rothman, 1971) concluded that, when farmed out or sold, people who were poor were often subjected to abuse and neglect. But when left to their own devices in the community, they were thought to be susceptible to temptation, dissipation, crime, and/or laziness. No longer could the church, family, or network of social relationships be depended upon to counteract these problems of the community. As Rothman (1971) related, the almshouse–workhouse became the centerpiece of U.S. public policy regarding people who were poor and "for the first time made incarceration central to the program of support" (p. 180).

Community exclusion was a common experience for people with disabilities. Although many of these people were institutionalized initially for rehabilitation (using a structured regime of daily activities that was called *moral treatment*) and/or protection from the stresses of society (Rothman, 1971; Wolfensberger, 1975), others were placed in community almshouses along with people who were sick, infirm, and older (Stone, 1984). Among New York's almshouse residents, for example, "the deaf, dumb, blind, and insane" (Rothman, 1971, p. 291) made up one fourth of the total population.

Almshouses–workhouses were created to isolate people from their communities, ostensibly for moral and social instruction. In theory, almshouses–workhouses were supposed to rehabilitate people who were poor in the same way that penitentiaries reform criminals or asylums cure people with mental illness. As Rothman (1971) observed, "The reaction to the problem of dependency paralleled the response to the issue of deviancy" (p. 180). Specifically, almshouses were supposed to protect people from the "corruption sure to ensnare them within the community . . . as a prerequisite to recovery" (Rothman, 1971, p. 188).

Although exclusion was the universal medium of treatment, "The most striking aspect of the nineteenth century Poor Law is that . . . a formerly undifferentiated mass of paupers came to be understood as comprising several distinct elements, based upon inability to work" (Stone, 1984, p. 39). According to Stone (1984), the "internal universe of paupers" (p. 40) was made up of the following categories: able-bodied males, females, and children and people classified as sick, "defective," older, or infirm. Each category was supposed to be housed in a separate building and accorded treatment appropriate to its own condition. All were deemed deserving and helpless and were exempt from employment (Stone, 1984). Treatment was therefore considered to be care, not punishment, and custodial, not instructional. For these people, the almshouse was supposed to be a place of relative comfort and protection from life's difficulties.

Alongside the almshouse proper was the workhouse, which was for able-bodied people who were poor and lacking visible means of support. Here people were rehabilitated 1) through an exacting routine of moral treatment consisting of daily order and discipline, and 2) by "a regular course of life" that would prepare them for "a better career when restored to liberty" (Rothman, 1971, p. 189).

In practice, it was likely that people with disabilities remaining outside of asylums and large institutions were treated comparably to those classified as undeserving of institutionalization, despite elaborate classification systems and rhetorical distinctions. In Boston, for example, a combination almshouse–workhouse served all people who were poor whether they were deemed worthy or not. The important point is that regardless of whether people with disabilities were actually treated as deserving or undeserving, they were considered unable to work. Thus, few cared whether the concept of moral treatment was a dismal failure as a tool for rehabilitation because the almshouse was considered first and foremost a place to segregate troublesome people. Apparently, people with disabilities were regularly assigned to workhouses for rehabilitation programs that were no more effective than are those of modern workshops in simulating a "regular course of life" or preparing people for a "better career when restored to liberty." As Rothman (1978) noted, people who were poor, criminal, insane, and delinquent were grouped together as appropriate targets for custodial treatment. And from the mid- to late 19th century, community exclusion for people who were poor, including those with disabilities, became a well-entrenched societal tradition.

Even as almshouses–workhouses assumed a more coercive, repressive character while discrediting people who were poor, their basic premise still was endorsed by economists, social critics, and people who considered themselves humanitarians and concerned citizens. As Rothman (1971) related, many urged the improvement, not the abolition, of almshouses–workhouses. "The public policy was to incarcerate all these groups, and the decision would not be quickly or easily changed" (Rothman, 1971, p. 294).

Progressive Influences

In the late 19th and early 20th centuries, the Progressive movement took hold in the United States and persisted through the 1960s. According to Rothman (1978), the Progressives were the first reformers in the United States to recognize and protest the wretchedness of the modern industrial system, which included almshouses–workhouses.

Modern sheltered workshops are described most frequently as emanating from Progressive beliefs such as the centrality of the individual, the value of work, and the societal obligation to help those in need (Nelson, 1971). However, under the banner of reform, the

Progressives sustained the exclusionary traditions of workhouses regarding people with disabilities, justifying their activities on the basis of individual need. As Rothman (1978) observed, individual need replaced punishment but was accompanied by a kind of professional coercion all its own:

> No group more energetically or consistently attempted to translate the biological model of the caring parent into social action than the Progressives . . . Progressives were far more attentive to the "needs" of disadvantaged groups than to their "rights." Needs were real and obvious—the poor were overworked and underpaid, living in unhealthy tenements and working in miserable sweatshops . . . But the concept cut two ways: those in need were more or less like children. The disadvantaged were the objects of care, they were to be done for. (pp. 69–70)

As the language of the Progressives spread and the concept of charity replaced that of punishment at the beginning of the 20th century, workshops in various forms gradually emerged as employment "retreats" (Best, 1934) and increasingly replaced almshouses–workhouses for people with disabilities. It should be noted, however, that the idea of retreat, although not evident in practice, is implied in the definition of almshouse relative to people with disabilities in the 19th century. It seems that the workshop idea of the early 20th century was a recycled concept that, although newly applied, was structurally consistent with the traditions, practices, and attitudes of the almshouses–workhouses of the 19th century.

The First Official Workshops

Proponents of workshops do not identify contemporary workshops closely with the concept and practices of almshouses–workhouses of the 19th century. They prefer to see the two as quite distinct, if not in structure, then certainly in intent and effect. In addition, there is disagreement regarding exactly how and why sheltered workshops took root in the United States.

It is generally agreed that the first formally designated workshops for people with disabilities arose as extensions of schools for people who were blind. Reportedly, Samuel Griddley Howe imported the idea from Europe in 1837 in order to train students graduating from the Perkins School for the Blind, as well as adults from the surrounding area, for community jobs. Thus, the initial thrust of Howe's effort was integrative (i.e., to assist individuals "to become members of general society and not a society of blind people" [Nelson, 1971, p. 182]). However, Nelson (1971) reported that "the blind workers preferred to remain in the shop where they could live and work under the same roof" (p. 18). Consequently, Howe established the workshop as an entity separate from the school, and the concept of a separate workshop facility spread to other states.

TenBroek and Matson (1959) described the emergence of workshops somewhat differently. They related that, like Howe, most directors of schools for students who were blind were initially optimistic about finding jobs for their graduates in the competitive labor market. However, employer resistance, not the resistance of workshop participants, caused school directors to concede that "they had been wrong in believing the blind capable of competition and self support" (tenBroek & Matson, 1959, p. 251).

Regardless of whether workshop development and growth was caused by workshop participants or the general public, most people who were blind were blamed for their employment problems and were treated as if they needed protection more than community employment. TenBroek and Matson (1959) concluded the following:

> It was soon generally agreed that the solution to the problem could only be found in the creation of subsidized shelters where the blind might ply the simple skills learned in school, without danger of competition—or contamination—from the sighted. "The proper preventive," concluded one report, "is the establishment of a Retreat where their bread can be earned, their morals protected, and a just estimate put upon their talents." (p. 251)

This rationale spawned workshops that advocated a clearly exclusionary intent more characteristic of almshouses–workhouses than of the Perkins School. Workshops such as those of the Society of St. Vincent de Paul, the Salvation Army, the Volunteers of America, Goodwill Industries, and the Deseret Industries offered primarily long-term, sheltered employment and moral treatment combined with personal salvation (Nelson, 1971). Nelson (1971) also pointed out that the director of the first workshop to operate independently of a school, the Pennsylvania Working Home for the Blind, championed the idea of combining a workshop and a home for men who were blind under the umbrella of a working home. In so doing, he both echoed clearly the old almshouse–workhouse idea and promoted a policy of segregation that was to last for many years. The similarities between sheltered workshops and the old workhouses for people who were poor were noted by workshop critics tenBroek and Matson (1959):

> The historical relationship between the workhouse for the poor and the sheltered workshop for the disabled has frequently been pointed out (Chouinard, 1957); but the issue of the present day relationship is generally glossed over. Yet it should be evident that modern work-

shops still preserve, albeit in a more kindly spirit, the essential characteristics of the old style workhouse. In short, the workshops must still finally be evaluated in terms of the extent to which, in structure and function, they have moved away from—or continue to reflect—the old fashioned workhouse. (p. 261)

WORKSHOP CRITICISMS

Sheltered workshops have attracted some vocal critics. Numerous authors (Albin, 1992; Bellamy et al., 1988; Conte, Murphy, & Nisbet, 1989; Mcloughlin, Garner, & Callahan, 1987; Nisbet & Vincent, 1985; Parent & Hill, 1990; Parent, Hill, & Wehman, 1989; Rusch, 1990; Whitehead, 1979) have argued that sheltered programs have demonstrated 1) limited effectiveness in achieving employment outcomes, particularly for people with severe disabilities; 2) questionable effectiveness in achieving rehabilitation goals such as heightened vocational skills, psychological functioning, and social behavior; 3) a history of financial exploitation of workers; and 4) a lack of sound business practices, relevant commercial equipment, training, and similarities to the real employment community, As Rusch, Johnson, and Hughes (1990) indicated, by the late 1970's, there was a heightened recognition that the vocational services system for people with severe disabilities was "broken" (p. 6).

This book does not review comprehensively all the criticisms of sheltered workshops. Readers are therefore directed to other works cited in this chapter. Selected studies and issues as well as some major themes that have emerged recently are reviewed in the following sections.

Sheltered Workers Are
Competent and Do Not Need to Be Sheltered

Critics of workshops believe that protection and shelter create rather than alleviate employment barriers for workshop participants. They argue that shelter is neither a needed safeguard against vocational incompetence nor an answer for public prejudice and discrimination.

Since the mid-1970s, a plethora of evidence has accumulated that proves the vocational competence of people with severe disabilities. Early studies have shown that people considered to have severe mental retardation can perform complex vocational tasks that were once considered to be far beyond their capabilities (Bellamy, Peterson, & Close, 1975; Brown, 1973; Gold, 1972, 1976; Rusch & Mithaug, 1980). Subsequent research has demonstrated that systematic, community-based instruction, on-site supports; and consistent follow-along services can enable people "whose productive capacity had been considered inconsequential" (Kregel & Wehman, 1989, p. 293) to obtain and maintain competitive employment (Brown et al., 1984; Paine, Bellamy, & Wilcox, 1984; Rusch, 1990; Wehman & Kregel, 1985).

Workshop opponents acknowledge that people with disabilities have been discriminated against. But in many cases, such discrimination is related to their differences, not their deficiencies. However, as Vash (1980) observed, the extent of employer discrimination is not well documented. Furthermore, the discrimination that does exist may occur for reasons other than simple prejudice and may be ameliorated by tougher legislation, enhanced employment incentives, and better vocational training and placement methods.

The answer to employer and public discrimination is not to isolate people with disabilities in sheltered workshops. Such isolation perpetuates the denial of people's civil rights, hinders the development of positive public perceptions and relationships, reinforces existing employer and public perceptions of people with disabilities as deficient and in need of special work settings, and obfuscates the need for more systemic solutions to problems.

Readiness Can Be Achieved Through Community Support

Proponents of workshops claim that people with disabilities need to be prepared for community entry by progressing through a graduated series of restrictive employment settings until they are deemed ready for community work. Opponents have countered by stating that years of poor outcomes indicate that people have spent far too much time in workshops and have very little to show for it. For example, one frequently cited study by Bellamy et al. (1986) calculated that an individual progressing through an adult day activity program would spend an average of 37 years getting ready for the next step in the continuum—the work activity center. He or she would then spend an average of 10 years in the center before being deemed ready for a job in the community or in a sheltered workshop. If the person was unlucky enough to be assigned to a workshop, he or she would spend another 9 years preparing for community employment. Assuming that the person began this process at age 21, he or she could expect to spend the next 47–56 years getting ready for community employment. He or she would begin his or her first job between the ages of 68 and 77. In order to give these figures a normative perspective, consider that in an equivalent amount of time, another person could have completed all the educational requirements for a Ph.D. from elementary through graduate school, pursued a career for between 24 and 33 years, and, in some cases, retired.

Workshop critics also point out that the idea of preparing people for the real world of work by assigning them to a sheltered setting where they are isolated from the realities, requirements, and relationships of that world is wholly contradictory. Bolstering their arguments is a host of studies that show that sheltered employment hinders people from learning appropriate social and vocational behaviors because they have been isolated from competitive standards regarding work training, modern equipment, job requirements, behavioral expectations, and social relations (Bernstein & Karan, 1979; Greenleigh Associates, Inc., 1975; Nisbet & Vincent, 1985; Pomerantz & Marholin, 1980; U.S. Department of Labor,1977, 1979). Consistent with these data are those of Whitehead (1979), who found that workshop participants who obtained community employment were those individuals who did not need extensive skills training.

Workshop training and placement activities have been criticized for many years. Greenleigh Associates, Inc. (1975), the U.S. Department of Labor (1977, 1979), and Whitehead (1979) all concluded that workshops have achieved poor placement rates of between 0% and 12% and have offered low pay ($.34–$1.40 per hour, on average), few working hours (between 0 and 30 hours per week), minimal instructional success, and almost no benefits for workers. These outcomes were essentially duplicated in a 1983 study conducted by the New York State Office of Vocational Rehabilitation (now called Vocational and Educational Services for Individuals with Disabilities). In this study, it was found that of 16,000 sheltered workers, less than 2% were placed in competitive employment. Moreover, the people remaining in workshops earned very low wages. On average, those with mental retardation earned $.85 per hour and those who were blind received $1.96 per hour.

Low-wage levels were reinforced rather dramatically by national figures cited by the AILCNY in 1993 (Association of Independent Living Centers in New York, 1993). These figures indicated that individuals in sheltered workshops who worked full time (i.e., approximately 30 hours per week) earned an average weekly wage of $22.87, as opposed to people in community-based supported employment programs who worked mostly 20-hour weeks and earned an average of $72.63 per week. Citing figures from the New York State Interagency Council for Vocational Rehabilitation and Related Services, the AILCNY reported even more disparate wage differences for the state of New York. In fiscal year 1990–1991, the average weekly wage of people with disabilities in New York in supported employment programs was substantially less than that earned by those in sheltered workshops (Association of Independent Living Centers in New York, 1994).

Studies have shown improved but still unsatisfactory and inconsistent workshop placement outcomes. Kiernan and Cibrowski (1985) reported that between 12% and 13% of people with developmental disabilities served by sheltered workshops between October 1983 and September 1984 found competitive employment. Bellamy et al. (1986) noted, however, that only 3% of these individuals were employed after 2 years. Apparently, the arguments of tenBroek and Matson (1959), two early critics of workshops, are still valid:

> The evidence of history and contemporary practice alike is compellingly against the proposition that sheltered workshops can adequately combine the functions of competitive rehabilitation training and terminal employment in noncompetitive and routinized tasks (p. 263). . . . The fact is undeniable that for large numbers—if not the majority—of its clients the sheltered workshop is still a place of terminal employment. (p. 261)

In sum, it appears that a long-standing justification for sheltered workshops—that they provide vocational readiness training—has been debunked. Sheltered employment has been shown to be a much better medium for preparing people to continue sheltered work than to begin competitive work.

Real Choice and Control Reside in the Community

As the preceding criticisms gained momentum, workshop proponents countered with the argument that people with disabilities should be able to choose between sheltered and integrated employment. Concern about choice and control goes beyond the sheltered workshop question and has been controversial in the vocational rehabilitation field for many years. People with disabilities and their families feel that they have not had adequate choice regarding or control over any of the services they receive. Furthermore, they are often discredited as decision makers by the professionals who supposedly serve them (Ferguson & Ferguson, 1987; Hahn, 1991). This situation is especially pervasive for people with severe disabilities and their families (Moseley, 1989; West & Parent, 1992) and has persisted despite federal legislation that has mandated heightened and formal consumer involvement in education and vocational rehabilitation decision making since the early 1970s. It is therefore ironic that workshop advocates have now begun to emphasize individual choice and control. Though severely criticized for ignoring individual choice and assuming control of people's activities in the past, workshops have heretofore largely ignored such criticism.

Whitehead (1987) reported that when people with disabilities and their families are asked about their employment choices, they express strong preferences for integrated employment options. Whitehead (1987) further noted that this sentiment represents a prominent change in employment expectations, preferences, and advocacy since the 1970s when people with disabilities and their families placed greater emphasis on safety and protection.

Vash (1980) asserted that service recipients rarely call for more and/or better workshops. She observed that the topic of workshops is usually introduced by professionals, not by people with disabilities; the latter group considers the issue to be peripheral to the larger employment picture. The conclusions of both Whitehead (1987) and Vash (1980) seem well supported by 1) the intensive lobbying efforts of organizations of people with disabilities for the passage of the Americans with Disabilities Act of 1990 (ADA), PL 101-336, and the Rehabilitation Act Amendments of 1992, PL 102-569—legislation that enhances community employment opportunities; 2) surveys of people with disabilities and their families dating back to the mid-1980s that indicate their concerns about many employment issues and strong preferences for integrated work, but never mention the need to increase or improve sheltered work opportunities (Harris & Associates, 1986; Whitehead, 1987); 3) the evident movement toward more integrated employment policies; and 4) the beginning of aggressive grass roots campaigns, such as the one in New York, to declare a moratorium on sheltered work.

As the vocational rehabilitation field moves away from segregated services and outcomes, the issue of choice will likely take a different direction. Presently, many people who have limited community experience and may never have worked outside of a sheltered setting are being asked to make a vocational choice between community employment (with which they are unfamiliar) and sheltered work (with which they are very familiar). This choice may be influenced by professional pressures, family concerns, lack of information, and peer experiences, all of which favor selecting what is known and regularized. However, as young adults and their families become more familiar with their rights and available options, experience years of inclusive school services, participate more fully in decision making, and develop skills in negotiating with professionals for desired services, they will be far less willing than their predecessors to accept only segregated options or to settle for framing the choice question around segregated versus integrated alternatives. It is unprecedented to require a group of people to choose a work setting that includes only a particular class of people. Restricting options based on race, gender, ethnicity, or national origin, for example, would not only be politically inconceivable, but discriminatory and illegal as well.

Given these trends, people with disabilities and their families will increasingly take for granted that choice and control regarding employment options will entail the same things for them as they do for all other citizens: community-based training and employment. They will understand that real choices lie in community options, options that offer sufficient diversity to realize one's preferences and supports and accommodations that can further individualize working situations to maximize success.

This is not to say that some people will not want or need some of the support, security, and safety offered in sheltered workshops. The challenge to professionals is obvious: Offer the required supports without segregation. Certainly, segregated programs will not disappear overnight. Workshop critics believe, however, that when people realize that community employment is not one option but an opening to many employment options, the demand for workshops will disappear almost completely. Just as institutions are no longer offered as a choice in some states, workshops will also be abolished as a viable option.

REFORM NOT CLOSURE

Although early criticisms of workshops were quite pointed, they were suggestive of reforming workshops, not eliminating them. Such criticisms actually reinforced the value of workshops and perpetuated their basic structure.

Power and Marinelli (1974) articulately criticized sheltered workshops, saying that workshops are harmful to the people who work in them. They contended that workshops offer an environment of deviancy, poor training methods, dull and menial work, "subhuman expectations" (p. 69), poor outcomes, and a denial of physical and social integration. They proposed, however, that workshops required relatively minor reforms such as providing service recipients with more challenging work, higher pay, better professional supervision, more realistic job settings, and more choices. Power and Marinelli (1974), like other critics before and since (Bernstein & Karan, 1979; Brickey, 1974; Nelson, 1971; Olshansky, 1972; Pomerantz & Marholin, 1977; Whitehead, 1987), considered workshops to be indispensable sources of refuge for people with disabilities despite serious flaws.

In asking whether workshops could become obsolete, Riscalla (1974) called for dramatic change at a time when few others had. She wanted professionals to find alternatives to sheltered workshops, believing that "it could eventually be possible that a place [in the community] could be found for anyone who wants it" (p. 36). However, she was quite explicit in noting that workshops "have and could continue to provide a useful service in rehabilitation, especially for those individuals who are unable or prefer not to engage in competitive employment" (p. 36).

Redefining Shelter

In addressing the need for change, some early critics expressed a perplexing distinction between segregation and shelter, supporting the latter but not the former. For example, Vash (1980) contended that

> There appears to be good consensus among American writers that there will always be a group of disabled workers whose handicaps to job functioning are so severe that they cannot exceed 30 percent productivity by ordinary standards. I don't know how this relates to the old truism that the average worker is about 45 percent productive. In any event, there is a "low group" which definitely needs shelter, not just accommodation. Whether they also need segregation is another matter. (p. 108)

Operationalized, the separation of shelter from workshops has come in the forms of enclaves, work crews, and affirmative industries. Enclaves and work crews, which are described earlier in this chapter, were originally promoted as desirable alternatives to sheltered workshops for people with severe disabilities (Brickey, 1974; Mank, Rhodes, & Bellamy, 1986; Rhodes & Valenta, 1985). In fact, these forms of sheltered employment have been defined by the Rehabilitation Act Amendments of 1992, PL 102-569, as being integrated supported employment.

For some writers, however (Brown et al., 1991; Conte et al., 1989), the concepts of shelter and segregation are inseparable. Brown et al. (1991) argued that enclaves and work crews are merely forms of segregated work; Conte et al. (1989) linked enclaves to many of the workshop's weaknesses such as low pay, poor training methods, limited employment options, lack of individualized services, poor placement outcomes, and social segregation. These writers contended that, like workshops, congregate work programs (i.e., enclaves and work crews) basically have a separatist character.

They not only limit people's inclusion in community employment situations, but they have proven no more effective than workshops in assisting people to move into competitive jobs.

Affirmative Industry

Affirmative industry (Durand & Durand, 1978) represents an attempt to congregate people with disabilities and people without disabilities under one employment roof. According to Conte (1983), affirmative industries differ from workshops in that they employ a significant number of workers without disabilities who function as exemplary models for their co-workers with disabilities. They may in turn compensate for the lower production of employees with disabilities. Affirmative industries also operate exclusively as businesses without the level of government support or the adjustment and counseling services of workshops. They may reject the assembly, packaging, and/or manually intensive jobs of the workshop, instead using updated, efficient business methods and equipment to perform the kinds of real work found in commercial companies profitably.

Though growing in numbers, the collective performance record of affirmative industries is not well established. Presumably, they serve as permanent places of employment for people with disabilities; therefore, their competitive placement record would not be seen as relevant to their overall mission. Affirmative industries, however, skew the natural proportion of people with disabilities to people without disabilities and offer limited, preexisting jobs to which they are assigned and must adjust. In this regard, such settings present problems similar to those of other congregate work programs. In response, advocates might argue that although assembled in large numbers, people with disabilities in affirmative industries are working in more typical employment situations, are performing high-level work that is valued, and may receive better wages than typical workshop employees. Of course, given their skills, the question might be raised as to why such workers are restricted in their choices of employment, are not employed in community jobs of their choosing, and/or are not earning competitive wages and benefits.

Supported Employment and Reform

Despite the strength of workshop critics, the idea of eliminating workshops is still not widely accepted. Although many of the sentiments expressed by TASH and the AILCNY were incorporated as federal policy into the Rehabilitation Act Amendments of 1992, PL

102-569, and although the success of supported employment has been demonstrated amply since the early 1980s, recent studies indicate that supported employment has not been seen as an *alternative* to sheltered work, but as *one more option* within an essentially segregated system of vocational services (McGaughey et al., 1993; Revell, West, Wehman, & Kregel, 1994; Wehman & Kregel, 1994; Wehman, Sale, & Parent, 1992). Apparently, the recent growth of supported employment has come from the addition of new services rather than from a reallocation of resources away from segregated programs. Specifically,

> Less than 10% of all adult day programs [activity centers and workshops] have actually reduced the size of their segregated programs and reallocated those resources toward integrated supported employment options. An even smaller percentage [less than 5%] have totally eliminated their segregated programs and replaced them with integrated employment alternatives. (Wehman & Kregel, 1994, p. 17)

It appears that Wehman and Kregel (1994) were correct when they concluded that "With a few notable exceptions, most states and localities have refused to wholeheartedly embrace integrated community-based employment as the primary outcome of adult vocational programs for individuals with disabilities" (p. 17).

The obstacles to eliminating workshops are numerous and complex. One factor evidently contributing to their continued existence is that a large segment of the population still believes that they are basically good and necessary, although perhaps poorly executed. It is still widely believed that some people with disabilities require workshop employment for indefinite lengths of time and that others need a significant period of sheltered preparation before entering community work. In the remainder of this chapter, it is argued that sheltered workshops meet only the least desirable of their societal mandates: vocational segregation of people with disabilities for indefinite lengths of time. Moreover, it is contended that proponents of workshops have largely ignored some very compelling historical analyses of workshop programs, thereby failing to uncover the underlying reasons for workshops' inability to meet their goal of community preparation.

THE ARGUMENT FOR REPLACING WORKSHOPS

Segregation has been a consistent and integral part of the structure and function of sheltered workshops just as it was for their predecessors. Community inclusion, although an often-stated objective of workshops, has not been achieved even when societal conditions are conducive to the effort. Historically, both workhouses and workshops have shown themselves to be far more effective at segregating than integrating the people they serve, despite rhetoric to the contrary. Moreover, throughout the historical evolution of workshops, professional decision making and policy making have remained consistent and dominant features of the workshop model.

Such historical evidence, combined with technical arguments and statistical outcome data, renders the professional arguments that attempt to defend the continuation of sheltered workshops unconvincing. Workshops hold minimal financial, social, and psychological benefits for people with disabilities; provide minimal entry to the competitive job market; and offer neither financially nor psychologically fulfilling quality of life. TenBroek and Matson (1959) contended that

> Sheltered workshops, by virtue of their very existence as segregated outlets of special employment, are an encouragement to the permanent placement of the disabled within them. (p. 263)
>
> It is difficult to escape the conclusion that the only real justification for [the workshop] is a psychology of human nature derived from 17th century Puritan ethic; namely that idleness is a sin, and that work— however routinized or demeaning, unproductive, or unrequited—is a virtue sufficient unto itself. (p. 15)

TenBroek and Matson (1959) added that the deficits rendering sheltered workshops inappropriate mediums for vocational rehabilitation are determined by well-entrenched structural elements that inhere deeply within their historical traditions and remain central to their continuing operations. These deficits cannot be eliminated by retaining workshops in their present form or by infusing them with more money, improving their equipment or contracts, and/or enhancing their staff's training.

Nelson (1971) dismissed much of this criticism as exaggerated, premature, and inadequate. He argued that workhouses are not the true predecessors of modern workshops because workhouses failed to operate in the best interests of the people they served and were designed both to discourage people who were poor as well as people with disabilities from seeking assistance and to reimburse benefactors for the services they rendered.

It may be argued, however, that whether or not social programs operate in people's best interests depends upon who is defining what those interests are. Almshouses–workhouses were designed to address what were defined as the best interests of people who were poor. However, as Caplan and Nelson (1973) and Rothman (1978) pointed out, even the most well-meaning and best-planned social programs "have sometimes yielded incalculable, unintended negative consequences for policy recipients" (Rothman, 1978, p. 66).

Nelson (1971) believed that many criticisms of workshops ignore the fact that people with severe disabilities need special adjustment training to enable them to work. Even if this is true, workshops are not places to obtain such training. As Whitehead (1979) concluded, even the relatively few people who are successfully placed from sheltered workshops are those who need no skills training. In fact, recent and successful community employment and school-to-work placement services using supported employment techniques operate on the primary assumption that no special adjustment or workshop readiness training is needed in order to find community employment.

The most recent data on sheltered workshops and community employment seem to confirm precisely what tenBroek and Matson contended in the 1950s (i.e., that workshops are inappropriate means of finding community jobs). And the record is even worse when examined in relation to people with severe disabilities. Moreover, although some people claim that the placement record of workshops may be improving (Whitehead, 1987), there is no evidence that people who are placed in workshops find more or better jobs than those who are not.

Finally, Nelson (1971) criticized opponents of workshops for offering no program alternatives other than competitive employment. He considered competitive employment impractical because of the severity of some people's disabilities and the negative attitudes held by the general public and the employment community toward people with disabilities.

Perhaps Nelson's (1971) views reflect the general tendency to grossly underestimate people's vocational abilities and the employment community's willingness to hire people with disabilities. Certainly, negative public attitudes and employment discrimination are still important obstacles facing people with disabilities. More recently, however, vocational expectations have risen on all sides, and those individuals previously considered inappropriate for community employment have been shown to be not only appropriate, but fully capable of finding and holding competitive jobs.

Disability should not be viewed as something fixed and predictable that in and of itself determines the potential, capacity, or behavior of individuals or the social reactions of those with whom they interact. Rather, disability is an interactive, dynamic concept that is determined less by people's physical, emotional, sensory, and/or intellectual characteristics and more by the ongoing, ever-changing relationships and contingencies within a person's social, political, economic, and physical circumstances. As a young man interviewed by Frank (1988) remarked, his disability is "the way people respond to my disability" (p. 108).

In short, individual attributes alone cannot predict a person's employability or other such complex issues. Such things must be determined empirically and individually. Finding a community job is theoretically possible for everyone because everyone presumably can find the personal motivation as well as the settings, people, and tasks that may be combined to achieve a successful employment effort using physical and social accommodations and supports.

DISPLACING INTEGRATION RHETORIC

Despite their segregationist practices, many workshops claimed to be transitional and continued to espouse an ideology of integration through the 20th century. However, as Scheer and Groce (1988) indicated, although segregation of people with disabilities was still a very recent policy, the general population increasingly lost the familiarity it had with disability in preindustrial society, dropped its familial and social support networks for people with disabilities, and came to see separation as the traditional and appropriate way of controlling people whose societal roles were not considered to be productive. In effect, workshops were unable to practice what they preached. And, in many instances, in order to legitimate their unsuccessful performance, they had to displace their philosophical goals. Two examples of this are described below, one by Hobson (1981) in her agency-sponsored history of Community Workshops, Inc., and the other by Scott (1967) in his analysis of workshops for people who were blind.

Community Workshops, Inc.

The Community Workshop in Boston, Massachusetts, is one of the oldest workshops in the United States. At its inception in 1875 and during its earliest years, Community reportedly emphasized a community-based, preparatory workroom program for women who were poor that was designed to get away from the almshouse concept. Although some women came to the workroom to do sewing, most received services through home visits. Gradually, however, the workroom gained more prominence. In 1904, the name of the organization was changed from the Cooperative Society of Volunteer Visitors Among the Poor of Boston to the Cooperative Workrooms for Handicapped Women. Despite the name and program changes, Community still did not define itself as a permanent employment setting but as a place of transition where women (and later men) who were considered to be handicapped could learn skills that would enable them to find jobs in the community.

Apparently placements in the community rarely materialized, and the workroom became the primary place of employment. This change in focus was explained in terms of the increasing severity of people's disabilities. At first, the workroom served primarily people who were poor. It later served people defined as handicapped and who, at one point, were referred to as "exceptionally difficult cases of mental and physical handicap" (Hobson, 1981, p. 24). Finally, after merging with an organization that had "severely disabled" workers and "a different orientation and a population requiring more specialized attention" (Hobson, 1981, p. 24), the facility changed its name to Community Workshops, Inc., and increasingly reconciled its rhetoric with its practices. By 1977, Community was no longer emphasizing its community placement intent but its ability to simulate the outside world within its walls. Describing Community's philosophy through an in-house account of its history, Hobson (1981) wrote the following:

> A sheltered workshop's value is measured by its ability to approximate the real world of work . . . In order to achieve this a sheltered shop must provide complex and challenging work tasks; the more the worker has a sense of useful production, the more pride he or she takes in the work performed. Thus, articles made in the shop should not be sold as charity items or labeled "made by the handicapped." Finally, wage rates should be equivalent to those of regular industry on the theory that in our society wages reflect worth and provide incentives. (p. 66)

Describing the workshop ideal, the long-time director of Community noted that "The concern is with work and the work role, the relationships are those that characterize any place of work. The worker is expected to dress as a worker and carry himself as a worker" (Olshansky, 1972, p. 155).

Community also cited several other reasons for replacing its community placement goals with more segregationist objectives. The first was the claim that workshops, because of their nonprofit status, could pay higher wages than comparable commercial businesses. Second, it was argued that a workshop was like a person's family, "giving meaning to lonely lives" and representing a welcome "change of scenery from the starkness of meager home or boardinghouse surroundings; in many instances the agency was the only home they had" (Hobson, 1981, p. 19).

Workshops for People Who Were Blind

Scott (1967), studying sheltered workshops for people who were blind, also reported that despite their stated mission, the structure and function of workshops hindered the achievement of community integration. Scott (1967) reported that in 1905, commercial employment of people who were blind was stated as public policy at the annual convention of the American Association of Workers for the Blind. Speaking at that convention, the then head of the Massachusetts State Commission for the Blind proclaimed that "Every able-bodied blind person . . . can find work of some kind side by side with seeing people . . . if efforts are persistently made in this direction" (Scott, 1967, p. 238).

Despite the rhetoric, however, most people who were blind were thought to have disabilities that precluded their working in competitive industry. They were enrolled in sheltered workshops where, as Scott (1967) indicated, they received primarily social services, not training for community jobs. Scott (1967) also revealed that as workshops for people who were blind grew in number, they became more prosperous but functioned more as factories than as training programs. In fact, as time went on, workshops adopted policies that increasingly subverted their stated mission of finding community jobs and exacerbated community attitudes that led to the need for employment programs for people with disabilities in the first place.

In order to survive, it was essential for workshops to find a market for their goods. The federal government established such a market in the 1930s through a policy of providing preferential contracts to workshops for people who were blind. Reportedly, the work required precision and speed, and, to meet the government's demands, workshops retained their most competent workers. Less productive workers and presumably those most in need of vocational and social services were eliminated or rejected, and the preparatory functions of workshops were minimized in favor of establishing efficient, running factories.

World War II created not only burgeoning government demands for workshop products, but worker shortages in the private sector as well. This increased community employment opportunities for people with disabilities dramatically. However, rather than pursuing these opportunities, workshops elected to pursue their own financial interests and went from filling lucrative though relatively modest government contracts to doing big business (Scott, 1967). Workshops became more concerned with retaining rather than placing workers. Thus, even when societal conditions were aligned properly for workshops to fulfill their purported mission of community integration, they were unable or unwilling to respond. Yet, most still claimed to emphasize vocational training as their primary goal. As Scott (1967) reported

> The first fact to be recognized is that the original, official goals of employment programs, as these were stated in the early 1900's, remained the official goals through the entire process . . . Even during the period when sheltered workshops were enjoying their greatest expansion, workshop managers and others continued to espouse the original and official doctrines of integration of the blind with the sighted in work settings, and of the virtues of commercial employment. (p. 173)

Despite the rhetoric, workshops subverted their mission of securing competitive work and furthered the impression among the general public and community employers that workers who were blind were best suited for segregated employment settings. As stated above, this consequence only exacerbated the conditions that led to the need for special employment programs for people with disabilities in the first place.

The discrepancies between workshops' espoused mission and actual practices created controversy among professionals, policy makers, and people who were blind who recognized and criticized these contradictions. Responding like their predecessors—asylums, almshouses, and large institutions—workshops defended their activities by pointing to the severity of people's disabilities and the pervasive negative public attitudes facing people who were blind seeking employment. As Scott (1967) concluded, workshops reduced the contradictions that existed between their stated mission and actual practices by proposing a new ideology that 1) questioned the virtues of integrated employment for all people who were blind; and 2) emphasized the need to protect people who were blind from the negative attitudes of sighted people, especially employers. At last, the rhetoric of workshops began to match more consistently the realities of their practices.

SUMMARY

In this chapter, it is argued that, historically and functionally, workshops are not designed to 1) meet individual needs and interests, 2) offer the varied employment and social opportunities typically available to other people, or 3) provide people with disabilities and their families with the level of personal control over their own lives that they increasingly demand. Moreover, workshops send out a contradictory public policy message. On one hand, people with disabilities are increasingly being recognized as capable employees having the same rights as people without disabilities. On the other hand, many people with disabilities are still being assigned to exclusionary workshop programs in which images of deficiency, difference, and deviance predominate.

In this chapter, numerous historical, ideological, social, political, and technical arguments are presented in opposition to sheltered workshops. One of the most compelling of these arguments is the close historical linkage of workshops to a strong tradition of societal exclusion and professional dominance. Stemming from the almshouses–workhouses of the 19th century, these characteristics of exclusion and dominance inhere deeply in the workshop concept, are defined as integral to its activities, and are not amenable to technical reform. Thus, despite the community integration rhetoric that has often surrounded both early and contemporary workshop development and operation, workshops have consistently segregated people and, as Scheer and Groce (1988) indicated, furthered a lack of societal familiarity with disability and reinforced community exclusion as the traditional way of managing people with disabilities. In so doing, workshops often have had to displace their espoused goal of inclusion. Furthermore, exclusion has persisted even during periods when societal conditions have been most favorable for community employment of people with disabilities.

Although shedding the overtly coercive dominance of the old workhouses for people who were poor, contemporary workshops legitimate professional control under the mantle of paternalism at a time when people with disabilities are demanding full social equality and inclusion. Using their power to define people with disabilities as incapable of choosing their own vocational directions, in need of adjustment and protection, and incapable of participating in the competitive employment world without a period of employment readiness training, workshops have it both ways. They perpetuate themselves by exerting powerful control over the employment services people receive and the directions their lives can take, yet they proclaim their allegiance to individual choice and vocational integration for those who are ready and able to make choices and be integrated. Such control, however legitimated, is increasingly incompatible with the self-defined interests of people with disabilities.

Sheltered workshops as well as recent variations thereof, such as enclaves and other congregate work groups, do not operate in the social, psychological, political, or economic interests of people with disabilities. Although some workshop participants achieve community employment and many find important friendships within workshops, no one *requires* sheltered workshop experiences. Furthermore, professionals have no legitimate basis for differentiating between who should and should not be assigned to sheltered workshop facilities.

It seems clear that sheltered workshops cannot meet the rapidly changing demands that people with disabilities, their families, and a growing number of professionals are making regarding personal choice, control of services, and integrated work. Because exclusion and professional control are so integral to the workshop concept, they render workshops culturally, structurally, and functionally anachronistic. Thus, many advocacy groups are calling for an end to sheltered workshops and other employment options that, under the banner of integrated work, still congregate, isolate, and limit people with disabilities.

The remainder of this book attempts to describe how workshops are being abolished completely. Beginning with a small workshop that converted itself from a segregated to a completely integrated employment service and by referring to examples from across the United States, this book describes the actions and reactions of those involved in workshop conversion as well as the overriding issues, practical realities, and problems that accompany workshop conversion.

2

Workshop Assumptions, Functions, and Outcomes

A Case Study of a Sheltered Workshop

The following excerpt was taken from a *Buffalo Evening News* article that described the demise of a sheltered workshop and the hardships that caused for the workshop's participants:

> The legally blind and multiply handicapped young woman sat at her work station recently, counting out eighteen screws to put into a cellophane bag, and explaining why she is happy with her life. "I come to work everyday. That's something I couldn't do back home. I've met alot of friends." [Ms. Durston] has a fierce pride in her job. She earns one cent for every bag she fills. . . . Since she moved two years ago to the Pioneer Center, a private agency for blind and multiply handicapped adults, a whole new world has opened up to her. She has moved from "my little girl to a beautiful responsible young lady, capable of living and working independently," her mother wrote.
>
> But her expanding world may be closing again, starting next month when the Pioneer Center—absent any last minute reprieve in state funds—will be forced to close its doors. If the Center should close its doors, that would force 28 clients . . . to find new facilities to meet their needs. . . . The clock is ticking on the facility where she is learning the independence she craves. (Warner, 1986)

When this story appeared, the clock was indeed ticking for Pioneer and the people it was serving. The agency was plagued with difficulties. Its mission and identity had become obscured; its constituents, such as workshop participants and funding and referral agencies, were increasingly dissatisfied; and its financial viability was questionable. Some kind of change was inevitable.

Beyond the specific circumstances of Pioneer not reflected in the newspaper accounts was the fact that the clock was also ticking on the entire concept of sheltered work in the United States. As noted in Chapter 1, this concept has come under heavy criticism by opponents who have reported its failure to serve people's community employment interests adequately. Thus, the story of Pioneer is more than merely an account of one agency's experiences and characteristics; it is a description of the plights of people considered different and deficient and of the changes that have occurred in the way they are viewed and treated.

Revealed in this chapter is an account of how participants in Pioneer's workshop, like many other people with disabilities across the United States, became separated from their surrounding communities; isolated in a separate social world; and divorced from the typical experiences, expectations, relationships, resources, risks, supports, and protections afforded people without disabilities. Although Pioneer was a unique agency and its participants were unique individuals, the general experiences of those who attended the workshop and the conditions that led to its complete transformation from a segregated to an integrated employment service could exist anywhere. Thus, it is hoped that readers seeing aspects of themselves or their programs in this account will review their activities and practices and work toward dramatic and significant change.

PIONEER'S HISTORY

Pioneer was founded in 1950 and was described in one of its early brochures as an innovative, multipurpose day activities center for people with multiple disabilities, people who were blind, and older people. After merging with another workshop in the early 1960s, Pioneer reappeared several years later as a specialized program for people who were blind. Reportedly, the agency was reconstituted because its original director did not believe that people who were blind were receiving adequate attention as part of a larger, generic workshop program and felt they needed a program all their own. In 1966, Pioneer was certified by the state of New York to operate as a social-recreational day activity and work training program for people who were blind.

In 1975, Pioneer amended its certificate of incorporation to include a domiciliary care facility for adults who were blind and had multiple disabilities, an operation funded by New York's Department of Social Services. With the addition of this 10-person community residence, Pioneer emerged as a unique agency in the region and a true manifestation of the segregated vision espoused in 1874 by Hinman Hall at the Pennsylvania Working Home for the Blind. Under one organizational roof and in one locality, Pioneer now could congregate people classified in the same way and offer them a place to live, work, and recreate away from their communities. Many individuals were uprooted from their families, neighborhoods, and friends, and some moved hundreds of miles to attend Pioneer's facility. In fact, slightly more than 70% of those enrolled at Pioneer came from locations more than 50 miles away. Ironically, in its brochure, Pioneer described itself as having a "wholistic approach" to rehabilitation that met the "developmental needs of the total person." Apparently, proximity to social networks of family and friends and access to familiar community activities, businesses, and facilities were not considered integral to the growth and development of the people served by Pioneer.

In practical terms, Pioneer's approach meant that people were being prepared for a separate social world of their own, a world inhabited primarily by other people who were blind and paid caregivers. Although some individuals attending Pioneer occasionally participated in community activities such as church functions and family gatherings, most socialized as they had since childhood. Many at Pioneer were living and working with the same people and under the same segregated circumstances as when they were children. Many attending Pioneer also had been assigned to the same state-operated residential schools for children who were blind where they lived and went to school for their entire educational careers.

Of the people enrolled in Pioneer's workshop who did not live at its community residence, some lived in large, local proprietary residences catering to people who were old or poor and/or had disabilities. Others were placed in area boarding houses. None of the people attending the workshop lived with their families.

Several basic assumptions seemed to prevail regarding the treatment these individuals received. One was the notion that people who were blind were so different physically, socially, cognitively, and psychologically from people who were not blind that they required a plethora of specialized educational and instructional services. Meeting the needs of people who were blind was viewed as being so far beyond the capacity of typical parents, teachers, and community organizations that they required separate environments and specially trained professionals. A second important assumption that prevailed regarding the treatment of people who were blind was that professionals knew what was best and needed to assume most of the life-defining decision making for service recipients and their families.

Given these assumptions, it is not surprising that Pioneer, an organization that orchestrated people's social and working lives under one roof, appealed to many professionals who enthusiastically communicated to families and other agencies the advantages of such an arrangement. Pioneer was described as a place where families could find comprehensive, protective, and congregate care and to which other agencies could refer people who were unable to obtain needed services in their areas. Thus, people who could not find such all-encompassing services elsewhere were referred to Pioneer by agencies and families across the state of New York.

Participants attended the workshop Monday through Friday from 9 A.M. to 3 P.M. Most spent their free time at their places of residence watching television or listening to the radio or a stereo. Occasionally, Pioneer or its residence groups went on community excursions to area shopping malls, parks, parades, the state fair, and/or recreational facilities. The agency had its own singing group called the "Out of Sight Singers" that performed on holidays and special occasions in order to raise money for the agency.

During the late 1960s—the years of peak enrollment—Pioneer's workshop served approximately 50 people, 21 of whom eventually participated in its conversion. Many of those attending the workshop had multiple labels, some of which remained long after their behaviors had changed. Only those people with visual disabilities were assigned to the workshop. Of the 21 individuals attending the workshop at the time of the conversion, 14 were totally blind, and 7 had some residual vision. Many participants also carried developmental disability labels—usually mental retardation—although 6 people were classified as having cerebral palsy alone. Four individuals used wheelchairs. A more detailed breakdown of the diagnostic classifications of the workshop participants is given in Table 1.

People attending Pioneer's workshop ranged in age from 23 to 51 years, with the average age being about 35 years. At the time the conversion began, individuals spent an average of 7.1 years in the workshop, with the range being 1.4–16.1 years. A further breakdown of these figures is given in Table 2.

PIONEER'S PHILOSOPHY AND SERVICES

As noted in Chapter 1, sheltered workshops have a long history of disparities between philosophy and practice, and Pioneer was no ex-

Table 1. Diagnostic classifications of workshop participants

Number of people	Diagnostic label
21	Visual disabilities
11	Mental retardation
8	Developmental and physical disabilities
4	Hearing impairments
4	Psychiatric disabilities
2	Seizure disorders
2	Visual disabilities only

ception. Like many other workshops, Pioneer espoused one philosophy and practiced another. Its brochures described its mission as preparing people with multiple disabilities, people who were blind, and older people for community living. This implied that Pioneer assisted people to acquire the necessary social and vocational skills to enter and function successfully in community jobs. However, this was rarely the outcome. In fact, it was scarcely attempted. Once admitted, the vast majority of people never left the workshop. The various reasons given for this lack of progress vividly illustrate the rationale used consistently by proponents of sheltered work (see Chapter 1). Specifically, Pioneer staff believed that workshop participants 1) had severe impairments and were in need of protection, 2) were in need of extensive social and vocational readiness training, and 3) were socially tied to the workshop because of their lack of social connections outside of the workshop.

Severity of Disability

There was a veiled condition to Pioneer's espoused community mission: People's disabilities could not be *too* severe. This condition of service, which largely negated its purported mission and dominated its everyday practice, was only implied in its policy manual:

> Though it is true that certain severely disabled blind, multiply handicapped individuals will probably not be able to engage in competitive work in the community because of low productivity or poor work behaviors, the primary goal of the agency is to provide services that maximize growth which leads to integration in the community.

Although workshop participants were often described as not ready for community employment, the vast majority of those referred to Pioneer were never actually considered employable at all. In fact, the expectation that an individual could not progress beyond sheltered work was a criterion for his or her referral to Pioneer.

Table 2. Length of time in the workshop

Number of people	Time in the workshop
8	< 5 years
8	6–10 years
4	11–15 years
1	> 15 years

One young woman was admitted to Pioneer and described by a clinical psychologist as having "untapped intellectual potential, but whether she can ever fully utilize these capabilities is very questionable. In all likelihood, she is at her best level of vocational adjustment." A young man, also seen as appropriate for Pioneer's services, was described by a workshop supervisor as not fit for the demands of even sheltered work. According to his case notes, the young man was said to be "best suited for work in a work activity program where the requirements are not as great as those for a sheltered workshop." According to one psychiatric report, he had reached a "functional plateau"; when faced with stressful situations, he "just drops in his tracks." The report added that the young man recognized and adjusted to his shortcomings: "Within his own limits, he has made the adjustments necessary to realize his role in society."

Apparently, both individuals had more ability and higher expectations for themselves than the professionals around them thought. Both eventually became employed successfully in the community after Pioneer completely transformed its service philosophy and methods.

Readiness Training

Another often-stated reason for retaining people in Pioneer's workshop was their purported need for *readiness training*. Workshop participants were said to lack the prerequisite skills necessary to enter and successfully function in community employment settings. Pioneer's tasks were 1) to identify and teach appropriate skills, and 2) to decide when people had learned these skills adequately and were ready to begin community employment.

One woman was diagnosed as having visual and hearing disabilities and spent approximately 6 years in Pioneer's workshop. Although she was described as an excellent worker, she was deemed by a vocational evaluator as not ready for competitive work because she could not communicate with others due to a lack of ability both to learn sign language and to write legibly. She also was thought to be emotionally immature with a low tolerance for frustration because she whined and stomped her feet whenever she wanted something or was frustrated. This was a particularly prevalent behavior in the workshop because she was a good worker and often ran out of work to do. In order to stop this problem behavior, her workshop training plan called for her "to learn to write legibly using a template and to use signing or hand signaling as a way to communicate with her supervisor" when she wanted more work.

Another person was described as "being trusted to work alone if the job was easy enough" even though he was not very productive because he "socialized too much with others during work." This man, who attended Pioneer's workshop for about 10 years, was also viewed as lacking appropriate social skills. It was thought that he could progress to community employment if he was given a training plan "to reduce his socializing and voice volume during conversations." These individuals and their vocational successes after Pioneer's conversion are discussed later in this chapter.

These examples demonstrate that vocational evaluation and existing workshop tasks were key ingredients in Pioneer's readiness training. Evaluation provided the framework for people's identities within the workshop and a blueprint for the direction of their rehabilitation; existing workshop tasks provided the medium through which rehabilitation could occur and people could prove their vocational eligibility for community employment. Unfortunately, this readiness approach was compromised seriously by financial self-interests and flawed instructional practices.

Vocational Evaluation Like most workshops, Pioneer had a vocational evaluation unit that operated in conjunction with its sheltered workshop. This arrangement deserves criticism for several reasons. First, the validity and appropriateness of the facility-based vocational assessments used by Pioneer and most other such agencies in the United States has been challenged vigorously, especially for people classified as having severe disabilities (Gold, 1980; Murphy & Hagner, 1988; Rogan & Hagner, 1990; Rudrud, Ziarnik, Bernstein, & Ferrara, 1984; Schalock & Karan, 1979). Second, having both an evaluation unit and a workshop constituted a serious conflict of interest for Pioneer and other such agencies. Because arguments questioning the validity and reliability of traditional vocational evaluation practices have been articulately presented elsewhere (see preceding citations), this section focuses on the conflict of interest issue that was particularly relevant to Pioneer but that has been critiqued far less frequently in the literature.

At the beginning of their programs, people were referred to Pioneer for vocational assessments by the state funding agencies charged with their vocational rehabilitation. The stated intent of these assessments was to evaluate people's vocational abilities and potential. After their assessment periods elapsed, these people were consistently referred to Pioneer's sheltered workshop for "vocational adjustment" services, ostensibly in preparation for community employment.

In reality, Pioneer had vested financial interests both for agreeing with the wishes of the funding agencies (because they were the only source of referrals for Pioneer's evaluation unit and workshop program) and for placing evaluation referrals in its workshop. In essence, such referrals, like contract work, were the lifeblood of Pioneer. Referring agencies, not people with disabilities, were Pioneer's real service consumers. They were the agency's paying customers.

The conflict of interest inherent in this arrangement was never really scrutinized by those receiving or providing services because 1) Pioneer was the only agency that accepted individuals with visual disabilities routinely, leaving service recipients and families with few alternatives; 2) the vocational evaluations couched people's problems in terms of behavioral deficits and negative employer attitudes—difficult claims to refute because they were generally perceptions shared by the surrounding lay society; and 3) the arrangement was generally supported by area professionals who did most of the referrals and whose bureaucratic and professional interests were furthered by programs that served circumscribed, specified groups of people, many of which were considered troublesome.

Sheltered workshops have a clear conflict of interest when they are charged with giving people with disabilities and funding organizations supposedly objective, neutral vocational information and service recommendations while at the same time offering the very services they recommend. This practice was not unique to Pioneer; it is a widespread, rarely questioned routine used throughout the human services system for people with disabilities. Research and critiques of this practice have been conducted and published (Murphy & Hagner, 1988; Murphy & Ursprung, 1983; Rogan & Hagner, 1990; Wolfensberger, 1967) with little appreciable effect on the way in which vocational evaluations are done across the United States.

Workshop Tasks In addition to vocational evaluation, workshop tasks were an important part of Pioneer's readiness training. Because the tasks and conditions in the workshop were presumed to approximate those of the competitive work world sufficiently, an individual's behavior in the workshop and his or her performance of assigned tasks were viewed as accurate projections of his or her competitive work potential. But the tasks offered in Pioneer's workshop were neither necessarily consistent with people's interests and skills nor close approximations of the work available in the community. Thus, performance of these tasks did not accurately predict community job success and was not a good instructional strategy.

Typically, the workshop accepted the usual array of assembly, stamping, bagging, collating, building maintenance, and small construction contracts that most workshops across the United States accepted. These jobs were done by workshop participants for area businesses. Consistent with the vocational continuum, the more skilled workers were assigned the complex tasks in the wood shop, book bindery, or chair caning and repair shop. Those participants considered to be less skilled were given work activities that consisted mostly of stapling, stamping, and bagging—activities that could be performed at a low level of productivity.

People were paid a piece-rate wage or an hourly wage depending upon the amount of work they produced as compared to a person without disabilities. Wages were very low. It was estimated that the average pay for Pioneer's workshop participants was about $22 per week.

Contract work, like referrals, was essential to the workshop's success not only because it provided a very flexible form of income for Pioneer and served as a way for service recipients to earn wages, but also because it was viewed as the medium through which workshop participants became vocationally rehabilitated. Contract work was limited, however, to those jobs that could be secured by the workshop from area businesses. In some cases, the work may not have been well suited for certain workers who neither liked nor performed certain jobs particularly well because of their disabilities.

Also, contracts came in cycles. Sometimes there was plenty of work, but at other times there was little work and people received even less pay than usual. During slow times, workers did *make work* or participated in counseling or job-seeking groups; some people refused to do anything because they were not being paid what they believed they deserved.

Even when people wanted to work and worked very strenuously, they were often unable to perform the work well enough (or they ran out of work too quickly) to earn much money or develop a liking for the jobs. Consequently, they could have become very discouraged and stopped trying to do well, which may have led to a downward, self-perpetuating spiral of negative expectations. Workers who were demoralized and expected little of themselves were expected only to produce at low levels. Their poor performance and lack of interest in jobs were then cited as clear indications that they were poor community employment prospects and in need of more readiness training.

Many of Pioneer's workers internalized such negative perceptions of themselves; this was reflected in their belief that the performance standards for community employment were too high for them to succeed. Therefore, they described themselves as incapable both of finding jobs and of being ready to meet such standards. It might be legitimately argued, however, that the readiness training itself led to workers' personal discouragement, low expectations, and poor performance.

Many employers contracted with workshops to complete jobs that were not major parts of their businesses. Most frequently, such jobs were more profitably performed by workshop participants than by their own workers who received higher pay. Thus, the work performed by Pioneer and other similar workshops across the United States was not necessarily prevalent or even available in the surrounding community job market. Even if one accepts the merits of segregated readiness training, it may still be argued that the type of work performed in the workshop did not translate easily into competitive jobs. Moreover, because many workshop tasks were not well matched to individuals' abilities and preferences, doing such tasks did not necessarily lead to the vocational self-confidence, motivation, and proficiency often ascribed to the sheltered workshop experience.

The shortcomings of readiness training may be illustrated clearly by returning to the examples of people cited earlier in this chapter as needing such training. The young woman was described as not ready for competitive work because she was socially immature, disruptive when frustrated, and lacking in communication skills. After Pioneer's workshop changed its focus to community employment, however, she became successfully employed with a large assembly and packaging company. The behaviors that were seen at the workshop as obstacles to community employment and the skills she learned to overcome those behaviors were irrelevant to her obtaining community employment successfully. At her community job, this woman had no time and little need to communicate her needs to her supervisor. Her supervisor's job was to anticipate her work needs and keep her well supplied with work materials. Thus, the need to demand more work occurred very infrequently. And though her foot stomping was socially atypical, it was not considered an impediment to her employment. In fact, it was interpreted by her supervisor as a sign of high motivation and served as a reminder for the supervisor to attend closely to her need for work.

The man who was thought to require modification of his socially inappropriate behaviors before he could become employed was given a training plan "to reduce his socializing and voice volume during conversations." After several months of such training, his workshop supervisor recorded that the plan had succeeded in modifying his behavior to the point at which he limited his socializing "to a few instances per day" and spoke at a "comfortable volume 75% of the time over a 13-week period." He was then deemed ready for community employment, and a temporary job was found for him in an industrial setting where, ironically, the background noise precluded socializing and high voice volume was necessary to be understood.

Through these examples, the fallacy of readiness training is illustrated. Such training, often conducted using a continuum approach (i.e., people are taught certain skills as they are promoted from most to least restrictive work settings), has little to do with successful community employment. The reality is that readiness is not a fixed attribute but a setting-specific state whose presence may be viewed differently depending upon the surrounding circumstances, people, and requirements. Until professionals understand and apply this reality, they will continue to focus restrictively on person-centered characteristics, deliver services that are irrelevant to community life, and waste the time of those they intend to serve.

Of course, at Pioneer, a person's being deemed ready for community employment was no guarantee that a job would be found for that person. In fact, according to case reports, between 1985 and 1987, eight people were judged to be ready for community employment. At the begining of 1988, however, only two had become competitively employed. Because readiness was such an ill-defined, open-ended concept, and because people receiving services were characterized as being seriously deficient, Pioneer could continue to provide what it claimed to be well-accepted preparatory and therapeutic services and receive at least minimal financial support for an indefinite period of time.

PIONEER'S PARTICIPATION AND CONSTITUENCIES

Despite their general lack of enthusiasm for the daily tasks, most people attended the workshop regularly. This occurred for social rather than vocational reasons and because workers had little choice and few alternatives.

For many, the workshop filled a social void. Geographic distance from family and a lack of transportation, spending money, staff support, and community contacts contributed to the socially isolated lives led by many people. In the absence of options, people came to the workshop to be with their friends. Although this arrangement perpetuated a very narrow circle of associations, especially because many people attended the same residential schools as children and adolescents and lived together as adults, it was their one stable, consistent social activity.

People also attended the workshop because they had to. Because people with disabilities were often required by state regulations and the agencies to which they were assigned to participate in a regularly scheduled day program, they were often assigned to a workshop as a condition for living in a particular residence. Workshop and residence staff monitored these people's attendance closely in order not to jeopardize their funding.

Day programming regulations did not require that people attend a sheltered workshop. In the state of New York, any regularly scheduled, meaningful activity could fulfill day programming obligations if it occurred for at least 6 hours per day. But most residential service organizations were set up for workshop attendance in that staff schedules, transportation, and residence routines revolved around workshop hours. In addition, workshop programs were not susceptible to the vicissitudes of the community job market. Workers were rarely laid off and almost never fired; even when contract work slowed down or expired, people were expected to attend. Such consistency was an important incentive cited by residential service providers for the perpetuation and even enforcement of workshop attendance even though individuals and/or family members might have preferred more integrated, individualized services. The workshop could virtually guarantee predictable daily programs for indefinite periods of time, which allowed for easier staffing and administration of community residences.

Illustrating the general point made in Chapter 1, professional control and service efficiency rather than program merit can become the driving forces behind human services actions. Also, as with vocational evaluation, the most valued recipients of workshop services are not necessarily people with disabilities, and serving a professional constituency is not synonymous with serving the best interests of people with disabilities.

Financial Arrangements

In the years prior to Pioneer's changes, financing for its workshop came from several sources. Referrals came primarily from New York's Commission for the Blind and Visually Handicapped (CBVH). Long-term funding for people in the workshop came from the state Office of Vocational Rehabilitation's Sheltered Employment Program (SEP). Other financial sources included the New York legislature in the form of two large, short-term grants (one administered through New York's Department of Social Services and the other through the state's office of Mental Retardation and Developmental Disabilities [MR/DD]) and private donations through fund-raising events.

From the time of its inception, Pioneer was supported financially to provide segregated vocational services. Despite its publicly stated goal of preparing people for community living, Pioneer was never expected by its funding sources to find competitive jobs for people as a condition of funding. Pioneer's real role could be determined easily based on its poor record of vocational placement. This role was described clearly by a local CBVH official who referred many people to Pioneer's programs and had his own definition of community living:

> Truthfully, Pioneer was not seen as a real vocational program. Its workshop was always pretty weak. It was seen as more of a therapeutic program where people could go to learn a little more about work, develop some social skills, and have recreational activities which they could not ordinarily get anywhere else. It was seen as a way to give people a total program which could help them psychologically so they could return to their own communities, enter a better workshop, earn more money, and feel better about themselves.

Clearly, Pioneer was recognized and supported by the surrounding community of professionals for providing a narrower range of vocational services than was outlined in its program descriptions and brochures.

Traditional Staff Roles

Pioneer's staff resembled the staff of a traditional workshop. Aside from the administrative staff consisting of the executive director, secretary, bookkeeper, and development officer, the agency employed a rehabilitation counselor, a vocational evaluator, a part-time social worker, a placement counselor, a peer counselor, a workshop director/contract procurer, and an average of 4^1/$_2$ workshop supervisors (including a chair caning supervisor). Pioneer's organizational structure at the beginning of the conversion is shown in Figure 1.

As in other sheltered workshops, the primary focus of Pioneer's staff was internal. Staff time and effort were directed toward assisting people to function more effectively within the workshop. Agency staff taught workshop participants the tasks necessary to complete contract work and worked on eliminating behaviors that they felt interfered with the performance of in-house work and the orderly operation of the workshop. Most workers had attended the workshop for a long time, were quite familiar with the contract tasks that they had done for years, and were able to learn new contract tasks quickly. Thus, supervisor instruction was often routinized and minimally intensive. It was disrupted mostly by 1) periods of contract slowdowns during which staff had to ration work and improvise activities, or 2) interpersonal conflicts that occasionally arose among workers or involved staff and workers.

Minimal staff were assigned to spend time in the community finding jobs or instructing people in community living and/or leisure situations. Although all agency positions were described in terms of helping people to become more independent, only one, the placement counselor, actually pursued community work opportunities. Based upon the record of placements, however, it is evident that the placement counselor rarely found such opportunities. When he did, they were usually short-term, temporary positions that involved using a crew from the workshop to complete a job during a business's busy period. For several weeks, a group of workers under the supervision of a Pioneer staff member would travel together to a jobsite; operate as a separate unit apart from the business's workers; and receive their paychecks from Pioneer, which was paid by the business. After the job was completed, all of the workers would return to Pioneer's workshop.

In the 3 years prior to Pioneer's conversion, community jobs were found for only two people. Both had worked in Pioneer's group

---

Board of directors
Executive director
Secretary   Bookkeeper   Development officer
Rehabilitation counselor   Vocational evaluator   Social worker
Placement counselor   Peer counselor
Workshop director/contract procurer   Workshop supervisors

Figure 1.   Pioneer's organizational structure.

placements, but neither was hired by employers who had used those placements.

The workshop was a primary medium for teaching a variety of behaviors that staff believed would transfer successfully to community settings. Workshop participants were taught mobility, social, and job-seeking and interviewing skills as part of their workshop routines. These skills were required rarely in the workshop, however, and because people had little opportunity for community contact, they had few chances to apply such skills in sustained work situations.

For example, the rehabilitation counselor's duties included running job-seeking skills groups in which 1) skills such as job finding, interviewing, and résumé preparation were taught; and 2) individual counseling that involved discussing work interests and experiences as well as problem behaviors and situations was provided. Although these activities seemed to be useful, workers rarely had the chance to use what they learned because almost no one was given the opportunity to apply their instruction in community situations. The few jobs that were found were not discovered by workshop participants, did not specifically address participants' interests and preferences, and most often did not require an interview or a résumé. Thus, people were taught things they never used. Moreover, instruction was routinized; individuals were rotated into and out of skill-building groups regardless of whether they asked for such services or were deemed ready to apply the skills in the community. In fact, there was often a gap of months or even years between the time a person received training and the time that he or she was classified as ready for community entry. In the rare cases when a community job was found for a person who was deemed ready, staff frequently had to repeat instruction quickly in order to prepare that person for the job application process.

Accounts from Pioneer's case records indicate that the vast majority of staff activities were directed toward enhancing workshop socialization and adjustment. Individual and group counseling and behavior management techniques focused on eliminating problem behaviors and assisting people to manage personal, social, and production problems in order to function more effectively in the workshop. Even when instruction was directed toward mitigating workshop difficulties, however, successful outcomes were rare. Case records repeatedly reflect unsuccessful staff efforts to eliminate or reduce what was described as acting out or socially inappropriate behavior.

For example, following her admission in 1979, one woman was described in her records as having "low frustration, poor attention and work habits, [a] rigid and inflexible personality, and need for constant supervision," all of which were said to require staff services. After 8 years in the workshop, however, her annual treatment plans reiterated the same problems and similar staff interventions. In August of 1987, it was noted that she needed instruction to facilitate "appropriate social behavior" and to improve "her on-task attention and work habits." Another worker was described in 1980 as "stubborn and rigid, refusing to try new workshop tasks." Seven years later, the same individual was to be taught "three new tasks in the next 13 weeks [which coincidentally was the same amount of time allocated for work adjustment training by the referring agency] in order to improve his adaptability."

Although the preceding problems almost always were characterized as serious, disability-determined impediments to people's vocational functioning, they were not problems that could be viewed apart from the context in which they occurred, whether that context was the workshop or a community job.

As noted earlier, the conditions and tasks of the workshop setting often reinforced certain emotions and behaviors in workshop participants that led staff to conclude that they were not ready for community employment. Moreover, it was in the best interests of the staff to find inappropriate behaviors to treat in order to justify their own work and jobs. Why would people be referred to the workshop for evaluation and treatment unless staff found deficiencies that needed specialized remediation? Thus, the workshop setting not only reinforced atypical behaviors in those who attended, but it actually created a need for staff to find deviance because their livelihoods depended upon the workshop's continuation.

Pioneer staff did not set about the task of finding deficiencies in the people receiving services maliciously or even consciously. They simply took for granted that people referred to Pioneer had deficiencies that required workshop services. It may never have occurred to staff that they might be imagining more deviance than actually existed or perpetuating deficiencies inadvertently for their own needs and interests. Interestingly, when workshop participants found appropriate community jobs, they lost or were affected minimally by the deficiencies that staff had considered serious obstructions to community employment success.

Family Involvement

Based upon their actions over the years, families of Pioneer's participants generally supported the agency's activities. In fact, many family members were grateful to find a program like Pioneer's that provided comprehensive care for their adult offspring or siblings. Families were told by the professionals with whom they consulted that their family members needed a specialized program that would address the particular needs of people who were blind. Families believed these professionals and based their evaluations of Pioneer's services on what they were told was best for their family members. Families also found few agencies in New York that would accept people who were blind with other disabilities and provide for their living, working, and social needs under one organizational umbrella. Thus, even though Pioneer was often hundreds of miles from their homes and communities, families were encouraged to send their offspring or siblings there. Families rejecting Pioneer faced the formidable task of searching for another program or perhaps going to another state to receive comparable services.

Either because of geographical distance or families' own dispositions, most families maintained only sporadic contact with their offspring or siblings at Pioneer. Monthly telephone calls and holiday visits were the norm, and, unlike those attending other workshops in the area, no Pioneer participants lived at home. Thus, there was far less direct, daily interaction between participants and their families and between families and agency staff than there was in situations in which participants lived with or near their families. Only four families maintained more than monthly contact, and 8 of the 21 individuals attending the workshop at the time of the conversion had no known contact with their families after enrolling at Pioneer.

Pioneer did very little to build or strengthen people's ties with their families. It is not surprising that many families became disconnected from their loved ones at Pioneer given Pioneer's geographical distance from their homes; its assurances that people needed specialized, comprehensive services; and the fact that people were receiving the important professional attention and nurturing they would need as adults. What little correspondence families received from Pioneer came very infrequently, and families were not asked to participate in plans or decisions involving workshop participants except in medical situations.

Families were called upon quickly, however, when Pioneer was threatened financially. When problems occurred, Pioneer's executive director blamed them on inadequate state support and urged families to protest the situation to New York's politicians and officials. In fact, the letters written by family members and the publicity they generated helped Pioneer to secure the emergency funding needed at one point to continue. This legislative reprieve lasted for only 3 years, however, and even families' continuing advocacy became less effective when Pioneer was unable to show fiscal and programmatic improvement to the satisfaction of local funding organizations.

The Board of Directors

Pioneer's board of directors consisted of 18 members, all but one of whom were middle-age, Caucasian men. About 75% of the board's members were area businessmen. In addition to these businessmen, there was a social worker, a minister, a retired military officer, and a parent who was an industrial worker. Three members had visual disabilities, and about one half could be described as active, attending meetings regularly, serving on committees, and organizing and running fund-raising functions. The other half attended meetings only two or three times per year and were involved minimally in the staff's ongoing activities.

Ordinarily, the board deferred to the judgments and recommendations of the agency's executive director. As Pioneer experienced financial difficulties, however, board members became more critical of the executive director and involved themselves actively in implementing agency changes. Through all of the agency's turbulence, board members retained the same paternalistic philosophy toward the people being served that had guided their actions since the 1950s. People in the workshop were perceived as being deficient, dependent individuals who had to be carefully protected from themselves and the harsh realities of the outside world. Many board members referred to people in the workshop as "kids" even though all the participants were over 21 years of age; some were as old as 50. Thus, board members assumed that any changes would require retaining the basic features of Pioneer's workshop and improving, not replacing, what the workshop had been doing.

When Pioneer's situation did not improve after about 2 years, the board terminated the executive director and began a search outside the agency for a replacement. Even though board members realized that significant administrative and program changes were necessary, they had little idea about what those changes should involve or how they should occur.

SUMMARY

Although Pioneer was certainly not an exemplary human services agency, it was similar in philosophy, structure, funding arrangements, staffing patterns, and even placement outcomes to many agencies of its kind. It provided its participants with circumscribed social and vocational opportunities and found community jobs for almost no one. Like other workshops across the United States, Pioneer assumed that people with disabilities needed professional care in protected settings.

The structural and financial patterns of Pioneer were constructed around presumptions of deficiency and low achievement. The workshop was designed to provide instruction to facilitate community entry for indefinite periods of time. And as long as the agency espoused a preparatory philosophy and engaged in even nominal readiness training, it could legitimate its limited success in terms of consumer deficiencies. This is the same rationale used not only by sheltered workshops but also by advocates of segregated services of all kinds.

Such a rationale reinforced the prevalent public opinion that people thought to have severe disabilities were capable only of very limited functioning and needed to be insulated from the risks, challenges, and failures (and potential triumphs) of their surrounding communities. Modest success was the rule rather than the exception.

Agencies such as Pioneer have been lauded for achieving 10%–15% placement rates and granted regulatory exemptions from glaring contradictions between stated goals and actual practices.

In Chapter 3, it is shown that much of the protectionist ideology that was integral to Pioneer's history and segregated approach to employment services was more a function of the needs and interests of the agency and its professional constituents than of the characteristics or preferences of the people it served. Pioneer's staff completely changed the types of services that Pioneer offered. In so doing, they also had to reverse the ways in which they perceived the people receiving services. This required substantial modifications in nearly every facet of the agency's operations. The ensuing results not only demonstrated the misguided nature of the workshop system, but also the myriad of ways in which the interests of people with disabilities can become obscured by the competing needs of social services agencies for efficiency, control, and self-preservation.

3

Closing the Shop

This chapter describes the process by which Pioneer reversed its service philosophy to provide community employment for the people receiving services. Changing its most basic assumptions about people with disabilities, Pioneer formulated a whole new way of operating that not only caused upheaval among its staff, but created a ripple effect throughout the surrounding community as well.

BEGINNING OF CHANGE: THE DECISION TO CLOSE THE WORKSHOP

Between January 1988 and April 1990, the Pioneer Activities Center became Pioneer, Inc. But the modifications to the agency went far beyond a name change. During that period, Pioneer was converted from a sheltered workshop to an integrated employment service for people with disabilities. The major objective of the conversion process was to use a natural supports approach to supported employment to assist people in finding community jobs of their choosing (Hagner, Murphy, & Rogan, 1992; Nisbet & Hagner, 1988; Rogan, Hagner, & Murphy, 1993).

The 2¹/₂-year project represented a unified commitment to change that was reflected by the involvement of local and state human services professionals, families of people with disabilities, workshop participants, and Pioneer's board of directors and staff.

Reform versus Closure

The decision to close rather than maintain, improve, or downsize Pioneer's workshop was made in order to avoid incurring the contradictions and dilemmas inherent within agencies that offer both segregated and integrated services. The leadership at Pioneer believed that it was important for agency staff and community constituents to understand clearly what Pioneer stood for and was trying to become. Such a sense of identity would be important for staff as they conducted their daily work and decided upon new agency policies. It was also important that Pioneer's constituents, such as service recipients and their families, funding organizations, and other community professionals, understand the kind of agency that Pioneer was, or was becoming, and the values that underscored its policies and practices.

Almost immediately after the new director took over, Pioneer's staff were informed of the pending changes. Most job descriptions were rewritten, and new positions were created that conformed to the agency's new community-centered mission. Staff were encouraged to apply for the newly created positions if they felt qualified. The director noted that as people in the workshop moved into community jobs, workshop supervisor positions would be phased out and reassigned as community employment staff. The gradually diminishing workshop population would eventually decline to zero because there was to be no backfilling after people left.

Underlying Agency Philosophy

From the start, the director pursued the goal of community employment for everyone in the workshop. It was this vision that he presented to workshop participants, agency staff, family members, funding organizations, job applicants, and other community constituents. Underlying Pioneer's service changes, however, were philosophic tenets that needed to be made explicit so they could serve as points of reference for staff as they considered new policies and practices.

After the nucleus of the new staff was hired, the director drafted a statement of philosophy that was circulated among staff for comments. After some discussion, a general statement was adopted to serve as the basic philosophy of services under which Pioneer would operate. This was an important step because this philosophy was 1) the agency's ideological foundation upon which its specific operations and methods would be built, and 2) the preeminent reference for future agency policies and staff activities. Thus, besides serving as Pioneer's primary operating criterion, this philosophy was designed to establish a clear and consistent identity for all of Pioneer's constituents, including service recipients, families, agency staff and board members, referring community organizations and professionals, funding sources, and the general public.

The philosophy included the following major tenets:

1. People with disabilities have the same human similarities and differences that exist among all individuals.
2. Disability should be viewed as being as much a function of setting-related factors as of individual characteristics.
3. People with disabilities have the right to the same community opportunities, risks, relationships, and activities experienced by other members of the community using, if necessary, individualized sources of support to achieve such participation.
4. Having the opportunity for valued, integrated employment and community participation of one's choosing is a right, not a privilege to be earned.

These philosophic principles were operationalized into the agency practices discussed below.

Unconditional Inclusion/Zero Rejection   Because employment was considered to be a right, not a privilege to be earned, and because disability was viewed as being as much a function of setting-related factors as of individual characteristics, no one was asked to satisfy predefined eligibility criteria or to complete a series of professionally constructed placement tests successfully. Anyone who wanted a community job was eligible for services regardless of the severity of his or her disability or what his or her employment prospects were purported to be.

Individualized, Person-Centered, Community-Based Assessments   Individual choice and control and community inclusion were values underlying Pioneer's services. Therefore, individual assessments emphasized community functioning and settings and individual choice. Thus, staff did not refer people to evaluation centers or conduct traditional, norm-based assessments of work samples. Vocational evaluations focused on personal interests, preferences, and strengths and people's actions in familiar, desired community settings. Staff went with individuals to typical community settings that they liked and selected. These settings might have included parks, restaurants, shopping malls, libraries, and homes. Agency staff participated in the activities of these settings and got to know individuals outside of professional situations. Staff developed positive relationships with individuals through informal activities and spontaneous conversations and, if necessary, by talking with their families and friends. These activities formed the nucleus of vocational evaluation.

Because setting-related factors were viewed as being as important as person-centered variables in defining disability and achieving employment success, assessments focused heavily on analyzing the work and social settings that people would potentially be entering. Thus, if a promising job was identified, staff and job seekers would examine carefully not only the tasks to be performed, but also the routines and social characteristics of the job setting to see if it constituted a good match. In addition, a major assessment activity occurred after placement when an individual's reactions to his or her job tasks, social situations, and on-site supports could be observed more closely and, if necessary, modified.

One Person, One Job This concept of one person, one job was based on active individual involvement, personal preference, and service continuity. Because individual choice and control were so important, all placements were individualized. Pioneer did not employ staff to do only job development. The same staff who got to know individuals personally also looked for available jobs and arranged for on-site training and support. This practice encouraged service continuity and individualized attention. Interests and preferences were also assessed through postplacement interviews and/or observations to determine if job changes or alterations were necessary.

Individual, Varied, and Valued Placements Consistent with the principles of individual choice and control, community integration, and individualized supports, all jobs were individual in nature. There were no group placements for assessment or employment. Also, there was an attempt to secure employment in a wide variety of culturally valued settings, such as libraries, universities, and offices, according to individual interests.

Under certain conditions, two or more supported employees could work for the same employer in physically proximate locations. For this practice to be acceptable at Pioneer, however, employees with disabilities had to be physically separate from each other, and they had to receive at least minimum wage.

In an early endeavor, Pioneer found jobs for two people at the same business. These jobs were in close proximity to each other, and staff soon realized that the arrangement was less than ideal. Hired for similar jobs, the two employees worked under the same supervisor. Thus, they were often treated by co-workers and supervisors as a couple rather than as unique individuals. For example, it was assumed that they would take their breaks at the same time, and/or arrange their work schedules in the same way. In most cases, these actions were well intentioned, but they tended to highlight differences and reinforce disability as the defining characteristic of their lives even though they had many diverse and unique attributes that distinguished them from each other and linked them with other employees.

Natural Sources of Work Support with Maximum Social Continuity Because employment was viewed as a primary means of community inclusion, it was critical that an individual become an integral and active participant in his or her place of work. Traditionally, supported employment agencies have assumed major and direct responsibility, often for indefinite periods of time, for orienting, training, transporting, and supervising supported employees. The emphasis at Pioneer was to supplement or, better yet, replace these professional procedures with more natural sources of support. Thus, staff functioned as employment consultants and attempted to involve supervisors and co-workers in job orientation, training, social support, problem solving, and follow-along services. Rather than merely teaching the employee the necessary job tasks, Pioneer's employment consultants actively pursued ongoing instructive and supportive relationships with co-workers as soon as possible while remaining in the background as much as possible.

It should not be concluded that people were dumped or left unsupported in job settings or that employment consultants minimized their duties regarding follow-along services. Employment consultants remained in contact with employers and supported employees as needed, visited jobsites to observe supported employees at work and talk informally with them and their co-workers, and talked with supported employees after work hours about their jobs.

Consultants avoided becoming social conduits for either co-workers or supported employees and instead encouraged direct communication among all parties. Agency staff also served as ongoing sources of consultation to employers if any job changes occurred or problems arose that employers did not feel comfortable handling.

COMMUNITY EMPLOYMENT OUTCOMES

Every person in Pioneer's workshop was employable even though not everyone elected to pursue competitive employment. Some individuals had more difficulty than others in finding and holding community jobs. It should be noted that predicting who would prove easy or difficult to place in a job was a very risky and unproductive undertaking.

Of the 30 people formally enrolled in the workshop at the time of the conversion, only 21 were active program participants. The remaining 9 individuals attended the workshop very sporadically in the previous year and left before the conversion began. Six withdrew because of recurring medical or mental health conditions, and three moved to other locations. One of the 21 active workshop participants later withdrew because of his family's concerns about the changes taking place at Pioneer.

Of the 21 people who participated actively in the agency's conversion, 20 became employed in community jobs. Of these 20, 18 preferred community employment and did not want to return to the workshop, and 2 preferred sheltered work. One individual left the program before a job could be found for him, and he eventually entered a work activities group. Thus, of the original 21 individuals relegated to the sheltered workshop for an average of about 8 years each, 95% became competitively employed, and 86% ultimately opted for community jobs.

Of the two who initially worked in community jobs but later opted for sheltered work, one young woman and her family were afraid of her recurring seizures and, after leaving her job for non-medical reasons, requested enrollment in a workshop. The other woman did not like her community job and believed that it was too hard for her. Refusing to consider trying another job, she decided to enter another agency's workshop.

Summative information on the types of jobs found for people in Pioneer's workshop is contained in Table 3. Table 4 contains specific data on each of the 21 active workshop participants, including ages, years in the workshop, last jobs held, and weekly workshop and community wages.

Table 3. Types of jobs obtained for Pioneer's workshop participants

Job type	Number of jobs found
Assembly	8
Laundry	7
Clerical	5
Telemarketing	4
Food service	3
Human services	3
Maintenance	3
Reception	3
Housekeeping	2
Stocking	1
Total	39[a]

[a]The average number of jobs per person was about 1.9.

Table 4. Specific data on Pioneer's 21 workshop participants

Diagnosis	Age (years)	Years in the workshop	Job type	Earnings per week	
				Workshop[a]	Community (wage/hours)
Mild mental retardation; visual impairments	32	9.7	Clerical	$27.60	$105/18
Visual and hearing impairments	55	4.4	Assembly	24.10	135/20
Blindness; seizure disorder	34	7.5	Telemarketing	19.52	120/20
Blindness; cerebral palsy	35	1.4	Telemarketing	14.15	120/20
Blindness; mild mental retardation	39	8.9	Laundry	13.48	75/15
Blindness; deafness; mild mental retardation	51	7.5	Assembly	21.45	70/20
Blindness; cerebral palsy; quadriplegia	37	8.4	Self-advocacy	14.56	100/20
Blindness	33	11.5	Assembly	23.91	250/40
Blindness; mental retardation; cerebral palsy	35	10.3	Laundry	16.88	112/25
Visual impairments; deafness	36	8.9	Assembly	21.47	180/40
Blindness; mild mental retardation	26	2.6	Clerical	14.38	90/20
Blindness; mild mental retardation	38	10.3	Laundry	19.84	180/40
Blindness; deafness; cerebral palsy; psychiatric disabilities	37	4.0	Assembly	29.24	138/20
Blindness; cerebral palsy; paraplegia	36	16.1	Clerical	22.41	100/20
Visual impairments	28	2.1	Food service	30.76	240/40
Visual impairments; mental retardation	25	2.0	Clerical	28.60	77/20
Blindness	39	9.3	Reception	54.00	160/20
Blindness	35	7.3	Assembly	16.08	100/30
Blindness; cerebral palsy	24	3.5	Sheltered[b]	16.46	Unknown
Blindness; seizure disorder	24	3.7	Sheltered[b]	13.66	Unknown
Blindness; cerebral palsy	33	10.1	Work activities group[c]	18.00	Unknown
Mean totals	35	7.1		21.93	125/24.4

[a]These statistics were based on a 30-hour work week.

[b]These people held community jobs but ultimately chose sheltered work.

[c]This person elected to join a work activities group before a community job could be found for him.

Of particular interest is the extent to which these figures refute conventional wisdom regarding employment feasibility and the readiness approach to vocational rehabilitation for people with disabilities.

It should be noted that the weekly earnings of those who found community jobs increased substantially even though they frequently worked fewer hours than they did in the workshop. Workshop participants worked 30 hours per week, and community employees worked an average of 24.4 hours per week. Moreover, the weekly pay differences were not trivial: People earned an average of five times what they earned in the workshop.

Because participants did things other than work in the workshop, attendance did not guarantee active work. Contracts fluctuated, downtime occurred, and people participated in counseling and job preparation groups. Thus, although time spent in the workshop was often greater than that spent in community jobs, it is likely that most workshop participants engaged in active work for fewer than 30 hours per week.

These data appear to be consistent with data derived from workshops in New York and across the United States (see Chapter 1) as well as with supported work data derived from states such as Virginia, Illinois, and Pennsylvania (Ellis, Rusch, Tu, & McCaughrin, 1990; Kregel, Wehman, Revell, & Hill, 1990; Vogelsberg, 1990). Despite the difficulty of making such comparisons, these figures reinforce the reality that workshops could not guarantee a consistent stream of paid work for participants. Even if they could, many individuals would have earned far less per week than if they held community jobs and worked fewer hours.

COMMUNITY RESPONSES TO AGENCY PLANS FOR CHANGE

Most people in the community were very positive about the proposed changes. There were family members and professionals, however, who were concerned about people's physical and psychological well-being, believing that some workshop participants would be rejected or even abused by people in the community. Some contended that not all people in the workshop could find community employment because their disabilities were too severe and they were vocationally unprepared.

Several representatives from funding organizations argued that Pioneer should not abandon its sheltered workshop totally but should improve it in order to provide vocational options for those who could not succeed in the community. A revitalized workshop also was seen as a place that would offer financial resources with which Pioneer could supplement its efforts toward integrated employment.

Even some proponents of expanding supported employment services argued that a conversion effort should wait until supported employment was more firmly established fiscally and professionally. They pointed out that there were not enough financial resources or trained professionals to expand existing community-based options for those in the workshop. They also contended that Pioneer's financial difficulties were too serious to overcome and that its failure would discredit the viability of supported employment for people with disabilities. Interestingly, all of these concerns eventually proved to be either exaggerated or baseless.

In the following section, family responses and the reactions of select community professionals are described in more detail. The responses of workshop participants are addressed in Chapter 4 of this book.

Responses of Families

As might be expected, the responses of families were varied. Some families were particularly worried about safety and security. Many enrolled their offspring and siblings at Pioneer because of professional assurances that they were not ready for life in the community and needed Pioneer's shelter and training. Some parents were older and were concerned that with the workshop's closure, their sons or daughters would be coming back to their communities and homes, and they could no longer care for them.

Although many families were excited about the prospect of community jobs for their offspring and siblings, many were worried about the workshop actually closing. Whereas Pioneer had committed itself to reversing its service philosophy, it may not have employed the soundest strategy in publicly announcing its intention to eventually close the workshop. Many workshop participants and their families concluded that the workshop would close immediately, leaving them with no source of assistance.

To alleviate the concerns of workshop participants and their families, the director sent out letters and held meetings in which he emphasized that 1) community jobs would be found only for those who wanted them, 2) no one would be terminated from the workshop until a program or an activity of his or her choosing was found, and 3) the workshop would close only when a self-chosen alternative activity was found for each workshop participant. Families were assured that their offspring and siblings would remain in the same geographical area unless they requested services elsewhere, whereupon Pioneer would assist in finding programs or activities of their choosing.

Reactions of Contract Employers

In order not to waste resources improving a workshop that would eventually close, Pioneer attempted to maintain, but not expand, existing work contracts. Thus, the agency retained just enough staff to complete existing contracts and reduced or shifted staff hours and available positions as people left for community employment. If individuals returned, which was initially allowed, staff hours were increased.

When they heard the workshop would be closing, several businesses that had contracts with Pioneer were worried that the work would not be finished or would be done sloppily. The agency tried to assure these businesses that the workshop was not closing immediately and that any contracted work would be completed as agreed.

Pioneer was very careful about accepting contracts, even short-term contracts, unless staff felt confident that work could be completed on time. In order to avoid becoming overextended and possibly jeopardizing participants' opportunities for community employment because of the workshop's need for workers, the director opted to obtain subcontracts from other workshops. These contracts were usually for long-term jobs that the other workshops were having trouble completing or were willing to give up because they had enough work.

It is curious to note that when informed that Pioneer was changing its service philosophy and seeking community employment for all its workshop participants, none of the businesses for which Pioneer did contract work offered to hire anyone from the workshop. Many of these businesses had a long history of involvement with Pioneer and reportedly considered the agency to be a reliable source of work. Even when approached directly about hiring people from the workshop, only one third of these businesses were receptive to the idea. In the end, only one business actually hired an applicant from Pioneer. Interestingly, despite their long involvement with Pioneer and their assurances that the work produced was of good quality, these businesses apparently believed that the workshop participants were unable to perform competitively in a typical work setting.

Reactions of Professionals Serving People Who Were Blind

For most community professionals, the successful employment outcomes achieved by Pioneer in its first 6 months of operation after the conversion served as a compelling argument in favor of the workshop's new direction. Some professionals believed, however, that integrated employment posed high risks for people served by Pioneer. The idea of actually placing workshop participants into community employment seemed idealistic and premature to many professionals.

The most vocal critics of workshop abolition were professionals who defined themselves as specialists for people who were blind who focused on assisting these people in becoming independent. Many of these professionals held advanced and/or specialized degrees; had been taught that people who were blind differed from sighted people physically, socially, and psychologically; and believed that people who were blind required specific (and usually segregated) social, educational, and vocational services. Some of the services they provided included counseling, mobility instruction, and rehabilitation teaching.

Pioneer staff had no quarrel per se with specialized instruction such as mobility training and rehabilitation teaching. But the professionals providing this instruction seemed to be socialized into having a narrow and restrictive view regarding who could benefit from their services and when and how such services should be provided. Many such professionals held low expectations for people who were blind and had other disabilities, particularly developmental disabilities. Mobility instructors and rehabilitation teachers often provided specialized instruction in people's living and sheltered work settings. But because they believed that individuals with blindness and multiple disabilities could not and/or should not work in the community, they often resisted and criticized requests for specialized community mobility instruction and on-site job and mobility training. Their reactions were particularly acute if they had attempted such instruction previously in a workshop setting.

Part of the problem for professional specialists was their wholehearted focus on individual independence. They saw themselves as helping people to become totally independent and judged their services to be useful and successful only if people could apply them eventually without any assistance. Because these professionals deemed Pioneer's clientele to be incapable of totally independent community functioning, they did not see them as viable candidates for community mobility instruction or rehabilitation teaching. Apparently, it never occurred to them that 1) people could still benefit greatly from such instruction even though they could do only a small number of tasks independently, and 2) parts of tasks could be supplemented by supports and accommodations built into both the instruction and the person's everyday schedule.

Because of this apparent difference in orientation, the community's professional specialists complained to state funding agencies as Pioneer's staff persisted both in finding community jobs for individuals and in requesting specialized mobility instruction, work accommodations, and adaptive equipment. These professionals suggested that Pioneer's staff were exposing people to physical risk irresponsibly and doing psychological damage by setting them up for failure. Pervasive in the work of these professionals were the paternalistic beliefs that blindness created psychological fragility and individual deficiency and that many of the expressed wishes, preferences, and interests of people who were blind could be minimized as unrealistic coping reactions to their disabilities.

Specially trained professionals apparently thought that they knew what was best physically, vocationally, socially, and psychologically for the people they served and could accurately predict who could and could not benefit from their services. This orientation contrasted sharply with Pioneer's philosophy, which espoused working with anyone who desired services; pursuing employment options that people requested; and using supports, accommodations, and adaptations in order to stretch expectations, opportunities, and outcomes beyond what other professionals might have deemed appropriate.

Another problem posed by professional specialists was their lack of experience operating in integrated work situations. This inexperience, coupled with their very paternalistic orientation, often led them to impose their beliefs and orientation on employment settings without proper consideration for supported employees, employers, co-workers, supervisors, or employment consultants. This sometimes led to conflict among the involved parties. In one situation, for example, a rehabilitation teacher was asked to assist a new supported employee in restructuring a jobsite and learning to use adaptive equipment for a job in a telemarketing company. The teacher entered the situation and immediately stated in front of everyone that the employee's disability precluded her from performing the job successfully. This angered the job coach and work supervisor and upset the supported employee. The work supervisor told the rehabilitation teacher that the new employee had already demonstrated her ability to do the job, and she asked the teacher to leave the site. Although the employer rebelled against what she saw as undue interference in this case, employers more often tended to defer to what they believed was the specialized knowledge of the expert. This could have resulted in setting low employment expectations, ignoring the interests and preferences of people receiving services, and/or adopting atypical or inefficient methods of doing jobs.

Unfortunately, tensions and conflicts regarding the issue of people's employment competence continued between professional specialists and Pioneer's staff. It became apparent that their dissonant philosophies were not reconcilable and that they could not work together amicably. Thus, at the suggestion of a state funding agency, Pioneer sent one of its staff to train as a rehabilitation teacher. Pioneer also tried to work primarily with those mobility instructors who shared its community-focused employment orientation.

FUNDING COMPLEXITIES

At the time of Pioneer's conversion, funding sources for supported employment were not well established, plentiful, or secure. They were, however, sufficiently available through federal grants and federally sponsored demonstration projects (in New York) to allow Pioneer to undertake a vigorous initial conversion effort. More important, the conversion project itself worked as an incentive to search for and attract sources of funding that might otherwise have been ignored. For example, there were private sources of support for innovative programs from organizations such as the Dole and Mott Foundations. There were also federal demonstration grants designed to facilitate supported employment innovations of various types.

The most critical decision was whether to give up a secure and well-established source of financial support—sheltered workshop subsidies—in favor of supported employment funding that seemed less permanent and stable. As noted earlier, however, once a clear identity and consistency between agency philosophy and actual practice were established, the decision to eliminate sheltered workshop funding gradually became obvious.

Until federal funding was made available in New York through a statewide systems change project, Pioneer relied upon case services money to offer integrated employment services to its workshop participants. The case services money was provided by New York's CBVH beginning at the time the conversion began. As part of this funding arrangement, Pioneer agreed to offer integrated employment services to individuals from CBVH's general caseload who had been waiting a long time for placement assistance. Over the course of the 2½ years from the time the conversion began to the official closing of the workshop, Pioneer served more than 60 people who were referred not only from CBVH, but also from New York's Office of Vocational and Educational Services for Individuals with Disabilities (VESID). VESID began referring people for services after Pioneer received supported employment funding from a statewide change grant in June of 1988.

More is said about funding issues later in this chapter. In light of the general inadequacy of funding levels for most supported employment programs, it is virtually certain that supported employment will continue to be underfunded in the near future. Given the heightened demand for integrated employment initiatives, however, such services *must* be provided as adequate funding is pursued vigorously. Unless agencies affiliate themselves with consumer advocates and assume an ideological/political posture in service provision, their relationship with those who should be their most important constituents—the people they serve—will continue to erode.

Service providers should address existing funding constraints not by avoiding supported work services or by trying to screen for the most promising candidates, the latter practice being notoriously unreliable. Because funding levels are determined politically and are not professional or clinical issues, agencies must form coalitions with powerful constituencies of families and people with disabilities in order to document and address funding inadequacies.

STAFF REORGANIZATION, SELECTION, AND TRAINING

There were few trained professionals in the community who were prepared to enter Pioneer and embark immediately upon the kind of conversion effort being undertaken. In addition, there were existing personnel issues and an organizational schema that had to be addressed before any steps toward agency conversion could be taken.

Staff Reorganization

At the time of the conversion, Pioneer was organized in a way consistent with its traditional workshop program. Only the placement counselor position was designed to focus on community employment opportunities.

When the conversion process began, all staff positions were converted into one core position that reflected Pioneer's new philosophy and orientation. That position, initially called the community job specialist (CJS), was later changed to the community employment consultant (CEC) to reflect an emphasis on natural jobsite supports.

Employees were told that CECs would be the only direct service personnel as the agency moved toward conversion, and staff were encouraged to apply if they were interested and felt qualified. Other positions would be phased out, either immediately or gradually. The vocational evaluator, rehabilitation counselor, social worker, and workshop director/contract procurer would be converted immediately to CECs. Workshop supervisors and peer counselor positions would be changed more gradually as workshop participants left for community employment.

Two years into the conversion, Pioneer had an organizational structure that reflected its new orientation. This new organizational structure, which is shown in Figure 2, was very flat with a minimal number of administrative positions and supervisory levels. Everyone except the financial staff provided direct service. Even the executive director had a small caseload, although this was not reflected in the percentage breakdown, in which he was listed as administrative. In this way, staff shared common activities that connected them closely as team members and, more important, kept them in touch with the essential activities of the agency. During weekly meetings, staff could discuss issues and problems from firsthand knowledge on a very practical level.

Board of directors

Executive director

Receptionist   Bookkeeper (*part time*)   Secretary (*part time*)

Senior community employment consultant

Community employment consultant

Community employment consultant

Community employment consultant

Community employment consultant

Community employment consultant

Peer counselor (*part time*)

Figure 2. Pioneer's organizational structure after the conversion. (Total part-time staff = 9, clinical and counseling staff = 0%, workshop staff = 0%, administrative and financial staff = 33%, community-focused staff = 67%.)

Another change in Pioneer's staffing came through the elimination of *fragmented services*. Prior to the conversion, workshop participants went to different staff for various services. Thus, the vocational evaluator did assessments; the rehabilitation counselor ran job-seeking skills groups; the social worker did individual, personal counseling; and so forth. After the conversion, CECs worked together as a team and provided all the services a person received, from initial assessment and job development to on-site support.

Staff Selection

In order to facilitate agency conversion, the executive director had to find staff to develop and carry out his plan. One option was to retain existing staff and train them in the methods of integrated employment. This option was desirable in that it would prove least disruptive to existing staff and workshop participants. Moreover, staff and participants knew each other and had developed long-term relationships that could prove reassuring and helpful as changes occurred.

The proposed changes, however, required a distinctly different service philosophy and an entirely new orientation toward the people being served. This could have proved very difficult for staff to accept because they had long considered most workshop participants to have disabilities that precluded work in the community. In addition, staff had to learn new skills, many of which were antithetical to those they learned as employees of a segregated program.

For the sake of continuity, the director hoped to retain as many staff as possible. In order to attract and eventually hire the very best people he could, however, he decided to open the new CEC positions to anyone who wanted to apply from either within or outside of Pioneer. The CEC job description was circulated to all Pioneer staff, who were encouraged to apply, and advertisements were placed in local newspapers. Due to the dearth of qualified, available professionals, the director also solicited applications from those he knew to be interested in integrated, community-based services.

Three of Pioneer's direct service staff applied for the four newly created CEC positions. Of those, two were hired as CECs and one was retained as a peer counselor. The peer counselor position was retained at the request of several workshop participants who developed a close relationship with this staff member and felt that they might have trouble adjusting to the pending changes. The peer counselor position was discontinued after the workshop was reduced to just a few people.

Of the two individuals who continued as CECs, one had trouble adjusting to the new job and joined another workshop's staff after about 6 months. The other adapted successfully to the new position and became a valued agency employee, although she did require considerable initial training and supervision to make the adjustment.

In order to evaluate those who applied for the remaining staff positions, the director established a hiring committee consisting of himself, a current workshop participant, a faculty colleague, and a supervisor of a local funding organization, all of whom shared a philosophy that espoused community integration and an interest in Pioneer's conversion in that regard.

It was felt by the committee that the most valuable asset that a prospective employee could bring to the agency was not a solid educational background, human services credentials, or even supported work experience, even though these were also considered to be important attributes. Rather, the committee was seeking people who 1) had a personal commitment to community integration, individualized supports, and consumer choice and control of services; and 2) could discuss how to operationalize this commitment in terms of helping people to achieve their personal goals. Ideally, candidates could point to experiences they had in actually implementing this service philosophy.

After screening all applicants initially for appropriate background and experience and obtaining recommendations, the committee interviewed selected candidates using hypothetical case situations to elicit their values and experiences. Candidates might have been asked if they believed that people with certain behavioral characteristics or psychological profiles were capable of working in community jobs. Or they might have been asked to respond to specific circumstances involving family participation, job development, employer concerns, behavior disruptions, job dissatisfaction, and/or any other issue that would reveal their compatibility with Pioneer's core values and their creativity and intuition in applying those values. Applicants with supported work or vocational rehabilitation experience were asked to describe their activities, critique their own methods of providing services, and suggest ways in which they could improve their service practices. Applicants whose views and background experiences were most consistent with Pioneer's values were most highly rated.

Few of those hired within the first year had extensive educational preparation or much supported work or vocational rehabilitation experience. None of the six people hired initially had graduate degrees. Only one had credits toward an advanced degree, and just two had previous supported work experience. This did not concern the director because he planned on developing unique ways of serving people and believed that applicants with less experience may be more flexible and receptive to new service methods.

In an attempt to attract the best people, demonstrate the value of the work involved, and emphasize the high expectations that would be placed on staff, Pioneer offered salaries that were about 15% higher than those offered to previous staff or paid by other agencies for the same positions. This decision was criticized by other agencies that felt pressured to match these salaries or risk losing their best people. Funding organizations also wondered how Pioneer could afford to pay higher salaries given its limited financial resources. Certainly, it was a sacrifice to offer higher salaries and it meant hiring fewer staff. In order to attract the best people, show them that much would be expected of them, and assure them that they would be valued, however, the director felt that the higher salaries were warranted. Critics were somewhat appeased when informed that CECs had broader duties than were typically assigned to job coaches and that Pioneer's budget was not substantially increased but merely realigned to address new agency priorities. In the end, the staff's obvious dedication, competence, and success appeared to confirm the wisdom of the decision.

Staff Training

Staff training included three primary phases: a didactic phase, an experiential phase, and ongoing staff discussions. A fourth phase, conference travel and workshops, was important but more restricted because of the costs involved.

The Didactic Phase The didactic phase consisted of an overview of supported employment techniques through enrollment in an introductory employment training course. Later, when this course was not offered regularly, new staff were given an orientation manual that explained the history and philosophy of the agency, defined supported employment, and explained the roles and functions of CECs. The senior CEC reviewed the manual's contents with every new employee. The didactic phase of training also included periodic in-service training by area experts who led discussions on topics such as individual assessment, job development, and natural supports.

The Experiential Phase The experiential phase and ongoing staff discussions were the most important phases of staff training.

The experiential phase began almost immediately after new staff started working at Pioneer. Upon completion of the didactic phase, new staff were assigned to either the executive director or the senior CEC for practical supervision. Each new staff member observed one of these supervisors carrying out various supported employment tasks such as getting to know service recipients and their families and working with business personnel to provide on-site job training. New staff members were then observed doing these tasks and given additional instruction and suggestions. Within the framework of the agency's core values and operational methods, new staff were encouraged to develop their own styles of working with people. They were also encouraged to identify and consult with coworkers who seemed particularly adept at tasks with which they were unfamiliar or unsure. The experiential phase of training lasted until the supervisors felt confident that each new staff member had mastered the various aspects of the job. Usually, this phase lasted from 3 to 6 months, with periodic reviews conducted to assess each individual's progress and to suggest methods of improvement.

Staff Meetings   The third phase of training involved ongoing weekly staff meetings during which individual cases and specific strategies were reviewed and discussed by the entire staff. These meetings were devoted exclusively to individual situations. Staff discussed the people with whom they were working, shared success stories, and tried to resolve difficult situations. Group thinking was encouraged and directed toward developing specific strategies for solving the problems that were presented. Updates were given at subsequent meetings so that people could see the effects of their problem solving, and previous recommendations could be adjusted as situations changed.

Staff meetings served several purposes. They certainly served as an ongoing source of staff training in that personnel were exposed regularly to the activities and methods of their more experienced colleagues, were able to solicit suggestions for their own situations, and were able to follow case situations over a sustained time period and assess the outcomes achieved in light of the methods used. The meetings also brought additional resources to problems that might otherwise have been addressed discretely. Such resources could be particularly helpful when, for example, someone was having trouble finding job leads, transportation ideas, or adaptive equipment for a particular person. Because all staff were constantly making contacts and arranging services, they often had many ideas and resources to offer in such matters. In fact, as time went on and the staff became larger, their need for information and assistance became greater than this weekly meeting could provide. Thus, it became more important to use other, more experienced staff as resources. Larger staff meetings were supplemented by smaller supervision sessions run by the senior CEC.

Conferences and Workshops Another method of ongoing staff development involved sending personnel to conferences and workshops throughout New York as well as the United States. Although such trips necessarily had to be limited, they served several important purposes. Staff learned new ideas, presented and received recognition for their successes, and developed a spirit and identity as part of a larger movement for change.

RELATIONS WITH THE BOARD OF DIRECTORS

Because he had initially been candid with the board of directors regarding the conversion and workshop closure, the director was given considerable latitude in carrying out his program of change. The board was particularly concerned about Pioneer's deteriorating relationships with its funding organizations and the lack of financial support provided by those organizations. When these relationships appeared to improve and funding agreements were developed and implemented, the board was more than willing to allow the director almost total planning discretion.

Board members saw themselves as being responsible for ensuring the financial viability of Pioneer and left program directions to the staff unless they threatened the financial state of the agency. It is interesting to note that despite the dramatic changes that occurred, especially regarding the way that people in the workshop were viewed and treated, board members' attitudes toward workshop participants did not seem to change significantly. They still referred to the people in the workshop as "kids" and perceived them as being very dependent and needy. For example, although they acceded to the director's wishes to have several workshop participants on the board, they did not view these individuals as contributing members and were uncomfortable with and disdainful of the practice.

Consistent with their efforts to ensure Pioneer's financial stability, board members assumed an active advocacy role with local politicians and private funding sources. They sought to expedite previous funding allotments when those allotments were stalled in state agencies and to ferret out new sources of financial assistance from private philanthropic organizations. In an effort to supplement Pioneer's income, board members also became active fund-raisers.

PIONEER'S PHYSICAL FACILITY

One of the issues in which the board took a keen interest was Pioneer's changing physical needs and their impact upon the agency's financial situation. It was obvious that the agency would no longer need the large space formerly required for the workshop. The building was not designed to serve as office space, which would be required in light of Pioneer's projected mission. Also, because of its age, size, and openness, the workshop incurred significant heating and maintenance bills. Thus, although the agency owned and seemed to control the building, the maintenance, heating, and mortgage expenses seemed ominous. The building was characterized by some board members as a liability that should be jettisoned. They proposed selling the building and renting office space with the proceeds.

The positive side of selling the building was that the agency would reduce its short-term operating costs. In the process, however, it would lose control of the short- and long-term costs associated with that endeavor. As long as Pioneer remained very small and was willing to move in order to maintain low rental rates, it would benefit from selling the building. If staff wanted more control of the situation and desired housing flexibility and stability, however, they had to consider alternatives to selling.

Pioneer, like many other agencies that owned their buildings, actually had a financial asset that could be utilized if part of the building was rented out. In Pioneer's case, the building was located in a desirable commercial area and seemed ideal for several small businesses. Thus, the board decided to retain the building and explore the rental market.

As the number of people in the workshop grew smaller, space for contract work was condensed into an increasingly limited area. The agency projected the additional space that would be needed for future growth (e.g., staff office space, meeting rooms) and set aside that space for its use. The remaining space was then considered for rent as it became available. Any construction costs incurred while preparing space for a particular tenant would be negotiated with that tenant, and any costs paid by Pioneer in setting up a space for use would be added to the tenant's rent.

Because of the building's desirable location, Pioneer had little trouble attracting tenants for the available space. Within 4 months of its becoming available, the agency had rented the extra space to two commercial businesses. The first business moved in about 1 year after the conversion began, using space that was available immediately as the workshop limited its operations to a smaller area. About a year after that, as more people moved into community jobs and more space was freed up for rental possibilities, a second business leased the remaining space. Thus, about 2 years after embarking on a course of dramatic change, Pioneer had transformed its physical facility from a sheltered workshop into two income-producing rental spaces and an expanded agency office space.

With only three people remaining, the workshop operated in one of the agency's conference rooms. Pioneer's workshop officially closed $2^1/2$ years after the conversion began.

SUMMARY

Many conclusions and recommendations can be derived from Pioneer's changes. Certainly, the agency's situation had many unique features that likely cannot be duplicated in other agencies. There were some elements of the Pioneer experience, however, that facilitated the conversion and might therefore be helpful to other agencies considering such ambitious change.

Clear Values

One of the first and most important tasks of Pioneer was to articulate a clear set of values and principles around which agency services could be built. This created a source of identity and provided a unifying theme for staff as they conducted their work. These core beliefs enabled those within and outside of Pioneer to have a clear vision of exactly what the agency stood for and a specific point of reference for the agency's activities, policies, and outcomes.

Pioneer was often under pressure from funding organizations or other human services agencies to compromise its principles and adopt practices that contradicted its values. As the conversion unfolded, some staff (i.e., those who remained committed to the separatist/readiness approaches of the past) questioned the agency's new values and practices. In order to maintain its identity, heighten staff morale and unity, and conduct consistent service practices, Pioneer had to continually communicate its core values to those around and within it and structure itself so that its basic principles were developed, applied, and reinforced as part of the staff's daily activities.

This is not to say that Pioneer did not make occasional compromises. But if proposed compromises served to undermine or contradict its core values, the agency vigorously resisted.

Strong, Consistent Leadership

Although it may seem trite, the most important ingredient of change is the commitment to change. This commitment is embodied in the actions of a movement's leadership and is reflected in the vigorous pursuit of change despite the inevitable opposition and obstacles that occur along the way.

Those in leadership positions at Pioneer showed significant resolve not only to embark on the path of change when they were advised against it consistently for a myriad of reasons, but also to sustain their efforts when their activities were criticized, their competence challenged, and their funding threatened.

Pioneer's leaders were willing to immerse themselves in various levels of the agency's operations in order to understand and address the problems that arose at each level. For example, the executive director had a small direct service caseload that allowed him to observe the daily experiences of the CECs and understand firsthand the problems they raised during weekly staff meetings. This knowledge also enabled him to negotiate more effectively with representatives from local funding organizations who often had no recent field experience. In addition, both the executive director and the board of directors were integrally involved in the financial situation of Pioneer and were willing to lobby local politicians, solicit funding sources, engage in direct fund-raising, and write grants in order to secure the necessary resources to sustain the agency.

The preceding activities demonstrated to those within and outside of Pioneer that the agency's leadership was strong, consistent, persistent, and resourceful. This level of overt commitment stimulated and enabled agency staff to concentrate on the vital daily work that would serve as the catalyst for the agency's ultimate success or failure.

Quality Staff

It was very important that staff be receptive to or, better yet, invested in Pioneer's values and practices. Certainly, education about and experience in providing integrated employment services enabled several staff members to be extremely productive and to contribute immediately to the success of the agency. It was not imperative, however, that a person have an advanced degree or a sophisticated background in human services provision. In fact, traditional human services academic and practical preparation could have been more of a hindrance than a help.

It was important that staff have certain beliefs regarding people with disabilities, the services they should receive, and the process through which those services should be delivered. Thus, when hiring staff, Pioneer attempted to go beyond traditional hiring criteria and discover core beliefs that applicants held regarding people with disabilities, their right to community inclusion, and their role in making choices and exerting control over the services they receive.

An attempt was also made to pay staff respectable wages. Pioneer's newly hired staff received salaries that were higher than those of previous employees and other area professionals doing similar jobs. This sent a clear message to staff that much was expected of them and that their work was important and valued.

Training and Staff Dynamics

It was important not only to provide ongoing training through inservice sessions and conference attendance, but to integrate training into the everyday activities of the staff. Pioneer's staff met weekly and sometimes bi-weekly with the executive director and senior supervisors to discuss individual case situations. During these meetings, supervisors would attempt to apply the training lessons learned from formal presentations and at conferences. Also, training was seen as a team effort, and supervisors encouraged staff to work cooperatively on tasks with which they felt weak in order to learn more effective methods and to obtain assistance from colleagues who might be more proficient.

Pioneer expected each staff member to be able to deliver a variety of services in order to maximize service continuity. Although services had to be delivered in accordance with agency values, Pioneer recognized that they should be offered in individualized ways and that each staff member had unique personal dispositions and behavioral styles. In order to accommodate such diversity, staff were encouraged to pursue their duties in the ways in which they were most comfortable within a team structure.

Understanding the Uncertainties of Change

Almost no one believed that Pioneer could accomplish the kind and level of changes it sought. There were many unanswered questions about the agency's financial stability, current and future funding, staff recruitment and training, board commitment, director competence, and physical facility. But what may have been neglected as a critical element in the agency's successful conversion were the dynamics of change itself. Change creates change and causes an unpredictable chain reaction of altered perceptions and actions. Although most often characterized as a negative condition, uncertainty can be a positive precondition for successful change. In Pioneer's case, the uncertainties surrounding its conversion led to new perceptions and stimulated the staff to pursue new opportunities for service relationships, funding, success, and further change.

This is not intended to paint an overly idyllic picture of what change means for an agency and its constituents and staff. Pioneer's conversion also introduced upheaval, conflict, and anxiety. Because none of the people involved had previous experience with agency conversion, no one could offer credible assurances that things would settle down, become more predictable, or conclude satisfactorily. Furthermore, extensive organizational planning and contingency projections could not organize the elements of Pioneer's conversion in a way that was predictable or manageable. The agency apparently understood that change brought uncertainty, however, and it was willing to proceed despite the fact that the elements did not fall into place immediately.

The next chapter offers a different perspective on Pioneer's conversion. It describes the reactions of the people who were integrally involved in the conversion process—the workshop participants—before and after the conversion occurred.

4

Perspectives of Workshop Participants Before and After Conversion

This chapter is divided into three main sections. It describes the experiences, circumstances, and perspectives of Pioneer's workshop participants before, during, and after Pioneer's conversion. The data contained in the chapter are virtually nonexistent in the literature and were collected over a 6½-year period through observations of and interviews with workshop participants, interviews with staff, and analyses of individuals' files. Interviews were transcribed verbatim, and detailed field notes were written during and after observations and interviews. Videotapes and photographs were used periodically to record observations at the workshop and at several community worksites. Researchers analyzed transcripts and field notes independently, and they then identified jointly the major themes that are the headings of the chapter.

The chapter begins with workshop participants' descriptions of their experiences in the workshop, including the activities they performed, issues they faced, concerns they had, and relationships they developed. It further discusses participants' descriptions of the personal significance of the workshop in terms of training and friendships. A glimpse of the workshop's functions from a social systems perspective is also provided.

The chapter then examines the perspectives of workshop participants on the conversion process both as it unfolded and after-

The authors gratefully acknowledge the contributions of Marjorie Olney, a graduate student at Syracuse University, in writing this chapter.

ward. Participants discussed their anxieties and successes, their job interests and abilities, and their concerns about future assistance.

Finally, using individual examples, the third section analyzes how participants were perceived before the conversion began. Here, formal, professional assessments of workshop participants' attributes are contrasted with their actual community outcomes and achievements. In the second part of the section, participants discuss the lifestyle changes they experienced after Pioneer's conversion was complete.

WORKSHOP EXPERIENCES AND SIGNIFICANCE

When asked to describe their experiences in the workshop, participants often referred to things that they did each day, such as their specific job tasks and interactions with staff and co-workers. Many participants expressed some dissatisfaction with the workshop's routines, referring to the workshop as "boring," "something to do," and/or "better than nothing." One young woman reflected on the tedium she experienced: "At first I liked it there. But then after a while it was boring because the people were doing the same thing; the same type of work. Anyone would get bored doing the same thing; the same job."

Several people referred to the jobs they did as simple, demeaning, and unpleasant. One worker referred to some of the jobs as "crazy kids' stuff" and suggested that staff get rid of the unchallenging contract jobs and get better ones.

Overall, the jobs people described did not elicit much enthusiasm nor did they seem to motivate participants to perform at their best. In certain cases, people with severe physical disabilities said that they could not do the assembly work that predominated in the workshop. One participant who had difficulty handling small objects complained about the displeasing nature of the tasks that she had to do. She described the parts she handled as "little tiny things, raisins, ants, whatever you want to call them."

This kind of mismatch between the characteristics of participants and the types of contract jobs, coupled with the antipathy participants felt toward their jobs, likely contributed to the low participant production rates of between 8% and 25% of the industrial norm. Interestingly, these low production rates were the reasons often given for maintaining workers in the sheltered workshop. Thus, a vicious cycle of poor performance was perpetuated due largely to ill-suited tasks. This led to staff judgments of workers' inadequacy and therefore to extended workshop enrollments.

The people who were considered the poorest producers were not always provided with enough contract work to earn even minimal pay. These participants engaged in reading, knitting, or craft work, which were referred to as *downtime* activities. The better producers completed the contract work. Downtime was a period of time during which no paid contract work was available; however, participants were still expected to come to the workshop to engage in "productive activities" for which they were paid a very nominal amount. Because of the cyclical nature of incoming contract work, almost everyone in the workshop engaged in downtime activities at one time or another during the year. More is said about downtime in a later section of this chapter.

Daily Compliance

Despite their complaints, most participants followed their assigned schedules obediently. Those who refused to do so were considered to be adjustment or behavior problems and were provided with special therapies such as behavior modification and/or counseling, most frequently the latter. In fact, counselors were key members of Pioneer's staff, and personal counseling was a central feature of Pioneer's program. It was offered to anyone having personal, social, familial, and/or adjustment difficulties. Counseling is discussed in more detail later in this chapter.

Some workers described their daily routines in striking detail, citing times of arrival, activity changes, and even standard conversations with staff and peers. The immutability of the workday seemingly provided the backbone of the work experience at Pioneer. One man who worked at Pioneer since leaving high school described his daily routine as follows:

> Well, I mainly come in the morning, and then I put lunches away, and then I sit down . . . and I usually do latch hooking or labeling. . . . Then about 11 in the morning I usually go on break until 11:15, then come back and do a little more latch hooking, or whatever they have, you know, that could be done out back, then around [11:45] I usually go into the cafeteria to set up lunch. And then after lunch I usually go back to work and do some more work until 2:30, and then to break, and then come back and do more work until [3:45], and get ready for the bus and go home.

Workshop activities were considered to be training for the unspecified day when participants would be judged to have achieved the necessary skills and productivity levels to work in the community. This orientation prevailed regardless of how unusual, unproductive, or impractical the activities were or how infrequently participants moved into competitive jobs. Because almost no one left the workshop for competitive work, it seemed that teaching community readiness was assumed to be a morally desirable end in itself. This orientation was reminiscent of 19th century rehabilitation:

> Founders of all three institutions [almshouse, penitentiary, and insane asylum] insisted that the removal of deviants and dependents from the community was a prerequisite for recovery. . . . At the very least institutionalization would remove the poor from the corruptions sure to ensnare them within the community. . . . The new almshouse would insist on order, discipline, and an exacting routine . . . [and would teach] industrial habits. (Rothman, 1971, pp. 189–190)

Not all participants in Pioneer's workshop accepted the fact that they were being prepared for competitive jobs. Some saw themselves as workers, not trainees, and as Pioneer employees, not service recipients. One individual argued this way:

> I hate when some people here call these people clients . . . 'cause if they're working here, I think they should be called employees. Because we're working our butts off for the Center, and I feel we should be called employees. . . . If someone called me a client, I'd say, "don't you *ever* call me a client." . . . I've told everybody I hate that word. The only time I feel like I'm considered a client is when I'm seeing a lawyer or something. That's it.

Pay

Although many people did not know exactly how much money they made each week, almost everyone complained that their pay was too low. On average, wages ranged from several dollars a day to minimum wage, with most earning between $30 and $50 per week.

One young man who had his own apartment pleaded with interviewers to intercede on his behalf with the workshop management. He was having great difficulty affording rent and food, and he thought that an outsider might have some success in presenting his case. He expressed the problem as follows:

> Sometimes it's hard to meet my budget if [the pay is] not there. I used to get like $1.15 an hour, and then $3.35 . . . because, remember, I've got to meet my standards and put my food on the table just like anybody else.
>
> [My pay] varies. . . . Some weeks, since a few weeks ago, it's been like $40 or sometimes $30 [per week]. It differs. But, ah, I'd like to keep it with that minimum wage because it does help.

Others found that their paychecks did not even cover the $2 a day it cost to travel back and forth from work on the paratransit system. Some spoke wistfully about small amenities they could afford with a little extra money in their paychecks: "get stuff out of the [soft drink] machine, plus . . . go out to lunch again," "do stuff," and "buy something."

About half of those in the workshop expressed an eagerness to work competitively in order to "make more money than I have when I'm here." For this group, the advantages of leaving the workshop were obvious. They would receive a "bona fide paycheck" and feel better about working.

Not all participants believed, however, that they had to leave the workshop to get better pay. Some suggested that they would be satisfied if the staff would procure more and better contract work.

Downtime

One characteristic of the workshop that annoyed nearly everyone and contributed to the problem of participants' low pay was the occurrence of downtime. When contract work came in slowly or was unavailable, participants were supposed to be provided with productive activities, such as crafts, cleanup tasks, or "practice" bagging or assembly work, for which they received even lower pay than they earned doing contract work. During periods of downtime, staff attempted to maintain the workshop's appearance as a productive place of employment by adhering to a structured work schedule and referring to downtime as a skill-building opportunity.

Participants had few delusions about downtime, viewing it as "practice work that you do just to keep busy so you're not just sitting around doing nothing when the real thing is not available." One man described it by saying, "when there is not work, then I do downtime work, which is not [work]." Observed packing and unpacking small white objects that resembled hats, a young woman was asked by an interviewer what she was working on. She responded in an offhanded way: "Those hats are nothing; they just give you something to do." Another woman gave one of the more magnanimous descriptions of downtime work: "Sometimes we've got pieces of stuff around to practice our counting and stuff. . . . Sometimes we have what I like to call a·goof-off day."

Counseling on the Job

Pioneer had a full-time professional counselor on staff and a peer counselor, and it also contracted with external counselors as needs warranted. If a workshop participant had problems that were deemed long term or too complex for the in-house counselor, he or she was referred to a visiting counselor who saw people weekly during workshop hours. Participants often assigned much importance to counseling sessions. There seemed to be some personal prestige gained by those receiving counseling. One young woman, for example, took pride in naming a string of counselors with whom she was working:

> Well, right now I see Harvey. I used to see Helen, but I'm going to change and see Donna. At one point there [were] three counselors here. There [were] two I used to see, Harvey, and then if I had more problems I saw someone by the name of Carol, and then if I still had problems I went to . . . whatever the counseling center is next to St. James. And then, I saw someone there. . . . I could talk to someone up there and tell them my problems. If I had problems that Harvey couldn't solve, then I could go up there and talk to somebody.

Participants saw counseling as a logical, routine way to solve their everyday problems. It was described much like a formal job accommodation that was necessary to deal with daily work pressures. As one woman related, "I've got to have counseling once a week because I'm not right without it." Other participants saw counseling as a more temporary way to handle specific, stressful events. One woman expressed this viewpoint during a period of turmoil at Pioneer:

> It's been a pretty upsetting time. I'm trying to get myself, you know, I'm pretty good today, but I get pretty upset sometimes. For a while I was seeing Helen. . . . I think a lot of people needed it, and I think a lot of the staff needed it too.

Counseling was promoted heavily by staff as a way to deal with troublesome situations and people. Having counselors on staff was a tacit sign that workshop participants were likely candidates for social and emotional problems. In addition, although the mere presence of counselors ensured that problems would be identified and discussed, the selection of "problem" cases was highly subjective.

In some cases, problems that might have been interpreted as everyday or situational in nature (e.g., refusal to do boring or downtime work, consistent expressions of dissatisfaction, frequent conflicts with staff and co-workers) were called "adjustment" problems that required professional intervention. In other cases, virtually the same behaviors were either ignored or tolerated depending upon how incorrigible a participant was judged to be, how much resistance he or she might have to being counseled, and/or how comfortable the counselor felt intervening in a particular situation.

Several examples illustrate how subjectively the need for counseling was identified and pursued and how little understanding existed about the occurrence of problem behaviors and their possible solutions. For example, two women often left their workstations without permission, saying that they hated the work, needed a break, or were tired. One would enter the cafeteria or staff office area, sit down, and begin crying. The other would go to the same areas and spin in a circle slowly. The latter woman, who had been at the workshop for over 10 years and was seen as incorrigible, stubborn, and difficult to manage, was ignored until she returned to work. The other woman was attended to immediately by the peer counselor, who sometimes counseled her for an hour or more about what was bothering her. In both situations, the problem behaviors continued unabated, and they were viewed as primary reasons for these women's inability to enter community jobs.

Some staff said that counseling only served to provide people with time away from work and attention that exacerbated problem behaviors. Interviewers observed that participants were always eager to leave the workshop for almost any reason, and, although no participant ever said so explicitly, counseling broke up a daily routine described previously as boring, menial, and unprofitable. Thus, even though counseling was thought of as a means of addressing participants' personal problems, it also functioned as a way to alleviate the tedium of the workshop.

Training to Overcome Deficiencies

For most participants, the workshop was seen as a place they attended for work training in the absence of other options. As one individual said, "Well, I guess that I'm here because I needed to be trained; have training for a particular job . . . for any job in the community. [Staff] felt that I needed training before getting a job."

It was clear, however, that 1) almost no one left the workshop for a community job; 2) much of what people did was unchallenging, boring, and "babies' stuff"; and 3) the workshop existed in lieu of other vocational alternatives. For some, it was difficult to legitimate views of the workshop as a viable training experience because of the absence of participant success and stimulation. Pointing to such contradictions, one woman argued that staff treated participants like babies, "spoiling" them by not expecting quality work and good production but then expecting them to become competent workers. She noted, "Hey look, how can you expect me to act this and this and this way, when you are treating me the opposite way." A young man complained about staff "setting goals for the clients here, but when things remain stagnant, how can one even think about setting goals?" A woman who attended the workshop for 17 years had no delusions about the workshop's being a viable training experience: "They did a lot of damage to us. We would have been out in the community a long time ago if they hadn't taken that first director of Pioneer. We would have been out of here a long time and I wouldn't have been this dissatisfied."

Despite such criticisms, most of Pioneer's workshop participants sustained their image of the workshop as a training resource. And they often did so at their own expense, believing that they had been enrolled and retained in the workshop largely because of their own deficiencies. As one man lamented, "I've been here going on 8 years now. I don't know how much longer I am going to have to be here. It could be a permanent thing." Another individual described his resistance to the staff's remedial efforts:

> I used to make this weird noise and the staff would always tell me don't do that. Because if I do that noise then they wouldn't hire me out in the community and this and that. They were always saying to me do that, don't do this. When they'd tell me not to do it, I'd get mad you know and I used to do it more. The more they told me not to do it, I'd do it. But now I'm finally realizing that they told me this for my own good because they know that I do want to be put out in the community and work.

Relationships with Staff

Participants also assigned significance to the workshop because of their relationships with staff. Although some participants complained about being overprotected and restricted, most viewed staff as valued friends and the best sources of support. As one individual related,

> I mean, a lot of the staff are really understanding here and are very supportive, that's one thing that they do have. . . . And I really do appreciate all of the staff for their support and helping me out. And uh, Pioneer is really a good, good place. I really enjoy it here.

Another person thought that the staff's decisions for her were good ones: "Yes, I feel that whatever staff chose me to come here, I'm glad that I did come here . . . because I thought that the staff have used their [good] judgment on me."

As reflected by this woman, staff made many decisions for those attending Pioneer. In fact, given their limited ties with their families, participants depended on staff for virtually all major life decisions, ranging from when and what they ate to where they lived and worked. Moreover, the social activities and contacts of those attending the workshop were very circumscribed in that almost all work and leisure activities were agency sponsored and attended only by Pioneer participants and staff. As one woman noted, recreation and residential activities were all tied together in one package: "Well, I like the place, and there are a lot of recreational activities . . . like going to Blue Lake and the state fair. And the people here are very nice. Plus the residence. I like it there."

Given their tightly controlled social lives, it is understandable that many participants were apprehensive about the prospect of leaving the workshop. They wondered whether community employers would accept them, accommodate their needs, and give them adequate training and support when they needed it. Participants also worried about forming new relationships and getting back and forth from work—things that were not considerations in the workshop. One woman spoke about these concerns, confidently, although somewhat tenuously:

> It wouldn't be hard to make new friends or learn a job. It would be hard for them to break the ice toward me. And that means to understand me as a person, not just as someone in a wheelchair who cannot see who they're going to have to help in a lot of ways. . . . I'm willing to have patience with them as long as they're willing to have patience with me.

To many, the workshop meant security and predictability. This illustrates the kind of paradox that Pioneer created for its workshop participants. Although the workshop supposedly prepared people for community jobs, it actually provided the basis upon which participants' social and vocational lives rested, isolating them from the very people, places, and experiences they were purportedly being prepared to deal with.

Socializing with Friends

Pioneer, which provided both work and recreation activities, served as a major social medium for its participants. People mentioned things like "talking to friends I know," "finding how everyone is doing," "telling a joke my brother told me," and "catching up on everybody's news" as enjoyable activities.

Interviewers noted, however, that participants seemed less committed to their friendships than might have been expected given their long histories, shared experiences, and living situations. Very few workshop participants made attempts to stay in touch with their friends after workshop hours. People who lived in different locations rarely talked to each other, visited, or dined together in the evenings or on weekends unless they attended an agency-sponsored event. When individuals relocated to nearby cities, they were seldom heard from by their friends in the workshop.

It is hard to determine why these contacts were seemingly limited and so easily severed. Some participants claimed that they did not have close friends. As one man remarked, "I don't have any close friends. I have friends, but they aren't very close." When asked about close friends, another individual responded this way: "Oh boy, a long time ago maybe I could say, but right now I don't know. Maybe Martha."

Others referred to their reliance on external forces to gain access to friends, even romantic attachments. A young woman spoke longingly about her ex-boyfriend with whom she had shared a close personal relationship. His parents decided that he should come to their home about 80 miles away to live. Although the decision to move was unrelated to the relationship, it apparently served to terminate contact between the two people because of the high cost of long-distance telephoning and a lack of transportation. The young woman wondered whether she would ever find another boyfriend. Others referred to similar situations in which one partner relocated, and neither attempted to continue the relationship by telephoning, letter writing, or visiting.

Because of participants' restricted mobility, minimal financial resources, circumscribed living and working arrangements, and limited accessibility to communication opportunities, it is not surprising that the workshop assumed a dominant role in their social lives or that they had difficulty sustaining relationships outside of the workshop setting. It may be argued that external parties such as staff and family members actually controlled participants' social lives, for even simple tasks like making telephone calls and writing letters could be restricted by financial limitations, housing policies, and/or the need for assistance in transcribing or posting. Certainly the barriers to these tasks were not insurmountable. Nevertheless, pursuing an individualized social life was comparatively difficult and often discouraged by human services staff because of its incompatibility with preexisting schedules, activities, and resources.

Some participants were interested in pursuing social relationships outside of Pioneer, particularly with family members. Participants often talked about seeing their families more often or moving closer to relatives. Some had ongoing contact with members of their churches who often picked them up for Sunday services and invited them to church-sponsored activities.

A few people mentioned an interest in dating people who were not workshop participants. One woman thought she might have luck meeting potential partners when she got a job in the community. A man mentioned being interested in a woman at the adult home where he lived: "There's a lady [who] lives next door to me

. . . and she, uh, stops into my room every once in a while to talk, and likewise I do the same thing."

A woman—one of a handful of people who had worked previously in a community job—described the pain of losing her friend and co-worker when the person moved away:

> The Monday after the conference she came to me . . . and she said, "When you come back, I'm going to be gone," and I looked at her and I said, "Please don't say that to me"—it just hurt. . . . Then she says, "Pam, I hated to tell you this—I didn't want to leave, but I got transferred to California."

This relationship was unusual in that these friends did remain in contact with one another. Overall, however, very few people enjoyed sustained and consistent social relationships outside of the workshop. To do so would have required that Pioneer give priority, resources, and supports to developing and maintaining community relationships. As noted previously, however, Pioneer offered only circumscribed social routines and opportunities to its workshop participants and people in its community residence. Structured schedules and restricted resources dictated the intimate details of participants' lives, including how, when, with whom, and for how long they interacted. Consequently, many participants never experienced long-term, meaningful relationships outside of the workshop or aside from their immediate families and did not see themselves as valued, close friends or lovers. Apparently, the demands of the services system and, less frequently, the needs of families took precedence over participants' desires to form intimate social bonds.

Separation from Families

Most of the people who attended the workshop were sent from communities throughout New York. Professionals who knew about the workshop program considered it to be particularly well suited for people with blindness or visual impairments and multiple disabilities. As one professional who referred an individual to Pioneer from a city 300 miles away commented, "It was a wonderful program from our standpoint because it targeted specific disabilities and gave [people] a place to live and work all in one [agency]." Pioneer was one of the few agencies in the state that routinely accepted people who were classified as having both visual and multiple disabilities. As one workshop participant remembered, "My mother didn't know what to do with me, where to place me. After I left Batavia [a state school for people who were blind] she came here [to Pioneer] for a visit and seemed to like it."

Not all of the 21 people who attended the workshop at the time of the conversion lived in Pioneer's group home, but all 8 of those who lived in the group home attended the workshop. Other workshop participants lived in designated housing that often was arranged by Pioneer but supervised by other social services agencies. None of the Pioneer participants lived with their families. In fact, for all but three, family involvement was minimized by sheer distance, and most people went home infrequently. Family separations were early and consistent experiences of many Pioneer participants. Over half of the participants were separated from their families as young children to attend residential schools for people who were blind. The schools were often located far from home, and many at Pioneer knew each other from their days at those schools.

Remarks

Pioneer dominated people's lives, especially those who both lived and worked in agency-supervised settings. Even for participants who were involved with their families or had separate living arrangements, Pioneer controlled most essential elements of their lives. Although many workers disliked certain aspects of the agency or thought that attending the workshop was only temporary, their only consistent source of friends, income, and daily activities, however minimal or circumscribed, was Pioneer. The longer people stayed, the more such dependency served as security from the surrounding community. Some people came to think that they needed to be at Pioneer not only because it was their only option, but also because their disabilities required them to have a buffer from what they came to believe were the harsh realities of community life. Despite being in the workshop for years, earning low wages, and often performing boring or *make-work*, most individuals were generally accepting of their situations and trusted that staff knew what was best for them.

From the vantage points of some participants, families, and professionals, Pioneer was considered a dismal failure. From a public policy perspective, however, it filled a societal need by providing a sanctioned place to live and work for people considered to be incapable of functioning successfully or productively in their communities. As such, it served as a powerful socializing agent for people with disabilities, their families, and professionals in that it supposedly defined the proper roles of people with disabilities in society. A critical element of this socialization was Pioneer's bureaucratic and moral authority to relieve families of the troublesome financial, social, and psychological burdens of maintaining their offspring or siblings with disabilities at home.

DURING CONVERSION:
PERSPECTIVES ON WORKSHOP CHANGES

This section describes the diverse perspectives of participants on the workshop's conversion. They explained how they perceived the changes, identified what they saw as their primary employment interests and skills, and described what forms of assistance they needed to enter the competitive job market.

Worried About Change

When asked how she felt about the workshop's new direction, one woman remarked, "Oh, everyone else is thrilled. I'm the only one who isn't, you know." But she was not the only participant worried about change. The majority of her co-workers were equally concerned about the proposed conversion and its potential impact on their futures. Most had mixed feelings. Some were clearly skeptical; only a few were unequivocally supportive.

In some cases, participants' apprehensions were caused by the chaotic atmosphere created by the pending changes. Others equated the changes with past upheavals and promises that proved both upsetting and futile. In addition, many participants expressed a lack of confidence in the staff's knowledge, employer and community receptivity, and, in particular, their own abilities.

Chaotic Atmosphere   It is easy to understand the stresses felt by participants and staff when considered in light of the organizational upheaval that took place as part of the conversion. One woman complained that participants were being told over and over again that things were going to get better despite the fact that the situation seemed to be getting worse. The changes in management, mission, staff, and services were seen as sudden and dramatic, and a number of people talked about having problems adjusting to those changes. A handful of participants left the workshop, citing as reasons allegiance to the former director, uncertainty about future directions, and poor sleep due to stress. One young woman described the situation as chaotic and tense:

> It was stressful during the time when we had that other director . . . [because] there was no open communication with the board. Nothing. But when we had that open meeting [with the board], they never told us who the director was going to be. When the board told us things

were going to be good, when things began to be positive, I began to think positive.

Past Promises Unfulfilled   Numerous participants were openly skeptical of the proposed conversion in light of the broken promises they had endured in the past before Pioneer vowed to change. Participants complained that, over a period of many years, they were promised job placements that never materialized.

When the conversion began, a cadre of new staff whom participants did not know or trust were hired to implement supposedly new supported employment services. Many participants did not believe that new staff would do any better than did previous staff in fulfilling their promises. A number of participants did not trust that services would improve even if staff did pursue a new direction in service provision. Some were worried that they would not be prepared appropriately for, or would be "dumped" into, community jobs. As one woman said, "I have a fear of being left with nobody there to help me."

Lack of Confidence in People and Resources in the Community   Several participants clearly did not want to leave what they viewed as the secure atmosphere of the workshop. One young woman who had been at Pioneer for almost 6 years who worked in several short-term enclaves opted to go into another workshop instead of community employment. She expressed her feelings this way:

> When I heard the workshop was closing, I was scared. I knew I had to think of something quick. They wanted to put us out into the community. Some of those community jobs were OK, but they didn't always last that long. I just didn't want to be put out into the community. I had some experience with jobs in the community and I was not too thrilled with the jobs, and [employers] were not too thrilled with me either. I did not like working in the community.

Although most participants wanted to at least try community employment, many thought of change as frightening and the competitive work world as a difficult place in which to succeed. As one man put it, "Right now I feel it is time to get out of here, but going on interviews and stuff like that . . . sometimes it is scary." Some participants worried about the willingness of community employers to hire and to give them a chance to prove themselves. One man expressed his concerns this way: "My blindness is no real problem to me. My epilepsy is, and a prospective employer, I don't think, would want to take me on because of it. I'm not worried for myself, you see, people have all these stereotypes."

Not Being Ready Many people said that they were not ready to begin community employment. When asked how long he would need to get ready, one man replied, "about 10 years or so, 9 years, yeah." A woman responded this way to the same question: "I need a long time. I need a couple of years 'til I'm ready."

No one described clearly the kinds of skills they thought they would gain by remaining in the workshop. Many participants believed, however, that they lacked prerequisite skills and felt that they were being pushed into the community prematurely. One woman said that she was not ready to manage the strenuous nature of community work:

> The thing that I'm afraid of is the type of job that all of us that walk [are] placed on and not being able to hold [it] down, because like I said, I'm so accustomed to light jobs that can be done sitting down, and I'm not accustomed to the kind of jobs that those of us who can walk ought to be able to do because the kind of jobs that those of us who can walk ought to be able to do are more strenuous than what I'm accustomed to. And I'm afraid when I talk about it.

Another young woman complained that she just did not feel comfortable in the community, and she wished that staff respected her decision:

> I know I took a lot of people at Pioneer by surprise. They couldn't believe that I did not want to work in the community. My counselor kept telling me that I would be happier in the community because I would be making more money. I kept telling her that money could not buy me happiness. She just kind of turned her head. She didn't pay attention to me. It was more important for me to be in the environment that I was more comfortable with. Not everyone wants to be integrated back into the community. I sometimes think they forget about that.

Ready for Change

The sentiment expressed most often by participants about leaving the workshop could be characterized as cautious optimism. Most people were especially optimistic about trying something more challenging. One woman related that, "I can try. See, I would like to try and see how far I could get with [a community job]. . . . It sounds like it would be, I don't know how to word it . . . a lot of fun. You know, I want to try it and see how I can do." Another young woman expressed similar thoughts, adding that some changes might lead to others:

> It's the only way for me to see what life would be like . . . the best of all worlds, or the worst of all worlds. I want to start from getting a job

and then I would seriously think about if I would want to move out of the apartment. Maybe I never do, but at least it will give me the experience of where I tried something and it worked or it didn't work. But I didn't sit back and let it go away. I just kept right on doing it until, you know, there was nothing more to be done, and just, you know, say I tried, and just show people what kind of fighter I am.

Another individual was also positive about the chance for community employment if new opportunities were selected carefully and if she was provided some job security: "But I feel, you know, it's good to get out, find something that's worth my while. But I'd like to find something where I'm going to be happy, you know . . . where I'm going to stick. I'd like to stick there for awhile."

Few participants 1) embraced Pioneer's new direction wholeheartedly, 2) argued forcefully that the changes were long overdue, and/or 3) expressed unequivocally that it was "time to move on." Nevertheless, one woman applauded her sense that "This time maybe things are really going to shape up." Another individual noted confidently that, "You just have to show yourself. Just because you're multiply handicapped doesn't mean you can sit around and twiddle your thumbs." A third strong advocate for change expressed happiness not only for herself, but also for other workshop participants: "I've always wanted the change for me, but it's good to see other people get that kind of change . . . from the workshop to the community."

Job Interests, Skills, and Preferences Although Pioneer's workshop participants expressed some ambivalence about community employment, most were eager to discuss their job interests and skills. Despite what might be considered limited work experiences, everyone could identify potential jobs, tasks, or types of work that they thought they would be especially interested in or good at. Participants discussed a range of job interests. Some confined their interests to jobs they considered realistic and available; others discussed avocational interests, volunteer possibilities, and long- and short-term goals and concerns.

Participants' references to interests and skills overlapped. Comments about skills ranged from general assertions such as, "I'm good at doing most any kind of work" and "I am good at working with my hands" to more specific assertions like, "I have thought about doing clerical work, perhaps," "I'm real good with numbers," and "I'm real good at . . . typing." Some participants expressed their interests in terms of work types or environments (e.g., paperwork, work in a factory). Others thought of work environments differently. For example, a woman expressed a desire to find a job environment where she might indulge her avocational interests by "working in a . . . place where they have an organ." Others focused on finding jobs in relaxed environments with people who were friendly. One individual described his job interests this way: "either a musician's job, or a comedian's. I'd like to play rock-and-roll, or jazz, or folk music, or be a comedian . . . and tell jokes and that. Or is that more of a hobby?" A woman wanted to integrate her personal experiences into her employment goals, stating that: "Basically, my big thing now is to share my experiences with people that have been disabled, and to try to help them change their lives too."

Some workers drew routinely on previous work experiences within and outside of the workshop to assert their preferences. Both participants and staff referred to these limited work experiences as *potential job areas*. Some participants mentioned specific assignments they were given within the workshop, including receptionist, client aide, and work distributor positions. A woman who had been working for 2 months as the workshop's receptionist said, "I like it better out here [in the office area] . . . because it helped me to break out of my shell because I used to be real shy." Another individual described his work at the state fair this way:

> Well, I was at the state fair, which was August 28–September 7, and I was a rest room attendant at the fair and I made sure the bathroom was well supplied with toilet paper, paper towels, and soap and made sure that the seats were cleaned and the toilet and the floor [were] mopped. And I got a certificate stating that I had completed the job at the fair.

Reflecting on his potential job areas, this individual referred to his experiences at the fair, explaining that he would like to get "a job out in the community . . . for example, like at the end of the summer, I could work at the fair."

Because many of their previous community work experiences were brief, restricted, and/or infrequent, participants tended to be tentative and pessimistic when discussing their chances for employment in the community. One participant commented that, "Well, it could be a volunteer job," as if a paid job might be asking for too much. Perhaps as a result of her years of waiting, one woman said that she wanted to work "someplace where the people are friendly and they don't hang up on you"; she then added, "but that will take years."

Support Requirements Just about everyone in the workshop acknowledged that they needed some type or level of assistance to succeed in the community. Sometimes this assistance was considered modest; at other times it was considered substantial. As one woman said, "There are certain things that they need to know. I need aide assistance, I need transportation, and it's going to be an ongoing thing with me." Overall, support requirements fell into four broad and often overlapping categories: task support, moral support, equipment and adaptations, and assistance with transportation and travel.

A number of participants felt that they needed accommodations from their employers in order to do their job tasks successfully. One participant, for example, said that a supervisor would have to understand "the fact I am slow" or that "every once in a while I might lose my train of thought . . . and I might need somebody to tell me where I left off."

The perceived need for moral support took many forms, but the general consensus was that participants wanted to know that a support person would be available if one was needed. No one felt the need for much job coach assistance after getting started in a job. People generally hoped, however, that there would be someone whom they could call if they had questions or "when I am having anxiety attacks about these things."

Workshop participants had specific suggestions concerning their needs for equipment and adaptations. Word processors, braille equipment, and other high-tech devices were mentioned as potential aids. Some participants talked enthusiastically about the special features, such as memory and portability, of some of these devices.

Transportation and travel were also common concerns for those who talked about community jobs. Both staff and workers talked about the paratransit system with great frustration. People commented that the buses were unreliable and often late and that they broke down from time to time. In addition, the system was limited by a paucity of times and areas of service, and accessibility was a serious problem because users were required to make daily reservations, regardless of whether they had fixed schedules or not.

A few participants circumvented these problems by taking regular buses. One man literally took matters into his own hands. Like most other Pioneer participants, he could not obtain *mobility clearance*. This meant that a mobility instructor would not certify that he was able to travel alone. Unlike most others, however, he took regular buses anyway: "Well, Pioneer isn't too impressed with my mobility because, ah, I never really got clearance. . . . I was just going to teach myself, and I know how to get around downtown." One individual addressed the need for transportation assistance and the lack of a reliable transit system by insisting on getting a job close to home. "No trucking all over, excuse the expression, hell's creation" was how this participant put it.

In addition to citing concerns about getting to work, many participants said that learning to travel in a new environment would be "scary." Some mentioned that the specialized services of an orientation and mobility (O&M) instructor would be a necessary support for community employment. Others thought that O&M supports could be provided by job coaches.

Remarks

One of the major arguments against conversion was that people with severe disabilities require sheltered facilities as a choice in the continuum of services. Others contended that participants were not ready and did not want to leave the workshop. This chapter indicates that the issue of choice is very complex.

When real change began at Pioneer after years of rhetoric but no action, people understandably became anxious. For most, the familiarity, safety, and comfort of the workshop contrasted sharply with the sudden emphasis on employment, an end that for so long was described as unattainable. Although there were a few participants who argued forcefully that they were not ready for community entry and wanted to remain in a workshop, the vast majority ultimately expressed dislike for the workshop and did not wish to remain there.

Certainly, the workshop participants were frightened of change, uncertain of their abilities, anxious about the community's initial response to them, and concerned about continuing staff assistance in the future. The reasons for their apprehensions were, however, as related to the chaotic conditions surrounding Pioneer's conversion and past staff incompetence as to people's belief in the benefits of the workshop. Furthermore, most of those who initially expressed reluctance to leave the workshop changed their minds as they developed closer relationships with new staff and observed their colleagues as they obtained and became satisfied with community employment.

The next section illustrates that most workshop participants eventually proved themselves to be capable of securing and functioning in community jobs successfully. Moreover, despite their fears, their limited community work experiences, and the fact that they were often considered by Pioneer staff to be vocationally naive and needy, a surprising number of workshop participants were reasonably well informed and realistic about their vocational aspirations and support needs. This belied the view that individuals with severe disabilities could not make employment decisions, formulate realistic vocational goals, and/or pursue vocational choices successfully.

AFTER CONVERSION: CONTRASTING
IMAGES, EXPECTATIONS, AND OUTCOMES

In order to understand the impressions that staff had of workshop participants and to assess the legitimacy of those impressions in light of participants' eventual achievements, several case studies are presented along with a follow-up description of what participants accomplished as the workshop underwent conversion. Included in these brief studies are professional assessments of participants' psychological characteristics; perceived physical, social, and emotional attributes; and prognoses for successful transitions to community employment.

The contrast between what was written about participants in their files and their postconversion outcomes is not explored here to imply that placement in the community suddenly made participants' lives perfect. Instead, the purpose is to illustrate 1) the power of human services professionals, environments, and activities in creating negative images about people; and 2) the capacity of people to respond positively and dramatically when such external conditions change.

The chapter concludes with descriptions of the lifestyle and personal changes experienced by those who left the workshop and some of the concerns that participants expressed regarding the workshop's conversion.

Case Studies of Workshop Participants

William Adey   William Adey was described in his file as having "congenital blindness, mild mental retardation, hypertension, Cushing syndrome, and cerebral palsy." In 1986, a rehabilitation counselor wrote that although he was "well groomed and neatly kept" and always willing to please others, he was "easily excited and frustrated . . . verbose, easily discouraged, and uncooperative when asked to quiet down or stop talking. . . . We believe this is because [William] lacks good judgement and common sense."

The following statements were taken from a 1986 report written by Pioneer's vocational evaluator about this man:

- "Unable to focus attention for more than 30 seconds"

- "Though capable, decisions are usually shallow and based on incomplete knowledge"
- "Problems of more than one step . . . beyond his capacity to solve"
- "Trusted to work alone if task was simple enough"
- "No work tolerance for even slight pressure"

A 1987 report written by a workshop supervisor stated that William's "training plan indicated successful completion of stated goal [to reduce voice volume during conversations]. [He] spoke at a comfortable volume 75% of the time over 13 weeks. He then achieved [temporary] supported work placement at the recycling center." Ironically, William had to increase his voice volume at the recycling center due to the high noise level there.

Since this time, he has been employed in several jobs but has held a clerical position at a local university since 1989. His job entails working between 20 and 30 hours per week and performing a variety of tasks, including filing, photocopying, mail sorting, and other clerical duties. He lives in an apartment with a roommate. He indicated to an interviewer that he enjoys his job very much and would not want to return to the workshop:

> Oh, no. [The workshop] was so long ago. I'm here now. Everyone here are friends, and I really like it a lot. . . . Remember when I worked at the grocery stores. I didn't like those jobs at all. . . . But this [job] is perfect. I would go back to the shop to see everyone. But I would work here.

When he was in the workshop, most people called him Willy. Now he asks to be called William, which he sees as a more adult name. According to his supervisor, William knows his job; does it well; and speaks and acts maturely, appropriately, and with self-confidence. He still likes to socialize with his co-workers and is reminded occasionally to return to work.

Jerry Bern Jerry Bern's case file stated that he had congenital blindness and epilepsy. He was described by a clinical psychologist in this way:

> His overuse of denial and dissociation as coping mechanisms suggest that he should be directed toward a solitary vocational field where decision-making responsibilities are minimal. He clearly has untapped cognitive potential and verbal strengths to capitalize on beyond sheltered work. However, he is multiply disabled and so may realistically not be capable of progressing beyond same.

A social worker's case notes about the same man stated the following: "It is not believed that [Jerry] can be successful in a vocational training program, nor could he move on from a sheltered environment. It seems appropriate to close his case." In 1987, Pioneer's vocational evaluator wrote that Jerry "requires constant prompting and supervision in the workshop setting . . . exhibits resistive behavior in most areas."

Before initiating the proposed changes, interviewers shot videotape footage of people working in the workshop. The tape showed Jerry sleeping and doing make-work. What the videotape did not emphasize, however, was that Jerry is an engaging, inquisitive, and stimulating person who had taken some college-level courses, held high vocational aspirations, and could engage people around him in interesting conversations about world affairs, music, and books.

Luckily, one of Jerry's evaluators was correct in saying that he was "restive," which perhaps accounted for his accomplishments outside of the workshop. In the 6 years since he left the workshop, he has held several community jobs. After working in a newspaper office as a telemarketer in 1988 and for the Red Cross soliciting blood donors on the telephone in 1989, Jerry now has a job at a local insurance company. He works 20 hours per week answering incoming telephone calls for the company's agents. If the insurance agents are not available, Jerry takes messages. He also transcribes insurance interviews.

Jerry contrasted his views of sheltered work and community work this way:

> Well, sheltered work was a little different. All we did was put useless things together, take them apart, and start over again. That doesn't make you feel very good about yourself. [My] community job is OK. It gives me a paycheck at the end of the week. I wouldn't want to do it forever, but it's competitive employment. That makes a big difference. I need to have a reason to get up in the morning. It's much better now, even if the work can get difficult sometimes. As for me, I'm going to stick at this job for as long as I can handle it or until I find something better.

Although Jerry's work life has improved markedly since his workshop days, his living situation has remained stagnant. He lives in a rooming house that serves primarily people with disabilities and/or who are older. He receives medical supervision and is given meals. According to one of his friends who is a community professional, Jerry could be in "a lot better living situation." Reportedly, the reluctance of other housing programs to take him, the extended waiting periods for many housing programs, and Jerry's seeming unwillingness to change his residence all contribute to his current living situation.

Jon McConnel Jon McConnel, a man who was described as having blindness, mental retardation, and mild cerebral palsy, was in the workshop for 12 years. As a workshop supervisor wrote,

> Mr. [McConnel] is best suited for work in a work activity shop where the requirements are not as great as those of a sheltered workshop. Relatively simple, undemanding tasks are best suited for him to guarantee his continued sense of accomplishment and fulfillment as a person and worker.

The workshop's social worker wrote,

> Our consulting neuropsychiatrist feels that [Jon] has reached a plateau in terms of his functional capacity, and that when stressed he "just stops in his tracks." Now that [Jon] has reached a plateau in his development . . . we would reemphasize attention to ADL [activities of daily living] and recreational training, hoping that a spin-off effect would be our trying him in more complex jobs within the sheltered workshop.

Fortunately, Jon progressed beyond ADL, recreational training, and more complex workshop jobs to hold several community jobs. He held his first job in a motel laundry for several years before being laid off because of slowing business. He then began another laundry job in which he has worked for about 9 months. Jon described his laundry work as follows:

> There are washers and I load those and the dryers and unload them, and I fold stuff up. I like the work—it's good. The laundry is fun. I'll be working here for a long time, not just for awhile. I don't want to quit this job here.

In describing both workshop and community jobs that he has held, Jon related,

> Oh, [Pioneer] was all right, except that I wasn't making a whole bunch of money. But I don't know if I can compare that because I was at the shop for training to get another job.
> The workshop changes did change my life a lot. I was glad to get another job because of the money. It's made a difference having more money. I can put more in the bank for saving. I like to buy more clothes; go to the barber shop; go out for breakfast, lunch, or supper; or go to a movie. I like the clock I bought. Before I couldn't do much because I didn't have much money.

Although Jon has experienced some ups and downs during his community employment, he has left little doubt that he is capable of succeeding far beyond sheltered workshop levels. Moreover, his living situation has changed dramatically for the better and likewise reflects that Jon is a far more capable individual than his workshop assessments indicated.

For some time Jon expressed dissatisfaction with the group home in which he lived and requested a change. He moved recently to an apartment that he "loves." There he lives with a roommate of his choosing and receives 24-hour supervision from staff who live in a separate apartment.

Dashielle Vickers   Dashielle Vickers was described in her file as having congenital deafness, blindness due to retinitis pigmentosa (RP), and cerebral palsy. A psychiatrist described her in 1987 as "providing clear-cut behavioral evidence of ongoing psychosis. All the symptoms suggest that her reality orientation is imperfectly present." A staff member wrote that she was "preoccupied with physical symptoms, obesity, and overeating." Although she was rated as being appropriate for supported employment in 1987, she was still in the workshop 2 years later and was named by several staff as the person they felt would be hardest to place in a community job.

In fact, Dashielle was the first workshop participant to obtain a community job, a job that she has held since March of 1988. She works 20 hours per week at a check printing company putting checkbooks into plastic covers. She earns nearly $10 per hour and works virtually independently.

Dashielle's supervisors and co-workers had trouble communicating with her at first because they did not know sign language. She became socially isolated because of this. Consequently, some of her co-workers learned some tactile sign language so that they could communicate with her, eliminate the need for on-site job coaching, and minimize even the periodic involvement of Pioneer staff in work matters.

Several years ago Dashielle became very depressed and began to act aggressively toward housemates and staff. Following the recommendations of a psychiatrist, Pioneer staff reluctantly hospitalized her. She remained in the hospital for several months. During that period, her employer granted her a leave of absence, holding her job open until she could return to work.

Dashielle has expressed an interest in starting her own chair caning and repair business, services for which there is a great demand in her area. She is working presently with staff and area businesspeople to start this business.

Dashielle also has changed her living situation so that it is more to her liking. She resided previously in a group home with seven other people, but she now lives with a roommate in their own apartment. Both residents receive some support, but the amount of staff assistance has diminished to the point at which it will likely be terminated in the near future.

Len Redman   Len Redman was described as having blindness, encephalopathy, and mental retardation. He was in Pioneer's workshop for 11 years. The agency's vocational evaluator wrote,

> [Len] will find simple one-step assembly tasks challenging. I think these kind of tasks are best suited to his capabilities and limitations. Complicated tasks will only frustrate him and anyone trying to train him. Mr. [Redman's] overall assessment indicates his behaviors are appropriate for sheltered employment as opposed to competitive employment.

In 1988, Len began working in the laundry at a Marriott hotel. He remained there for over 5 years until he relocated to another town to be closer to his family. He said that he liked his job at Marriott better than Pioneer's workshop because he got benefits, including vacation and sick time. He also spoke of having money for vacations to visit family and friends in other parts of the state.

Interviewers reminded Len of some of the worries that he had expressed about getting a job and asked whether those worries materialized. He had been worried about transportation and the "people out there." When asked how those things worked out, he replied: "good; no problems."

Linda Chow   Linda Chow was described as "a neat worker who had good attendance and was punctual, highly intelligent, well coordinated, with good spatial, memory, and tactile skills." In addition, she was assessed as being "disruptive and guilt ridden," often because of poor work performance. She was also viewed as having "no mobility skills" and as "needing prompting on personal care and appearance."

Linda's most recent rehabilitation plan included goals to "replace her disruptive behavior with requests to see her counselor" and to "learn three new tasks at the workshop." Apparently, Linda was not considered a good candidate for competitive work by Pioneer staff because no plans existed to assist her in finding community employment. Linda herself also had some reservations about community employment, noting that "The community job thing was worrisome. I wondered what kind of a job they would place me in. I couldn't believe that I would keep jobs for a very long time. . . . I didn't know how I would do."

Interestingly, a letter from a consulting clinical psychologist written 13 years prior to Linda's getting a community job was contained in Linda's file. In it, the psychologist articulated that the major source of Linda's problems was her lifestyle as a consumer in the human services system. This reflected views far ahead of those operating at Pioneer at that time:

> Ms. [Chow's] fantasy orientation is not mental illness; it is an adaptation to sheltering, being idle and friendless. She will outgrow that orientation to the extent that she spends time involved in work, satisfying social relationships, reading and culture, and other more satisfying nonfantasy pursuits. She wouldn't sit around imagining her stories if she had something more satisfying to do.

Linda has held two jobs since Pioneer began to emphasize community employment. She did assembly work and, more recently, telemarketing for a local waste management company where she worked for 2 years. Currently unemployed, she was laid off by a newly hired supervisor who thought that she was not productive enough. Linda still wants to work and is looking for another job.

Her living situation has been more stable than have her recent employment circumstances. Previously, she lived for about 10 years with several older women who agreed to take her in after she left her apartment. When one of the women died, Linda had to move into a boarding home. Soon after she began a relationship with a man whom she met at the boarding home, and they expressed an interest in living together. This was arranged through a local housing agency, and Linda is living currently with her boyfriend and several roommates in a housing situation she likes.

Amy Lou Gronchick   Amy Lou Gronchick was described in a 1985 vocational evaluation as "an immature, childlike woman with extreme sensory and spatial deficits" requiring counseling and occupational therapy (OT). In the same year a rehabilitation counselor at the state agency of vocational rehabilitation wrote that Amy Lou

> [had] no outdoor mobility, [was] in need of supervision in most areas, [had] poor social adjustment, low frustration, poor work progress, habits and attention, [was] rigid, complaining, untidy, careless, and requiring constant attention.

On the positive side, she had a "good sense of humor," was punctual, and made "good progress in counseling, OT, and social adjustment training."

Despite her positive attributes, she was apparently not thought to be suitable for competitive work because there was no mention of her being considered for community employment. In fact, there was more evidence that staff had serious doubts about her ability to do even simple workshop tasks.

Amy Lou was not much more optimistic or enthusiastic than were staff about her leaving the workshop. This is not to say that she liked the workshop because she described Pioneer as "bugging her," particularly the staff and other workers. She nevertheless insisted that she "just wasn't ready to go into the community right now."

Amy Lou was convinced gradually to try a community job after many other participants left the workshop and could report their enjoyment. She was persuaded to accept an unpaid job at a nursing home playing the piano, one of her favorite activities. Once she was familiar with being outside the workshop and confident that adequate transportation could be arranged, Amy Lou agreed to try a paid job cleaning motel rooms. Reportedly, she liked the work but was only moderately productive. After returning to the nursing home, she was offered a 10-hour-per-week position preparing meals. She has been working at that job for over 2 years and told an interviewer that she likes the job a lot, earns a lot of money, and is no longer bothered by the people at the workshop who used to "bug" her. She added the following: "[I have] to go to work every day or [I'm] just not right. I can't stay at home all day, you know."

Amy Lou's living situation also has improved dramatically. She lived formerly in Pioneer's group home with seven other people. Most of these people worked with Amy Lou in the workshop, and she did not get along well with many of them. Amy Lou has since moved into her own apartment with one of the friends she had from the group home. They receive 24-hour supervision from Pioneer staff.

Remarks

Workshop participants underwent a variety of vocational evaluations regularly. Individuals' records revealed descriptions that were heavily deficit based, containing relatively few examples of individuals' abilities. Professionals most often recommended services to "fix" people, targeting isolated and nonfunctional goals with meaningless criteria to justify the continued placement of consumers in the workshop.

LIFESTYLE AND PERSONAL CHANGES AFTER CLOSURE

Almost all of the workshop participants felt that their lives had changed for the better as a result of leaving the workshop. Many spoke of experiencing personal growth and of having increased expectations of themselves and others, new opportunities, and better options and choices. Many also spoke about having money to do more of the things they liked. As one man said,

> I didn't make much money at Pioneer. You'd make around $1 an hour. Now I'm making around $5 an hour and working more hours. I never had some things like much money. But now I have some money to do things. I'm not the richest man in the world, but you never know.

Some participants emphasized that community employment entailed an overall improvement in working conditions as compared to the workshop even though community employment was more demanding. One woman put it this way: "Well, one good change was that I got a good job. I've got a preference. . . . I work from 8:30 [A.M.] to 3:30 in the afternoon and I am pretty tired. I was pretty wiped out from that."

Another individual referred to personal growth as he talked about his community job:

> I've grown from the inside and the outside. I've learned a lot and grown physically and mentally. Now I think I can do other things. If they hadn't got me started finding my first job I think I would still be there [in the workshop]. I've grown to do a lot more than I did back then.

A woman also described a growing confidence in her abilities and a heightened enthusiasm for her work:

> I thought I would never do advocacy work again. And now everything is coming about the way I wanted. And I'm pretty glad for myself. When I was at the workshop I started a self-advocacy group. But now I'm taking my experiences to the community so I feel really good about it.

Even though one former workshop participant won the *Salesperson of the Month* award, she decided to quit her job as a telemarketer. Apparently, working made her confident in the fact that she could be a productive person capable of getting a job that was better than telemarketing. She said that a key to improvement was more education. Describing her decision to complete her general equivalency diploma (GED), she said,

> I started going to school because I wanted a better job. Don't listen to teachers who tell you to quit school. I went to school for awhile and they said I couldn't learn any more. My parents listened to them and after that I was home for 17 years before I went to [Pioneer's] workshop and home.

Whether referring to starting a new job, returning to school, or learning something new about themselves, many participants exuded a sense of freedom as they discovered new options. As one man noted, personal power and control are implied in the uncertainty of new opportunities: "Maybe I'll stay at Denny's all my life. Maybe someday I'll do something completely different. You never know. It depends on how it goes."

Meeting New People, Missing Old Friends

Another lifestyle change that participants mentioned took place in their social lives. Many talked about meeting new people at work as well as about missing the friends they made at Pioneer. As Jon McConnel said, "The people [in my community job] are nice. They help me out, like with folding sheets and stuff. I talk to them but not during work, on break time." Another man mentioned going bowling with his co-workers, attending various get-togethers from time to time, and getting rides home from the cook on Saturday nights.

In reflecting on the importance of her friends at Pioneer, one woman said, "I want to keep in touch with all my old friends that I've worked with, and you know to be a part of them too. I don't want to let go of anything like that just because the shop closed. I don't want to lose friendships over it."

Negative Impressions of Change

Not everyone was thrilled with the changes that occurred in their lives. One woman objected to Pioneer closing its workshop and felt that too many changes took place too quickly. These changes affected her schedule, her daily activities, and the people with whom she worked. As one of two participants who opted to go to another workshop, this woman contended that, "I believe in supported work, but I don't believe in forcing everybody to go for it 100% if they're just not into it. Some people just aren't into community employment–type things." In describing her "new" life, this woman related that,

> [The workshop I now attend] is operated about the same as [Pioneer], but you get more pay. We stuff envelopes, do boxing and bagging of different things. Sometimes I get bored there, but for the most part it's OK. . . . My working situation could be better. Some of the people I work with really bother me and I feel as though I don't have any freedom there. Some of the [service coordinators] really push their people around and don't listen to their real problems. People are always telling me what to do and never listen to what I have to say. I just don't feel as though they care about me as a person. Sometimes I wonder if I should leave, but I plan to stay there for the time being. If [Pioneer were] still open I would still be there, that's for sure.

Some participants commented on specific aspects of their jobs that were problematic. Some wanted more working hours. Others did not like their jobs and had already quit or been fired. Several participants said that they were lonely in their jobs and did not feel like they were a part of their workplaces. As one woman said, "It's hard for them to break the ice toward me."

SUMMARY

Although some participants were dissatisfied with the changes at Pioneer and experienced difficulties in specific work situations, nearly every workshop participant demonstrated that he or she could achieve significant employment and community living success. This fact stood in marked contrast to participants' files, which contained reports that were overwhelmingly negative, highlighted shortcomings, portended community failure, and often neglected participants' perspectives.

Long-term staff impressions and stereotypes, restrictive settings and evaluations, and limited work opportunities and tasks created a self-perpetuating, self-fulfilling cycle of low staff expectations that led ultimately to workshop participants experiencing menial, low-paying, restrictive work; individual apathy; poor performance; and stagnant outcomes. Rather than viewing participants' problems as results of the workshop's environment, activities, and expectations, staff attributed those problems to participants' deficits. Consequently, staff initiated long, often futile efforts to ameliorate real as well as imaginary deficiencies through a nearly endless array of arbitrary behavior management and/or counseling programs. Such programs had little or nothing to do with better community employment preparation because they were more directed toward heightening workshop management and control. Therefore, they failed miserably to improve community opportunities for workshop participants.

When workshop staff became truly committed to achieving community-based outcomes and got rid of the paternalistic, deficit-laden, readiness mentality that pervaded Pioneer, previous assessments were refuted and significant changes occurred in the workshop participants. Participants who were formerly considered to be immature, intolerant, appropriate only for sheltered work, psychotic, disruptive, guilt ridden, and/or in need of constant prompting and prodding not only had insightful ideas about their own vocational interests and possibilities, but achieved significant employment success as well.

Those who did obtain community jobs found that many of their fears did not materialize. Once participants began community work, they felt much better about their employment potential, pay, supports, and skills. Furthermore, the quality of their lives improved appreciably. This is not intended to say that all facets of their lives improved as well. Although community jobs became the highlight of some participants' days, their lives outside of work often continued to be socially isolated and unsatisfactory. Therefore, it is shortsighted to think about converting or closing sheltered workshops without addressing the broader community and human services issues that continue to isolate and exclude people with disabilities.

There were two participants who opted to continue sheltered work and eventually were referred to another local facility. For those who may want to remain in a sheltered situation on a short- or long-term basis, the extent to which their concerns, interests, and issues can be addressed within the broad, diverse settings of the surrounding community must be determined. Isn't this the approach used by typical community members as they strive to find a place in their communities? The question to be asked is not whether individuals in sheltered workshops are ready to enter their communities, but rather are their communities ready to abolish the barriers, excuses, and policies that preclude their full-fledged entry and membership.

The pessimistic reports and restrictive practices that are documented in this chapter were not meant by staff to be intentionally cruel or malicious. In fact, most Pioneer participants were well liked by staff, and staff believed fervently that they were providing valuable services.

Indeed, inappropriate practices have not continued just because of staff inadequacies, but because a long tradition of societal devaluation, though often latent, is still implemented in existing human services agencies. As noted in Chapter 1, the idea of thinking about people with disabilities in terms of what they need has been perpetuated by cultural beliefs, economic values, political forces, and outmoded service traditions. The comments and descriptions that are presented in this chapter, however, articulately affirm their ability to speak for themselves and their right to be taken seriously. Chapter 10 of this book discusses in more detail why one-sided human services practices regarding people with severe disabilities continue, how the traditional human services system reinforces such misguided efforts, and what alternatives are available to realign the emphasis of the human services field.

5

Stakeholder Perspectives

Despite years of staff rhetoric about getting community jobs for Pioneer's workshop participants, once the reality and magnitude of the conversion were understood, many of the workshop participants were fearful and unsure about the agency's new direction. Individual fears were alleviated, however, as staff began to help participants think about, plan, and pursue their vocational preferences and as participants began to find community jobs. Becoming more comfortable with the proposed conversion seemed to be related to perceiving linkages between that conversion and participants' involvement in planning their own lives. It was imperative that each participant have an active voice in planning his or her future as well as an opportunity to take part in the process of agency conversion.

As with any significant change, people are often reluctant to embrace a new way of doing things, especially if they are still vested philosophically and practically in the old way. It was this way with many stakeholders as Pioneer's conversion process began. According to staff who had been with Pioneer for years, the proposed conversion was threatening and did not seem to be in the best interests of the people receiving services. For the small number of families who were involved in the lives of their offspring or siblings, reactions to the conversion were mixed and ranged from their being thrilled to their being so upset that they pulled their offspring or siblings out of Pioneer's program immediately.

Board members knew that change was necessary for Pioneer's survival, but they did not have a vision of what that change should entail or how it should occur. Most board members were overly protective of the workshop participants and did not believe that they could work in the community.

Representatives of New York's offices of VESID, MR/DD, and the CBVH were among those most supportive of Pioneer's changes.

Although they advocated for a shift to community employment, however, they had not envisioned total conversion for Pioneer and lacked confidence in Pioneer's ability to initiate such a conversion effort.

Just as it was important to understand the perspectives of workshop participants on the conversion process, it was also critical to know how others involved with Pioneer perceived the situation. Only then could their issues of concern, fears, and needs be identified and addressed. This chapter describes the perspectives of workshop staff, the board of directors, funding organizations, and parents during the conversion process. People's reactions to the initial changes are contrasted with later attitudes that were more positive and supportive. The factors that prompted the conversion and retrospective thoughts about the conversion process are described as well.

INITIAL REACTIONS TO CHANGE

Pioneer was under pressure from funding organizations, advocates, and some workshop participants to provide community employment opportunities, but no one was advocating publicly for total conversion to community employment. The only person espousing conversion initially was Pioneer's new executive director. Most stakeholders were skeptical about the agency's ability to undertake such a conversion effort.

Skepticism About the Board of Directors

Because state funding organizations had worked with Pioneer in the past and were aware of the agency's fiscal difficulties and board members' traditional perspectives on vocational services, they doubted the board's willingness to abolish the sheltered workshop in favor of community employment. In fact, the impetus for conversion ultimately came from outside the agency, and many people actually blamed the board for its lack of program leadership and preoccupation with fund-raising. As one funding organization representative put it, "[The agency] seems to be without direction from governing authority. Lack of commitment to anything but fund-raising is not sufficient. You have a board of fund-raisers, not a board of directors."

Skepticism regarding the actions of the board of directors continued, both internally and externally, even after the conversion process was underway:

I think most of the board has their own mission as opposed to what the mission of the Center is. The board sees itself as just fund-raising. The agency sees itself as supported employment and establishing a rehab program for clients to get into the real world, to get successful job placements, and to function. Other than belonging to the same organization, I don't see the two mixing.

Board Member Concerns

As the conversion to community employment began, board members realized that many people in the community and within the agency were scrutinizing their actions: "[Funding sources] were looking at us like we didn't know what we were doing. And maybe we didn't, to be honest about it. Maybe we were overprotective. We had a group of people [in the workshop] and we were trying to overprotect them."

For the most part, board members were supportive of the new direction not because they believed in the abilities of the participants, but because they knew that Pioneer had to change its practices in order to survive. A few board members actually believed, however, that conversion was right for the people receiving services. They observed participants in the workshop and felt that they could do more. But the workshop was not the place to train them. One board member concluded that "One of the things I noticed about the workshop was that there was never enough work. People really needed to move on to be trained in competitive employment."

Although they were acutely aware of the pressure to do something different, some board members were skeptical about conversion. As one individual said, "I wasn't that keen on it, to be honest about it . . . but it was a situation that was 'wait and see.' If somebody comes in with a new idea, when you're my age you normally don't support it. We resist change too, you know what I mean."

Other board members had doubts about the employment potential of people in the workshop because of the severity of their disabilities: "I'm still wondering, but [the executive director] maintains that everybody is employable. You're talking about unpredictable behavior problems, when someone goes into an emotional fit, that type of thing." The disabilities of some workshop participants were considered to be "overwhelming": "When supported employment was introduced to us, I just couldn't quite see where that thing would fit with people who have catastrophic handicaps."

Some felt that the business community would never accept the workshop participants: "There will never be a time when all clients will be able to be placed in positions in business. There will always be some that business will be incapable of absorbing." Most board members viewed the people in the workshop as members of a happy family who needed care, not as oppressed but capable individuals.

Skepticism About the Director's Abilities

Some stakeholders were unsure of the new director's ability to lead Pioneer through the conversion process. Because the director was a faculty member at the local university before taking over at Pioneer, some funding organization representatives, agency staff, and local service providers did not believe that he knew what he was doing: "Some of the staff were thinking: 'Oh boy, here's this professor from the college. He's going to come down and make things better, right? He's never run a sheltered workshop before. He doesn't know the first thing about it.' " The fact that he was taking over Pioneer, an agency with a troubled past, added to people's doubts about him: "Just wait until this academician is down here and tries to do things, especially with *that* agency."

Staff Concerns

Workshop staff felt threatened by the proposed conversion from the start. The question pervasive among staff was, "What will it mean for me and my job?" They were told that they would become primarily CJSs (later called CECs; see Chapter 3). They then took it upon themselves to decide whether they wanted to stay or leave. Some left before the new director even started. Many left because they did not want to, or felt that they could not, be effective CJSs. A new staff member reflected on someone who tried to make the job shift but eventually left the agency:

> I think he tried really hard to make it make sense for him. I think that he could understand the logic in it, but he still maintained a lot of his old values in terms of even some real basic issues like who is worthy of working or how much effort does this person deserve, and I think because of those conflicts it made it much more difficult for him to sell what it is we do here to the community.

Like some board members, staff expressed concern about breaking up the group in the workshop and losing the family atmosphere: "As a sheltered workshop, it is one big family." Others had doubts about the abilities of some participants to work:

> I think I thought different things on different days, depending on the morale in the shop. Some days I thought this is crazy—there is no way this is going to work. Other days when I really understood what it was all about I began to think differently. I could see some people in the shop in a regular job. Some people, I'll be honest, I couldn't see them being out.

Reactions of State Funding Organizations

Although personnel from state funding organizations were skeptical about Pioneer's conversion efforts, the regional directors of VESID, MR/DD, and the CBVH were supportive of the conversion to community employment. Community pressure from families, advocates, and people with disabilities for change to more integrated employment opportunities was cited as a positive force that pushed funding organizations toward supported employment: "We've had community pressure here that has been steady enough on everybody so that a lot of . . . [funding sources] have wanted to change."

Funding organizations spoke about their efforts to nudge other agencies in this direction:

> What we've been trying to do is to get those agencies who have decided to be entirely sheltered workshops to open up their services, to get job coaches in the community . . . putting RFPs [requests for proposals] out for the supported work money, all those things.

Although advocating for movement toward supported employment, none of these state funding organizations spoke about conversion. This may explain their skepticism when Pioneer's new director began to plan for a complete conversion openly. Some people believed that there would continue to be a need for a place to which people could go when they were out of work: "If anything happens that the economy worsens, where are [the supported employees] all going to go? It's a scare tactic, but I still think we're going to need an enclave or safe haven for in-between."

Despite the favorable dispositions of funding organizations toward supported employment, the funding situation was far from ideal for an agency experiencing conversion. Funding organizations acknowledged that supported employment in the community was underfunded in the state of New York at the time of Pioneer's conversion:

> We grossly underfund the real cost of supported work. We're paying probably close to half [of the actual cost]. We basically pay $15 an hour. The calculations of the local agencies [that] provide supported employment services . . . I think it comes out to $24–$26 an hour. And what agencies are finding is that the only way they can survive is to take in a mix of clients, some who need less follow-along.

So, in New York at the time of Pioneer's conversion, it was more profitable for agencies to run sheltered workshops, and funding organizations were thus aware of the uphill battle that Pioneer faced financially.

Concerns of Families, Parents, and Guardians

As discussed previously, most of the participants in Pioneer's workshop came from other parts of New York. This resulted in less family involvement than might have been expected if families lived nearby. There were, however, families who lived near Pioneer who maintained close ties with their offspring or siblings. A handful of other families maintained regular contact despite their living hundreds of miles away. After receiving a letter from the new director that described the proposed conversion for Pioneer, some families called or wrote to obtain more information or to clarify certain points.

Predictably, most families were skeptical about Pioneer's changes. Despite its purported mission to find community jobs for workshop participants, Pioneer had established its workshop firmly as a long-term sheltered setting. Most families considered this to be an acceptable situation, and, despite the director's letter, many reacted to unfounded rumors or were misinformed about the pending conversion.

Soon after the new director took over, he announced his intentions to convert the agency and eventually close the workshop. Families began writing, calling, and responding in protest. One family decided to remove their son from Pioneer's workshop and enroll him in another workshop closer to their home. Another parent, a man who lived nearby, came to Pioneer and demanded angrily to see the director. He reminded the director that he placed his daughter in the workshop for protection and security. Neither he nor his wife supported the proposed conversion, which they believed was not in the best interests of their daughter. He contended that,

> [She] lived at home for all these years and it was her idea to come here [to Pioneer], not ours. Now you're saying that you're going to close the shop and put everyone out there. If she could be out by herself, don't you think she would be there by now? Where will she go when this place closes?

Like this father, many families were as concerned about the closing of the workshop as they were about Pioneer's new focus on community employment. Some worried that their offspring or siblings could not get jobs and would have nowhere to go. Others were concerned that the workshop would close before their offspring or siblings could find jobs or that there would be nowhere to go if they lost their jobs. As one parent said, "What happens if my son can't find a job before the agency closes? It took us years to find a place for him and we are a lot older now. I don't know what we can do."

As implied by this statement, several families also believed that the entire agency was going to shut down overnight. Many were afraid that they again would have to search for an agency that would accept their adult offspring or siblings.

The new director explained that 1) the workshop would not close until every participant found acceptable community employment, and 2) another workshop setting could be found for those who wanted to continue in a sheltered setting. Although this allayed some families' concerns, it did not help to alleviate fears about community employment itself. One parent cited her daughter's continued participation at Pioneer as evidence that she needed to be in a sheltered workshop:

> I don't think my daughter can handle a real job. That's why she came to Pioneer and stayed here all these years. And another thing, I know other people can be cruel and she's not used to that. The people here have always been nice and I know she likes it here.

Another parent pointed to previous professional assessments regarding her son's inability to work in a competitive job: "[He] was tested in school and afterward by psychologists [who said] he should go to a workshop. Aren't you giving him false hopes?"

In every case, the director tried to alleviate families' concerns by reiterating that workshop participants 1) could continue to live in Pioneer's community residence for as long as they wanted, and 2) would not be coerced in any way to find community jobs.

Some families were not opposed to the idea of agency conversion and were in fact hopeful that their offspring or siblings might obtain community employment and earn decent wages. This is not to say that they did not have reservations about other matters such as safety and supervision. One family member inquired about her sister's security once she left the workshop. She wondered how her sister would get to and from work and who would be responsible for her while she was at work. She expressed relief when she learned that, for as long as necessary and through the use of CJSs, Pioneer would retain responsibility for people's safety and supervision when they traveled to and from work and while they were at work.

A local parent also had concerns about her daughter's safety even though she felt that the agency changes "were long overdue" and that the supervision in the workshop was "not all that good." Her doubts about her daughter's safety stemmed from an incident during which her daughter was scalded after spilling hot coffee on herself accidentally in the workshop lunchroom. This parent referred to that incident when she commented that, "Maybe the job coaches would be better supervisors than the workshop staff." She also expressed disappointment that her daughter, who had held a job in the community for a brief period, had to earn "such lousy wages" and "wait so long for another chance."

FROM SKEPTICISM TO SUPPORT

Although many people were skeptical as the conversion began, stakeholder perspectives changed as stakeholders heard about and saw evidence of positive practices and outcomes. Factors influential in soliciting support from stakeholders are discussed below.

Having a Clear Vision and Good Leadership

The director articulated clearly his values regarding and vision of conversion from the start. Although this up-front discussion of radical change was difficult for some to understand and accept, all of the stakeholders knew of the director's goals. According to a member of the board of directors, Pioneer's new direction was neither a secret nor vague: "His idea was to start right away to get the people out into the community to work and make a living by themselves, and that's what the object of it was."

Such clarification of values, along with the articulation of best practices, was critical in helping people to understand why conversion was necessary and appropriate. As one staff person admitted,

> We weren't doing what we should have been doing, but we didn't know it. We thought we were doing the right things because we're the professionals. We were running the center trying to be do-gooders, and maybe we weren't doing that well.

The strong leadership abilities of the director were key to obtaining the support of staff and the board of directors. A board member said, "He brought tremendous prestige and respect and credibility to the agency." He also had a good reputation in the community, and he established a network of state and local contacts. In addition, he instilled trust among consumers, staff, board members, parents, and community members by being open and forthright. As one state agency manager stated,

> It was important that the board had faith in him right from the beginning so he had immediate credibility with the board and with the community, with a little bit of question. He was not a practitioner, he was an academician. But everyone knew him and liked him and respected him. So that all made a difference.

Stakeholders Observing Immediate Successes

For the many who resisted the conversion, or did not believe that Pioneer's new direction was appropriate, seeing was believing. In order to win over "nay sayers," there were immediate demonstrations of positive strategies and outcomes. These demonstrations were sufficient to convince key stakeholders that total conversion could occur and that outcomes would be positive. As this representative from a funding organization said, "The thing that they did that was so great was they started getting people jobs right away. So luckily, we were able to go back statewide and say, 'See, it works.' We had really quick results and that was wonderful."

Families who always dreamed of their offspring or siblings working in the community finally saw their dreams come true. At the same time, those who were reluctant to allow their adult offspring or siblings to work also benefited from knowing that they were working successfully: "His daughter now has a job, so he's real happy. She did have some problems with the Pioneer family breaking up, but she's very content with her job now and she looks forward to it."

A person at one of the state funding organizations said, "Well, there are some people we didn't expect to get jobs, and interestingly those were among the first [to get jobs]."

A board member was equally impressed with the immediate results demonstrated by the agency: "When he told us what he could do, we hardly believed him at first. And we were very surprised that right away within the first month he had some of [the people in the workshop] out working."

One board member who was unsure about Pioneer's new direction changed his mind after seeing the impact of the changes on a person whom he knew from the workshop:

> He had a whiny, high-pitched voice, kind of [a] clingy-type kid who hung on everybody. And all of a sudden he got a job. When he came back in he was 4 inches taller, [his] voice was deeper, and he was talking to the clients. . . . That was the metamorphosis. This did it for me. I was convinced when I saw that take place in this young man.

Other board members also changed their views about the workshop participants: "This getting them out into the community now, it will get back something that they need, that they're worthwhile people, that they can make a contribution." People finally realized that the family atmosphere of the workshop bred dependence and segregation: "I feel that in general it was better for the clients. I think they felt [like] a family, but I think they were also isolated, and this has given them some new opportunities, more independence."

After the conversion began, community employment could be contrasted with the sheltered workshop, and the differences became obvious:

> You begin to realize. . . . You look into it and you become more exposed to [the workshop]. The people were dissatisfied. They were lumped together because they were handicapped people. They weren't happy, [and] they weren't making money. All these minuses. So, with the advent of supported work, I think what we've done is go from the dark ages into the world of light, and these people are working.

Staff members were revitalized by each new job placement. As workshop participants saw other workshop participants get jobs, they too wanted to get out and work. They began to ask, "When am I going to get out of here?" and say, "This is what I want." As one staff person recalled, "I felt the pressures coming from folks in the shop: 'We want jobs.'" Thus, successful job placements had a positive impact on all who were involved.

Networking with Key Organizations

It was important for people in state and local organizations to feel informed about and involved in Pioneer's conversion efforts. People from state funding organizations appreciated the fact that Pioneer's director kept them abreast of new developments: "He got in there and immediately went to work connecting with the people he had to . . . the community of human services people [and] funding sources."

Hiring the Right People

People were hired who were knowledgeable about supported employment and believed in the value of community inclusion. New staff played a significant role in influencing existing workshop staff by bringing enthusiasm and skill to their jobs, securing jobs for workshop participants, and generally convincing stakeholders that conversion could be accomplished successfully: "He got people to come work with him. They knew him—people who had a lot of faith in his ideas."

Words such as "unbelievable," "dedicated," "knowledgeable," and "positive" were used repeatedly to describe new staff and/or their efforts. They impressed this funding organization representative as being activists for change: "They don't see themselves as just passive counselors. I really think they see themselves as change agents who are out there to change the community."

This parent saw the difference between the attitudes and skills of the former staff and those of the new staff: "With the staff and their approach to the people, it's working. People said you'll never do it, and old timers said you'll never find places for these people to work. They did!"

Staff worked together in teams to assist people in getting and keeping community jobs. Frequent staff meetings were used for group sharing and problem solving and to continually hone staff skills.

Obtaining Funding

Pioneer's director immediately wrote proposals for and secured two supported employment grants from the state of New York. Combined these grants were worth approximately $90,000. They were instrumental in instilling confidence in funding organizations and board members about Pioneer's stability as well as the director's abilities.

As discussed in Chapter 3, as people moved out of the workshop, space was made available for lease by community businesses. The income thereby generated served as another source of funding for the agency: "Not having to use the building for a workshop, we are now leasing the building and have an income just from leasing. That's what we intend to do I guess—just keep one corner for offices for ourselves and rent the rest of it."

State funding organizations also worked to provide funding for Pioneer's new conversion. One organization solicited support to interpret regulations flexibly in order to allow the use of personal adjustment training (PAT) money in providing community supports: "It dawned on us that it didn't say anything anywhere in our personal adjustment training regs that that had to happen in the workshop. We had never thought about that before. So we wrote a proposal and talked to the directors in Albany."

EMPLOYMENT CHALLENGES

As the conversion progressed and more and more participants moved from the workshop to community employment, various challenges arose for Pioneer staff and the people for whom they provided support. Most of the challenges paralleled those experienced by supported employment agencies everywhere. They included things such as negative employer attitudes, lack of transportation, finding quality jobs, satisfying consumers, inadequate funding, workshop reentry, and striving to maintain quality. Interestingly, few challenges described by staff were unique to the conversion process itself.

Negative Employer Attitudes

As stated previously, most of the workshop participants were diagnosed as having blindness or visual disabilities with other intellectual, physical, and/or sensory disabilities. Staff were surprised to find that employers were most hesitant about hiring people with blindness:

> The major challenge that we've experienced here has been that the community has not . . . that the employment community is not yet able to think of people with severe visual impairments and blindness as competent workers. I was very, very surprised to find that employers were pretty uniformly reticent and negative about hiring someone with a visual impairment, citing all kinds of problems from liability to quality control. I was totally unprepared for that kind of reaction.

Therefore, staff became skilled at providing 1) examples of jobs that people with visual disabilities held in area businesses, and 2) names of employers who were willing to serve as references. Employers who hired former workshop participants were able to allay the fears of other reluctant employers.

Lack of Transportation

Pioneer staff had not been involved in transporting participants to and from the workshop, and they were not familiar with transportation issues faced by people with disabilities in the community. Few participants rode regular buses even after obtaining community employment. Most relied on a specialized transport service (i.e., the paratransit system) that was fraught with problems (see Chapter 4). Still, it worked better when everyone went to the same location at the same time on the same days. Thus, supported employment compounded transportation challenges because people headed in different directions and had different schedules: "Transportation is a problem with or without work, so I'm not sure that's an excuse. It just becomes exacerbated because now people are going in a thousand different directions."

Finding Quality Jobs

In their zeal to get people out of the workshop, staff were, at times, a bit hasty in moving forward with and maintaining job placements that may not have been the best matches for the workshop participants:

> Other problems are [that] we're too eager to accept whatever job placement comes along. I don't think we've gotten very sophisticated about saying so and so isn't working out. We're afraid to give up that placement for another placement. I think we've wedded ourselves to the service industry, but we haven't really attacked other situations like we should.

Staff were encouraged continually to take the time necessary to find jobs that met the expectations of the workshop participants. Unfortunately, funding organizations pressured Pioneer to find job placements for more people more quickly but discouraged multiple placements for any one individual. This "numbers game" and other funding issues are discussed further later in this chapter.

Satisfying Funding Organizations

Pioneer staff were up to the challenge of finding jobs for everyone in the workshop. However, their efforts to do so were sidetracked because funding organizations expected them to provide services for new referrals as well. Attempts to satisfy funding organizations and play the numbers game proved disheartening to staff: "Granted, there are tons of people out there who are just waiting to be served. But we're also trying to close a workshop. And if [VESID] could have waited say an extra 6–8 months, we could [have] probably had everyone placed."

Because of the need to provide services for new referrals, efforts to get people out of the workshop were stymied significantly. Funding organizations also discouraged staff from "re-serving" people after they quit or lost their jobs: "You have funding sources saying, 'Why . . . isn't this [supported employment] working? Why is this person in a third job?' Well too . . . bad, you cannot tell me that you have not had three jobs in your life." Thus, Pioneer staff struggled to meet the needs of their consumers in a climate of competing demands.

Inadequate Funding

At the time of Pioneer's conversion, the bulk of New York's VESID and MR/DD funding was used to support segregated services throughout the state. Therefore, both the start-up and the follow-along costs of supported employment were underfunded: "It isn't just start-up costs that are the real problem, it's the long-term follow-along costs. The dollars are not there right now."

Inadequate funding had a significant impact on the quality of supported employment services. First, it discouraged agencies that provided sheltered employment services from moving toward supported employment. Second, it forced agencies to screen people to determine who would not need intensive support; otherwise, the agencies would lose money by providing services for people with more severe disabilities. Finally, inadequate funding resulted in hasty job placements, less-than-adequate training, and insufficient follow-along support for supported employees.

Workshop Reentry

Staff encouraged workshop participants to try community employment by assuring them that they could return to the workshop for as long as it was in existence. "We've also had an issue of people coming back through. We've had a couple people who have left jobs who've come back in." Although this approach made it easier for people to leave the workshop, it stalled the process of closure. Staff were not as quick to assist workshop participants in finding community employment because they knew that the participants were "safe and sound" in the workshop. Conversely, workshop participants were less adamant about finding community employment because they were able to "relax" in the workshop for the time being. Having the option of entering the workshop may have even prompted some supported employees to put less effort into keeping their jobs in the community.

Striving to Maintain Quality

One of the distinct advantages that Pioneer had with regard to its conversion was its small size. Staff could work together as a close-knit team. They felt that this team structure was critical for supporting one another as well as the supported employees most effectively. They expressed a desire to maintain Pioneer's small size and not to grow too quickly: "The whole idea for us is to stay small so we can provide quality, so we can be a team. If we grow too big too fast you lose perspective." In order to meet the growing demands of funding organizations and others to provide services for more people, however, it became apparent that the staff needed to expand: "We put our foot down, saying we're not growing, we're not! Now we're at the point where our hands are tied and we need more staff."

The staff did indeed grow. With the hiring of each new CJS, the agency worked to regroup, build new teams, and establish a desirable work climate. Although all of this was necessary, it took time and energy away from helping workshop participants get and keep jobs in the community.

IN RETROSPECT

As the last few workshop participants were receiving job placements, staff discussed aspects of their work that they might do differently if they had to do it again. New staff brought positive attitudes and practices to Pioneer, but the conversion did not occur as quickly as they had hoped. This sentiment was expressed by this CJS:

> The major priority was getting folks employed from the workshop so that we could close the workshop. But at the same time we had started another grant, so it meant we had to pick up some new folks from outside the shop and be actively working to place them too. So what I experienced was a definite struggle in that we had to close down the workshop but because of funding we also had to serve new people.

Interestingly, a staff member who worked at Pioneer when it was strictly a workshop reflected on the ease and quickness with which the conversion took place relative to her expectations: "I think, well, the amount of people we've placed out of the shop went relatively easier than I thought it was going to be. I thought it was going to take a really long time."

Another issue dealt with the importance of finding job placements for those people with the most severe disabilities early on in the conversion process. The director noted the advantages of providing services for people with a variety of characteristics and issues, and he was disappointed that Pioneer did not do more of this from the start:

> Our plan was to mix the people who were leaving the shop and select some people who were going to be a little harder to serve. We did that somewhat but not to the extent that I would have liked. Anyone who's looking to convert, it would make a lot of sense to make sure that those people with greater needs and who are going to need more training go first for a couple of reasons: first of all because it's going to make the end of the conversion process a lot easier, and second, because it would motivate the people who are doing the placement and help them understand that everybody can work.

Many felt that some workshop participants had to wait too long for jobs. This was so partly because staff tended to fill job openings with the more skilled people from their caseloads:

> I think at this point we as staff have matured to the point where we understand what it requires to look for one job for one person and stay

at that task and not get sidetracked into placing someone who might be easier in a job that we're trying to develop. So that's what I would do differently.

A staff member from the workshop who stayed with Pioneer and became a CJS reflected on the changes that she needed to make in order to be successful as a CJS:

> I feel like initially being a professional was hard. I think the way I come across to people has to be a lot different than I used to come across. I think I would have taken some classes on how to be more assertive [and] persuasive.

In reflecting on their training and support, staff felt that they would have benefited from more formal training, but they felt comfortable with the informal way in which they learned their jobs and received support:

> Staff training was dealt with in a real informal way by getting together two [or] three times a week to talk about what we were doing and do a lot of group problem solving around an individual. We put a lot of energy into developing some group cohesiveness and getting this whole sense of mission and purpose throughout the staff so that we were all in the same place working together as a unit. . . . I think that was probably the right thing to do when I think back.

Staff realized that the CJSs could make or break the entire supported employment program. Previous experience with supported employment was not necessarily the priority when hiring new CJSs, however, as described by this veteran staff person.

> We had intentionally hired people who were bright and capable and able to pick up new skills very easily. We knew from the beginning the issues would be around philosophy and around a willingness to expend the energy to get the job done. As long as you can keep that energy high, we assessed that we would be able to accomplish what we set out to do, and that indeed did happen.

Staff were very proud of the reputation that Pioneer earned as a result of their efforts. They grew in their expectations of the people receiving services as they began to focus on quality placements and job and career growth for supported employees:

> When we first started we were perceived as a very marginal kind of agency. I think in 2 years we've completely turned that perception around and we're now probably perceived as the leader in terms of supported employment in this community. So that feels really positive. When I first worked here I was embarrassed to say that I worked at Pioneer. At this point I feel very, very proud to be a part of this agency.

SUMMARY

It is clear that stakeholder perspectives about Pioneer's conversion changed significantly from being quite negative prior to the conversion to being quite positive after the conversion process began. Many lessons were learned because of Pioneer's conversion. First, agencies that are interested in conversion do not need the blessings of all stakeholders before undertaking a conversion effort. Second, it is impossible to wait for everything to be in place because any one change alters the situation and subsequent actions. Third, people's attitudes can and do change if they are provided with concrete evidence that refutes previous thinking solidly. Fourth, demonstrations of success are particularly powerful in changing attitudes and perceptions. Fifth, it is apparent that the human services system and its key participants provide few incentives for change and in fact inhibit innovation.

Total conversion was completed successfully at Pioneer. If it can be done under adverse conditions, just think what could be done if disincentives are nullified. The impact of Pioneer's conversion could be felt across New York and, to a lesser extent, the United States. The regional director from a state funding organization reflected on Pioneer's conversion and the effect that it had on the system:

> I would say Pioneer did do that—gave us the impetus. But something else I think Pioneer did for . . . agencies is it checked an amount of complacency. People were so used, for so long, to—I don't mean hand-holding exercises—but just really set ideas. It was still like, "We really know what's best for you." Anyway, it did make them sit up and say, "Well we can't say it can't be done."

II

LEADERSHIP FOR CHANGE—EXAMPLES OF AGENCY CONVERSION

6

Kaposia, inc.

Founded in 1963, Kaposia, inc., was a day activity program located in St. Paul, Minnesota, that provided services for about 65 people whose disabilities were thought to preclude their entering sheltered workshops. Kaposia had about 10 staff who operated three programs, each at a different location. One was a home living and apartment preparation program that consisted of an actual apartment in which people learned cleaning and other skills that would enable them to live more independently. The second program consisted of a workcenter in which individuals performed subcontract work or work activities. The third program was administered in a community center in which small groups of participants learned daily living, social, and recreation skills by engaging in such activities as going swimming at the local Young Men's Christian Association (YMCA) and attending social and recreation events in the community.

The chief executive officer (CEO), who was interviewed, has been with the program for 21 years. She began as an instructor and moved into the CEO position in 1977. She described Kaposia as being very self-contained during the early years. By this she meant that staff worked on the periphery of the community, having minimal contact with the employers, neighbors, businesspeople, human services professionals, and citizens of the surrounding area.

INITIAL IMPETUS FOR CHANGE

In 1980–1981, the CEO and some staff were influenced by several factors that led them toward major change. According to the CEO, this period was marked by public disenchantment with high taxes, particularly when those taxes were earmarked for social services programs that were increasingly characterized as wasteful, expensive, and ineffective. Many citizens did not feel that they were getting their money's worth. This forced human services professionals to scrutinize their programs more carefully. Some Kaposia staff attended workshops conducted by Lou Brown of the University of Wisconsin and Wolf Wolfensberger of Syracuse University, both of whom were vocal critics of the traditional human services system for people with disabilities; they were calling for dramatic change.

In addition to outside forces, there were internal factors at work to effect change. For example, many people attending Kaposia indicated verbally and behaviorally (i.e., by acting out in anger or frustration) that they wanted more work opportunities. This was interpreted by staff as an indication of the need for more meaningful activities. But the fact that some of the people whom staff felt could benefit from advanced work training were returned to Kaposia and classified as being inappropriate for community work because of medical or behavioral problems showed that the programs themselves were inadequate. Staff believed, however, that such individuals were not being given a fair chance to succeed.

Kaposia was also getting many referrals from schools and institutions. The latter were downsizing and sending more people to community agencies. Through its workcenter, Kaposia provided services for these people but experienced such rapid growth that the CEO felt the program was operating beyond its capacity to be effective. Many people were entering the program, but almost no one was leaving. As a result of this overload, many young people were not receiving the vocational rehabilitation services necessary to find employment. In frustration, some staff complained that "These individuals shouldn't be here. They should be working."

Taking all of this into consideration, the CEO noted that Kaposia's policies and practices were not making sense to her anymore:

> We knew it wasn't working. All of a sudden we looked at it and we thought, "Gosh, this is not making sense to us." We always had certain evaluation outcomes and considered people's level of satisfaction with our service. And we always mentioned how much [money] people made in a year. Everyone made $2,500 for the whole year—all 65 people. That wasn't making sense to us. It was the downtime too—all the waiting. We believed that there is a better life for people than that. So our thinking began to change. We started thinking differently. We would always refer to ourselves as a program. We changed our language so we would think differently. We no longer referred to ourselves as a program. Programs group people. We believe we are a service. Services look at individuals. We are not going to think of ourselves as an agency. We consider ourselves a company.

CREATING A NEW VISION

All the preceding factors led to a reevaluation of what Kaposia was and should be. As the CEO noted,

> We went back and we took a look at what our mission was . . . what our vision was, and what we believed in. We listed what we called our new set of service principles or guidelines that we believed our services should reflect. We wanted to be more integrated and not segregated. Our vision was to become a service without walls. That's what we called ourselves in 1983. . . . We didn't call it conversion. We called it a facility without walls. We used the word conversion probably in about 1985, because we thought we could be completely converted by 1988. That was our goal. But we needed 2 extra years. We were totally converted in August of 1990 when we closed our last [segregated] site.

How to Begin

After they decided to change, Kaposia staff developed a new philosophy and created a vision of what they wanted the program to become—a "service without walls" and a provider of supported employment services. But staff lacked a means of achieving these goals. As the CEO noted,

> We didn't know how to do [the changes] yet. We hadn't really worked out a plan. We decided we were going to start slow. We wanted to make sure that what we did, we did well. We had to gather a lot more information and learn how to work with the State Division of Rehabilitation Services [DRS]. We didn't even know they existed in 1983. We knew what we wanted to do but we didn't know how to do it.

One of Kaposia's first tasks was to establish a leadership team to plan its changes and draft new values and mission statements. These were later presented to the board of directors, and they were approved about 1 year later. Staff also hired a new placement coordinator and began supported employment activities. The CEO recalled having many meetings with staff and constituent groups such as parents, service coordinators, vocational rehabilitation counselors, and so forth. The process was described as a dialogue, but one that needed action as well as talk. According to the CEO,

> It was a transition process. I made the decision but I didn't announce [the changes]. [Staff] were part of a planning process. We had some directors, some senior program staff, and we talked a lot about it, but it was like we were just going to talk and we needed to act. We talked about 6 months. Talk about readiness! I mean there is only so much talking you can do. At one point I brought all the staff and board together and basically said that "we have to walk our talk." Then we began to . . . [change]. And that's when we saw some unhappy employees.

Kaposia's Planning

Kaposia's planning was constantly changing and uncertain. There were periods when outside help was called for.

> We only planned for about 120 days at a time. Our organizational structure changed so much over those years [of change] that we would only plan for about 4 months. I brought someone in from the outside to help us with some long-term planning and to make sure we were staying on track, because everyone around us was saying that [supported employment] was only a trend; it can't be done; people aren't ready. We had a lot of resistance, especially from our county [service coordinators]. The facilitator was someone the staff felt comfortable with. He also had the opportunity to go through PASS [Program Analysis of Service Systems] training at the same time I did, and he was a good match for me. He slowed down my pace sometimes, and he helped me when I had to pick [the pace] up again.

As noted above, the CEO relied less on formal planning than on concrete action, particularly after concluding that planning did not always lead to action, at least the level of action that she wanted. Thus, action at times preceded planning.

In terms of specific actions, the CEO began by working with people who wanted to receive the new services, stating that, "We started with people who wanted to make some changes in their [lives] . . . [not those] who were resistant. We thought we would let our actions demonstrate our success."

Services were provided by devoting available staff and financial resources to activities that were consistent with Kaposia's new philosophy and practices. The CEO further said that,

> I began by taking away all the things that were not age-appropriate, because I thought we might fall back on those things—worksheets and recreational equipment. They all went. We just took a day and got rid of all that stuff. If a staff person said, "This is what I want to do," and if it matched our service principles, they got the funds to do it. And [the staff] who wanted training got the training. One of the things we got started was a housecleaning crew which began from the apartment preparation program. We were teaching people how to take care of an apartment. So a staff [member] asked about starting a housecleaning service. At least the individuals would be paid. They know the skills already. [The crew] didn't allow for the level of integration we hoped for, but it was a step toward that. And it was more meaningful for people.
>
> We also came up with the idea of a recycling business in which people would go from business to business taking care of any recycling jobs. The idea was picked up by a workshop supervisor. We called it *Kaposia Can.*

In addition to changing the staff's activities, the CEO also modified job descriptions and expectations (e.g., staff would now have to work year round). As she indicated,

> We changed our job descriptions and all of our personnel policies because we weren't a year-round service. We were getting money to open 10 months of the year. We would have a break at Christmas and in August. We were a lot like the school program.

In order to change from an insular to a community-oriented program, Kaposia also had to become more widely known and recognized among groups important to its new activities; in Kaposia's case, this meant the business world. The CEO pointed out that this entailed not only getting to know individual employers, but also finding out firsthand how businesspeople thought and acted in order to relate effectively with them. She put it this way:

> To do supported employment, we had to become more businesslike. We weren't very well known in our community even though we had been around for 20 years. We were a pretty quiet little community program. We didn't work with the business community at all and we decided that we were going to need some help with that. So we got some employers together that we had worked with and bounced some things off them, like our name change. Do we call ourselves Kaposia Developmental Learning Center? They said the name sounded like a venereal disease! So we made it just Kaposia, inc., and they helped us look at . . . the features of this service for the employer and for the individual—the customer. We really went through a whole image change.

AGENCY CHANGE AND STAFF THINKING

Training

Staff training was viewed as a key ingredient to Kaposia's eventual success. The CEO said that "We had access to a lot of training, and I really believe in training. We had to get our staff the tools to do what they needed to do." In addition to acquiring specific job skills, staff also had to abate or eliminate some old habits and behaviors. The CEO reported that "Dress codes had to change. We were a casual crew. We had to make some changes in that. And people's hours had to change."

Training was also described as a way of introducing staff to the pending changes. Attempts were made "to offer [training] and market it [to staff] as an opportunity for them to become more marketable. We felt that this was going to be the job of the future. We were trying to prepare them for that."

The concept of training was considered and applied on more than just a staffwide or even an intra-agency level. Change was seen as something that needed to permeate the entire community and influence the functioning of other human services organizations. This was an important expansion of the concept of change because it recognized 1) the need for change both inside and outside of Kaposia, and 2) the implications of Kaposia's change for the entire community. As the CEO stated,

> We were able to bring together the [DRS] and county [service coordinators] and at first they looked at each other and pointed fingers, asking who was going to fund all this. But gradually they worked out new arrangements and funding streams using some new funding sources like [the] DRS and Medicaid.

The CEO described a process whereby people came together with little history of working together, differences in philosophy, and funding uncertainties and worked out some new relationships that are still being negotiated and modified.

Transitional Funding

About 1 year after Kaposia began its conversion, it started to receive funding and provide training to bridge the gap between existing services and desired services. The CEO, seeking new sources of funding, acquired several state and federally supported employment demonstration grants. The local Metropolitan Council and the McKnight Foundation recognized the growing enthusiasm for supported employment in the United States and offered funding initiatives to programs that provided supported employment services. The CEO wanted to participate in the initiatives: "I heard there were discussions going on in both of these organizations to learn the technology of supported employment locally—what it was and how it worked. And I wanted that information."

Kaposia subsequently received funding from both organizations to begin its supported employment projects. In addition to the funding from these sources, Kaposia also received transitional funding from a federally sponsored statewide supported employment project. As a result of funding from this project, Kaposia was able to provide supported employment services for the people remaining in its workshop; offer staff training; market the concept of supported employment to the business community; sponsor employer forums, breakfasts, and luncheons; learn about working in the community with people who had severe disabilities; and serve individuals with multiple disabilities with whom Kaposia had not worked previously.

CONSTITUENT RESPONSES

A common activity of the CEO's approach to Kaposia's constituent groups was to work more intensively with those groups and with individuals who were most interested in the conversion process. The focus of her efforts was on providing education about and a rationale for Kaposia's proposed conversion, initiating work with interested parties, and using previous success as a primary means of getting support from other groups and individuals.

Board Reactions

In order to make agency changes of such magnitude, the CEO required the approval of the board of directors. She began by presenting to them information that she termed *indicators for the need to change.* These indicators comprised data that she had gathered about 1) the outdated work preparation that people in Kaposia's programs were receiving; 2) the lack of acceptance of Kaposia's participants by other agencies to which they were referred; and 3) the dissatisfaction that people expressed about Kaposia's programs, particularly about the lack of work provided and the pay received. As she recalled,

> I talked with our board and shared with them all the indicators—things I saw, our program evaluation information, things that were happening [across the United States]—and I said we needed to make some changes. And they were supportive.
> My proposal was that we have to find real jobs for people because this subcontract work and the activities that we provide aren't making people's lives any better [or] adding any meaning to them.

The CEO also noted that Kaposia was interested in becoming a very different agency, and she stated this to the board during the initial meetings:

> In 1983 we didn't know how we were going to become a service without walls, but we still wanted to be that. . . . So we developed a new vision and mission statement. Our values statement and mission were adopted by the board of directors.

The CEO also described meetings that she called between the board and staff during times when progress seemed slow or when people seemed to be dragging their feet; she felt compelled to exhort them to action. She said that "We had board and staff meetings. It was painful. And I said this is what we need to do."

Family Reactions

In dealing with families, the CEO reportedly began by focusing on those Kaposia participants who were interested in change and whose families were generally supportive. By doing this, she felt that the chances for success would be maximized and that such success would serve as an incentive for others' participation. The CEO stated, "We had parent meetings. We started with people who wanted to make some changes in their [lives]. We didn't start with parents who were resistant. We thought we would let our actions demonstrate our success."

Reactions of Other Professional Groups

The CEO described her program's relationships with other agencies as being problematic at times. In some cases, Kaposia's difficulties stemmed from its years of isolation. As she indicated, "We had to learn to work with the [DRS]. We didn't even know they existed in 1983. . . . We weren't even acknowledged by the DRS at that time. Our people were not considered eligible [for DRS services]."

Some agencies established specific expectations regarding the types of services that Kaposia should provide. As the CEO remarked,

[Other human services agencies] kept thinking that we're a place for people where they are being taken care of. Let's not worry about them. We were saying, "No, wait a minute, we want to be looked at as a service, not a program or a place."

Some professionals disagreed with Kaposia's new direction and opposed its changes. On one hand, as the changes unfolded, the CEO was accused of working with people who had "less severe disabilities" and fewer problems. On the other hand, she was criticized for pushing people with severe disabilities too far too quickly:

County [service coordinators] gave us the most resistance. The heat came because [service coordinators] didn't feel that people were ready. It was the issue of readiness, and we said no more readiness criteria. We wanted to try training on the job and not in a simulated work situation.

In some cases, community professionals equated services for people with disabilities with the existence of a designated building or site. Without such a site, these professionals apparently had difficulty understanding and accepting Kaposia's new services. The CEO noted that,

Some people are still not comfortable with what we are doing. They believe that we should have a site for people. In fact, we are meeting next week with a group of people and I am going to hear from a [service coordinator] that she still believes we need to have a site for people.

Several agencies were more receptive to Kaposia's new ideas. For example, the CEO found that although counselors at the state DRS had not worked with Kaposia in the past and had little experience working with people with severe disabilities, they were open to trying new ideas and services. She attributed their cooperation to the federally funded statewide supported employment project, a project with which Minnesota's DRS was closely affiliated. Thus, staff at the DRS were committed to the idea of supported employment and were beginning to talk about it, even though they had not started doing much at that point.

Finding Professionals with Whom to Work

Assisting people in finding community jobs of their choosing required the cooperation and active participation of professionals such as service coordinators. Kaposia's staff realized that they would not be able to convince every constituent group of the value of their new community orientation. As the CEO observed,

> As more time went on, more meetings, and more work, [it became obvious] that [some people] didn't share the same values as we did. So staff decided that they were "not going to try to change people's attitudes [for whom] we have been beating our heads against the wall." We decided to just do what we could. And other people began to contact us. . . . So we started a list identifying the [service coordinators] who were willing to take the risk.

STAFF REACTIONS TO INITIAL CHANGES

Although the reactions of staff to Kaposia's initial changes varied, most described the new focus on integrated services as "scary." The CEO said that staff responses changed dramatically when the time came for action: "It's [OK] if someone else does it, but if [staff were] asked to do it, [they] weren't ready to do it. They had to make a decision for themselves if they wanted to stay with our company or leave."

Not only did staff have to learn new roles and methods, but they had to manage new working conditions as well. As the CEO described it, establishing a community orientation required staff "to go out in their own directions and limit their internal social network. That was painful for them." She further said that although she tried to ease the effects of the changes, she often had to advise people to leave Kaposia:

> I tried to reassure them that it was scary for everyone. I offered to help them develop other activities that were more age-appropriate . . . and that we would get lots of training and go see other places. And we did lots of training and lots of traveling, but the shift was beginning to happen.
>
> Three times a year we do performance reviews and during those we get people together and say this is where we are headed. [I advised some that] maybe we are not a good match anymore. Quite a few staff . . . left over a period—not in the first or second year, but 3 years later, most of the staff had turned over.

Staff Reactions and Changes in the Workcenter

Of all program personnel, workcenter staff had the hardest time with the changes. Several reasons were given for this. First, compared to other Kaposia programs in which even in-house work services were almost nonexistent, the workcenter looked good. Staff saw themselves as providing concrete, organized, needed vocational services. Therefore, although it was not consistent with Kaposia's new direction, the CEO viewed their work as generally acceptable and decided to focus on revamping other programs first.

Second, workcenter staff had formed their own definition of change and advocated for implementing that definition. Even though their definition did not match that of the CEO, it was difficult to dislodge once it was formed. As the CEO observed,

> The people at the workcenter were the hardest breed to make changes. That was one of the last areas that we made changes in, because there was some work going on there. . . . When I hired the placement person, the workcenter would lose workers because we began placing people out of there. The workcenter people felt, maybe, devalued. I tried not to devalue them, but we needed to make these changes. I probably didn't pay enough attention to them. . . . I think they needed more reassurance that what they did was okay, but we were just trying to find a better way.

The CEO noted that although she made some compromises in the pursuit of change, she could not approve the proposals of workcenter staff because they were really designed to improve and extend the workcenter:

> Instead of doing jobs, [workcenter staff] wanted to start a business, manufacture cards, do a prime product. They wanted our resources to go into developing the prime product . . . so that we would have work on a steady basis . . . bring in other people [without disabilities]. But that wasn't the same for me, because I didn't want to be the employer. I didn't want [workcenter participants] to get a [Kaposia] paycheck. We

wanted to be a trainer. . . . [The new placement coordinator] was somebody who was going to find jobs for people, not subcontract work. That was a real hot issue at the time for us because we had so many people waiting for work and still experiencing downtime. But that was the way it was going to be. . . . We are still the employer for many of the people we serve through some of our work crews and through subcontracts, but I saw those and still do today as small steps toward getting to natural supports.

One important change in the workcenter program was the hiring of a placement coordinator to find community jobs for workcenter participants. Interestingly, the individual who was hired was employed formerly at the workcenter but left because he did not agree with Kaposia's changes. When he returned for a visit, he was apparently so impressed with the changes he witnessed, especially with regard to new staff, that he applied immediately for the placement coordinator position. According to the CEO, the strongest credentials this man had were his beliefs in integrated employment and the need for agency change:

> The person I hired [to be the placement coordinator] had left because I had talked about making this shift to the community into real jobs and he didn't buy it. He left for a year, and came back to the area and did some work for us. He saw the differences in people and said, "I want this job. I can see the difference."

Managing New Admissions to the Workcenter Program

One problem faced by Kaposia was what to do about other agencies' continuing demand for its in-house work services. On one hand, staff wanted to abolish the sheltered workcenter program altogether. On the other hand, they were faced with a continuing stream of referrals from community agencies. The CEO saw the two circumstances as incompatible and felt that Kaposia had to make a choice one way or another:

> In 1985 we recognized we were not doing it right. Because even though we were starting to do supported employment and moving more people out, there were more people coming out of the state hospitals that needed to be served yesterday. . . . So we were taking them off the waiting list and [putting them] into our in-house services. And it took us about 1½ years to figure out that this just wasn't working. Because once some people got in they wanted to stay in. . . . We made a policy decision . . . and had to be a little stronger in our message that we were going to become community based and that people who need or want our services aren't going to receive in-house services anymore. We are only going to provide jobs for people in community settings. . . . So we had to say to the [service coordinators] who were referring people to us that we were only going to serve people when we have [jobs] for [them].

COMMUNITY LINKAGES

Partnerships and Affiliations

One of the most important lessons the CEO learned during the conversion process was the importance of developing and using community partnerships. Some of the affiliations that Kaposia pursued were described in some detail earlier. Affiliates included DRS counselors and select county service coordinators. Others, such as the local school system, also proved helpful. As the CEO noted,

> I learned through the [federally funded statewide] supported employment project the importance of building linkages [and] building networks. If anyone asked me what I learned, it's the importance of working with your competitors and your community and doing partnerships and joint ventures. With funding always being tight, we had to look at ways of pooling resources to help us get what we wanted. We had to become partners with other community agencies.
>
> We partnered with the school district, [the] DRS, and the county so that we could start working with students before they graduated. We developed a contract [so] we could begin working with students in their last year of high school instead of waiting until they graduated.

Publishing a Newsletter

Another way that Kaposia bolstered its profile in the community, publicized its actions, and provided rewards to its staff was by generating publicity about itself. Using a newsletter, Kaposia began a campaign to disseminate information to the community about its accomplishments. As a result of the newsletter, the CEO recalled that they

> got lots of attention from the state who liked what we were doing. We would be asked to talk with other groups about what we were doing. We were getting lots of "how-to" calls. So it became a real perk for the staff and for our company to be acknowledged like that.

SUMMARY

External as well as internal factors initially spurred Kaposia's movement toward integrated employment. Two leaders in the field, Lou Brown and Wolf Wolfensberger, spoke of problems with the traditional human services system for people with disabilities and clarified an alternative vision of how services should be delivered. Internally, the CEO and others became dissatisfied with what they increasingly perceived as congregating people with disabilities. This awareness led Kaposia to revamp its mission, vision, and service principles to focus on integrated work as a "service without walls."

Kaposia's board of directors was supportive of the new direction, but total conversion was not part of the original plan. Kaposia intended to hire a new placement coordinator and begin demonstrating success by finding jobs for those who wanted to work in the community. As can happen with attempts to change organizations, however, Kaposia got caught up in planning (i.e., talking), which in turn delayed action. Once real change began, staff and other constituent groups expressed concern. The changes were threatening because they were contrary to most of what staff and constituents believed in for years. Staff who wanted to participate in the conversion process were nevertheless encouraged to do so. Staff training was viewed as essential and was well supported by Kaposia. Despite this, most of the original staff left over a period of 3 years.

An outside consultant proved very helpful in keeping the CEO and program on course. Rather than invest in a long-term plan during this period of uncertainty, Kaposia only planned for about 4 months at a time.

Kaposia worked to change its image externally as well as internally. Age-inappropriate materials were removed from the workcenter, and staff roles and expectations were changed to present a more professional image as well as to meet the needs of consumers. Employer assistance was sought to advise Kaposia regarding a name change and other image-related issues.

Funding came from multiple sources, including state and federal grants. New relationships were developed with Minnesota's DRS and other state agencies in order to fund supported employment efforts.

A key decision in the process of the workcenter's closure was to disallow new admissions to the workcenter. By doing this, Kaposia reinforced its new mission and reaffirmed its belief that people with disabilities did not need a special, segregated place in which to work.

Kaposia closed down its workcenter completely and renegotiated the lease for the building about 6 years after the initial changes began. Fortunately, the landlord was agreeable to decreasing the length of time remaining on the lease from 2 years to 6 months. This allowed the workcenter participants adequate time to find community employment.

Staff now prefer to identify Kaposia as a customer-oriented company rather than as a human services program; the latter is now viewed as being too paternalistic. Kaposia serves about 150 people and received a grant recently to offer services to people who have been living in a regional treatment center in nearby Hennepin

County. According to the CEO, expanding into Hennepin County will be Kaposia's major challenge in the late 1990s. Not only will Kaposia staff be working in a new county, but they will be providing integrated employment services for individuals who have been institutionalized for many years and have almost no community experience.

Kaposia also provides community-based, school-to-work transition services for students with severe and multiple disabilities. Previously, these students would have been viewed as candidates for segregated day or workshop programs only. More recently, staff have tried to improve their transitional employment program by using more natural supports in providing their employment services.

The CEO also mentioned that Kaposia has undertaken an internal reorganization effort designed to improve the quality of services, heighten the satisfaction of consumers, and use increasingly limited funding more efficiently. She explained that staff used *backward chaining* to analyze services carefully. This meant that they began by studying the services that people received last, such as ongoing supports, and moved to services provided earlier in the process, like taking initial telephone inquiries. In scrutinizing each of these tasks, staff identified several areas for improvement. One problem, for example, was an overreliance on outside, untrained, back-up staff. This practice was financially inefficient, was not well received by consumers, and was unsuccessful in providing necessary services.

In order to address this and other problems, Kaposia changed its traditional, hierarchical staff structure to one comprising three self-managed teams. According to the CEO, the new structure allows direct service staff more flexibility in making daily decisions and especially in providing back-up supports internally. Each team is responsible for developing a back-up support plan for every consumer using existing Kaposia staff. According to the CEO, this team structure has been successful because outside people are no longer providing back-up support for Kaposia staff.

7

New Horizons

Located in a very rural area in Ashland, Wisconsin, New Horizons provides services for individuals with developmental disabilities and/or mental illness. These groups make up 75% and 25% of those served by the agency, respectively. New Horizons covers two geographically large counties, and, with the exception of one community with a population of 8,600, there are no communities with more than 2,000 people. Major industries of the region include logging and tourism, and local government is the largest single employer.

Established in 1968, New Horizons offered a day activities program in which 35–40 people came to a center and engaged in work, social, recreation, and skill-building activities. Employing nine staff, New Horizons offered 17 classes in subjects such as cooking, bed making, money management, first aid, and sex education.

New Horizons provided work and day activities. As the agency's executive director noted, "We never had a sheltered workshop because none of the people that we served were that skilled. They were all considered to be [at the] work activities or day services level." New Horizons provided work activities in areas like recycling, rug making, and woodworking. Staff did not focus on community employment. This was evidenced by the fact that only one person obtained a community job during the first 13 years of the agency's operations.

New Horizons also had a resource room where activities were conducted for people whose disabilities or behavior problems were thought to preclude their working in the workcenter. There they matched colors, learned to write their names, and went on outings or participated in other recreation activities. Friday afternoons were set aside for bowling, and all agency participants went to camp in the summer.

New Horizons also ran a community residence program consisting of two group homes housing four and eight people, respectively. The executive director had been with the agency for 7 years at the time New Horizons's changes began. She started as a part-time home training consultant and worked her way up to become the executive director in 1980.

INITIAL IMPETUS FOR CHANGE

The executive director attended a speech given by the former director of a statewide advocacy organization who was a strong proponent of community integration. The speaker impressed the executive director with her talk about the separate, segregated lives led by people with disabilities in contemporary society and her criticisms of existing human services programs that promulgate such separatist circumstances. This stimulated the executive director's thinking about what was happening at New Horizons and led her to call for a total agency self-evaluation.

Creating a Vision

The self-evaluation took the form of a combined staff–board of directors retreat during which staff, through their own PASS evaluation, and the board held a day-long meeting about New Horizons's mission and values. The purpose of the retreat was to evaluate the services provided by New Horizons with regard to whether they provided real opportunities for people to learn, grow, and be seen as valued members of their communities. Staff asked themselves, "What do we want our services to achieve for each person we serve?" After reviewing the people receiving services and the services being offered, staff concluded that the way in which they provided services reinforced stereotypic thinking already prevalent in the United States.

The board then passed a resolution that stated New Horizons's commitment to integrating program participants into the community. At that time, there was no thought of closing down the segregated day activities program. The executive director described the agency's changed vision as follows:

> What really facilitated actual change for us was the shift in our thinking about what was possible for people with disabilities. We stopped thinking about them as people who needed to be taken care of and started thinking that, given the right opportunities, they could make some valuable contributions. We stopped thinking that they needed to be kept busy. We started thinking that maybe we need to be providing

opportunities for them to be seen as valued citizens. We stopped thinking that people with severe disabilities can't do meaningful work and started thinking that they can work with support and training. We just have to figure out what that will be.

And we stopped thinking about all the reasons why things can't happen and started thinking: "Let's figure out ways to make things we think should happen, happen." So our focus moved from a focus on disabilities and obstacles to a focus on opportunities and abilities.

How Change Began

After the board committed to integrated employment, a new mission statement was developed. It stated that New Horizons was committed to improving the quality of life for people with disabilities by providing programs and services that facilitate their integration into the mainstream of their communities. The executive director then established a task force to consider how to implement and educate the local community about New Horizons's new mission. Representatives from the local vocational technical school, the state job service, the office of vocational rehabilitation (VR), and other local service organizations served on the task force. They reportedly got the word out about the New Horizons's changes and provided some initial community education about the agency's new mission.

The first step toward change involved eliminating nonwork activities from the in-house day activities center and focusing staff energies on community employment. This occurred over the course of a few years and included steps such as 1) teaching daily living skills at home instead of in the day activities center, and 2) moving people from the day activities center to the in-house workcenter in order to eliminate nonwork activities while community employment was being sought. This move was resisted by workcenter supervisors who saw participants in the day activities center as unproductive and potentially disruptive. In order to compromise, the executive director instructed staff to bring subcontract work into the day activities center. Staff there were told to focus on teaching the participants how to work instead of academics and daily living skills. Eventually, people from the day activities center gradually moved into the workcenter (which was located in the same building) with the day activities staff providing supports.

Another work-related reform involved making the workcenter more businesslike. In an attempt to help participants improve their self-images and make positive impressions in the community, the agency focused on assisting them to update their clothing and use age-appropriate lunch containers for work. In addition, people were now required to punch a time clock each day. No longer could program participants schedule medical appointments during work hours or take vacations without proper notice. The executive director also began a community education program through the local media to eliminate New Horizons's image as a charity organization. The agency gave up accepting ticket donations from charities. Through this media campaign the executive director emphasized the agency's business, production, and training orientation.

A final step taken to enhance New Horizons's image as a legitimate place of business was the renovation of its physical plant. As the executive director said, she received a community block grant and a Small Business Association loan to modify the facility inside and out:

> The building we were in was a shabby mess and we wanted to be seen as a business, so we needed to change our image. We needed to look like we valued the people we served by having a decent place for them to work. That was long before we ever thought of closing down. [After the renovations] it fit into the community. . . . It's kind of nondescript, but attractive, and you drive by it and say, "I wonder what kind of business is in there?" I sold the building in November of 1994, after leasing it for awhile to a light manufacturing company.

New Horizons began to focus on community employment, attempting to find competitive jobs for as many people as possible. Although initial efforts were unsophisticated, staff were clearly moving away from the day activities focus of the past.

In addition to changing its workcenter, New Horizons also began to address its segregated recreation activities. Friday afternoon bowling, group camping, weekly sing-alongs, and the Special Olympics were all either eliminated gradually or modified significantly.

New Horizons encouraged folks who liked to bowl to join regular leagues. Group camping activities were replaced with a more individualized approach through which people were asked where they wanted to go on vacation and then helped to make specific arrangements with staff support and accompaniment, if necessary. Gradually, staff were replaced by volunteers, and families and friends currently assume the major responsibilities for individuals' vacations. The Special Olympics, which had been sponsored by New Horizons, was stopped after the agency withdrew its support. Because no one else sponsored the Special Olympics it expired gradually with few objections from families or community groups.

Weekly sing-alongs at the workcenter were eliminated during work hours and rescheduled in the evenings. The executive director said that sing-alongs were popular events that involved a group of committed community volunteers. Staff, participants, and volunteers complained that evenings were not convenient because many participants could not attend in the evenings. It was left to the group to find a time that would not interfere with people's work schedules, but apparently no other convenient time was arranged and the event ceased to occur.

New Horizons also closed down its two group homes. Agency staff asked participants where and with whom they wanted to live and helped them to secure the individual living situations they preferred. This was the beginning of what today is a viable supported living service.

AGENCY PLANNING

As the changes began, the executive director recalled that everyone, herself included, experienced a lot of confusion and uncertainty. She could present no long-term plan or well-conceived vision for the staff, and she often improvised as the changes continued:

> One of the things that didn't go well is that I was unclear about what kind of staff structure or even what kind of employment service I wanted to set up. With so much uncertainty, I often let staff do what they were most interested in as long as all bases were covered. . . . If they wanted to try job coaching, they could. If they wanted to stay in-house as floor supervisors, they could. I remember [one staff member] asking me, "What am I supposed to do? What is my job?" And I didn't know. I would say, "Come back in a few weeks and hopefully I will have it figured out." Eventually staff got a feel for what they preferred, and I got an idea of who had the skills to do good job coaching.

Restructuring

After this period of uncertainty, the executive director developed a new structure in pursuing her supported employment goals. She wrote new job descriptions and asked staff to apply for the jobs for which they felt qualified.

After developing a vision, identifying procedures for realizing that vision, and filling newly created jobs, staff began working to place people in community jobs. The executive director said that initial efforts were very successful, but staff were promising too much to employers and then trying to deliver it. This led to more challenges and dilemmas. New Horizons was taking action on the staff's behalf, however, and that, the executive director felt, was the most important issue:

> It was real challenging operating a [workcenter] that needed workers and was simultaneously placing some of our best workers in jobs in

the community. As people left, the supervisors would say, "How am I going to [run the center] without them?" We said, "Well, we will just have to figure that out, and we did."

Implicit in the preceding comments is the dilemma faced by the executive director who, although planning for the dissolution of an old system, had to maintain that system minimally in order to build a new system on the same financial, physical, and staff foundations. As the executive director described her dilemma and her solution, it was evident that one system and staff would have to endure some neglect:

> The [in-house] staff said, "We don't get any attention here. This place is really suffering." And I said, "You're right. It is suffering, but we can't do both of these things well. So, for now it is just going to have to be that way." I think this is where [we had] to make short-term concessions for long-term results. I think that clearly one of our concessions was that while people were still working in-house, we couldn't give them all the attention they and we would have liked.

The executive director wanted to maintain only those work activities that she considered to be consistent with New Horizons's new direction and business image. The used clothing store that operated at the workcenter was a long-standing and popular endeavor for both the agency and the community. The store was not an integrated employment activity, however, and it perpetuated an outdated image of the agency to the general public. Despite some staff and community opposition, the executive director closed the clothing store.

But the executive director viewed the recycling center as a profitable and potentially integrated *affirmative business*. Affirmative businesses are businesses that 1) exist to make a profit, 2) attempt to operate as free-standing small businesses without social services subsidies, 3) do not offer vocational rehabilitation services, and 4) employ workers with disabilities and workers without disabilities. Most often, affirmative businesses operate as separate units under the administrative umbrellas of not-for-profit rehabilitation agencies and begin as successful subcontracts, enclaves, or work crews. She saw it as a commercial enterprise that could be "spun off" as a free-standing business. After developing a business plan, she decided to create a separate business development unit within New Horizons that would operate the recycling center and possibly other similar businesses. Five employees, three of whom had disabilities, were hired to run the recycling center. Four years later, the entire center was sold to a major recycling company.

Furthering the Commitment to Change

Several years after the changes began at New Horizons, the executive director hired an outside facilitator and held a week-long planning retreat to discuss possible future directions. During that retreat, it became clear that the agency could not provide both in-house employment services and community employment services because of the contradictions inherent in doing so. Following the retreat, the board passed another resolution stating that the agency would provide only community-based services. A new future vision was developed that reflected the agency's total commitment to community integration.

Closing the Workcenter

The executive director noted that staff were so focused on finding community employment for workcenter participants that they seemed as surprised as anyone when they realized that only 13 of the original 35 participants remained in the workcenter. Some returned when their seasonal jobs ended or when they were not working in the community, and many of those who returned did so out of convenience rather than necessity. It became obvious that as more people entered community jobs, there was less and less need for the workcenter facility. As the executive director remarked, "We didn't plan to close the [workcenter]. It just evolved that way."

Soon after the board passed its resolution to provide only community-based services, New Horizons closed its sheltered workcenter, leaving five people unemployed. Those five, all of whom were considered to have challenging disabilities, were placed in jobs within 4 months of the facility's closing.

When people lost their jobs or needed some additional work hours, New Horizons offered options such as joining others in existing community jobs, working with integrated work crews that cleaned rest stops along highways and included people without disabilities who were hired by New Horizons, staying at home, performing volunteer work, or increasing daily living skills through training activities. Volunteer placements at several local churches and a co-op are used currently as interim activities for people who lose their jobs.

New Horizons's workcenter facility was sold in November of 1994 after being leased to a light manufacturing company. The agency's supported employment division now provides services for 85 people and employs 16 staff. This amounts to a ratio of service recipients to service providers of about 4:1.

Individual placements and *dispersed cluster sites*—sites at which several people work in different areas of the same business—facilitate New Horizons's provision of supported employment services. For example, in one hotel, New Horizons has two people working in the kitchen, one in the laundry, and two on the main floor, with one staff person monitoring the entire site. These people do not work the same schedules but rather work at different times throughout the day and week.

Staff have attempted to address people's transportation needs using the most typical methods available. Individuals walk, use buses, ride with co-workers, or, as a last resort, are driven by agency staff.

In 1994, one third of the people employed through New Horizons were receiving at least minimum wage. All others were working for subminimum wages. On average, people worked between 16 and 18 hours per week. According to the executive director, some people worked 30 hours per week. Other people, particularly those with mental illness, only wanted to work between 2 and 6 hours a week.

STAFF TRAINING AND HIRING

The executive director recalled that when staff initially began community employment efforts, they had much enthusiasm but little technical knowledge. She indicated that they did job placement "backwards," starting out by finding jobs and subsequently figuring out who could do them. As she noted, "We would post these jobs and ask if anyone would like to try any of them. We were often out there finding jobs and placing people and promising the world to employers, then struggling to deliver it."

Developing Expertise in Job Placement

Because the people who wanted community jobs were generally the best workers in the workcenter, initial job placement efforts resulted in removing these participants from the workcenter within a relatively short period of time. This left a concentration of people in the workcenter who were considered less productive and more challenging. Thus, work with people who might have required more creative placement and support efforts was put off until staff gained more experience and skill. The executive director described how staff developed job placement skills gradually:

> We just decided as a staff that we better try someone we considered more difficult to place because we had to know if we could do this.

And so we picked an individual who [was] pretty severely impaired and just tried him in a nursing home volunteering. We just asked to try it for 6 or 8 weeks . . . and it worked out well. And then we started figuring out how to do a real jobsite. And I think our whole job development process changed then. We were really getting clearer about the fact that it [was] critical to get to know the individual first and that we had to go into the worksite with the goal of finding out what the employer's needs [were]. Once we started doing that, we would go into these worksites with someone in mind that we knew had some skills that could be used in that particular worksite. We would tour the site sometimes two or three times to figure out what the employer's needs were. We always [did] written proposals [for] the employer [that identified] the benefits of supported employment . . . and specifically how we [intended] to meet [those] needs.

Getting Technical Assistance

During the initial period of change, New Horizons received technical assistance from outside sources, especially from state agencies and advocacy organizations that were supportive of its changes. The executive director said that these agencies and organizations were useful in teaching staff the techniques of supported employment; helping staff to design a new program and organizational structure; and providing staff with values clarification, moral support, and a vision for the future. The executive director was not shy about seeking such assistance because New Horizons was one of the first agencies in Wisconsin to provide integrated employment services only. As she recalled,

I called them and said, "If you say this is the right way to go, and we are here trying to make it happen, then we need your help." Most of the training at that time was done by an outside consultant. I would call her and say, "You need to make another trip up here. We are stuck." And she would come, and we would figure out ahead of time what [she would teach] and she would do training on supported employment and give us moral support.

Now we have a very strong supported employment team. It is the strongest team in our agency. There are 16 people on that team, and they support about 80 people working in the community in about 35 businesses. We also send all new staff through PASS training to strengthen their values.

Hiring Good People

Training was apparently not the only means by which the executive director tried to assemble a competent staff. She also believed that the hiring process was critical. When assessing prospective employees for agency positions, the executive director emphasized applicants' values regarding people with disabilities before she considered their professional backgrounds and experiences. As part of the interviewing process, she also said that she asked prospective employees how they might respond to various scenarios. These scenarios were developed by her and were intended to demonstrate applicants' values as well as their technical knowledge.

TRANSITIONAL FUNDING

Soon after New Horizons decided to change its orientation, the executive director met with funding organizations and explained her desire to move toward agency conversion. New Horizons received contracts from two counties to provide work and day activities for people with disabilities in those counties. Although one county was very supportive of New Horizons's changes, the other was reportedly less agreeable because a parent opposed the changes. As the executive director recalled,

> The parent of one of our service recipients was vehemently opposed to our proposed changes and did everything he could to defeat us and harass us. I had to work with the county director, who was supportive, to give the appearance that we were putting money into sheltered services before this parent, who was on the county board, would sign the contract. He got really ugly with me publicly.
>
> With each of these boards I regularly presented what we were doing and why we were doing it. I talked to them about how we saw people with disabilities and how we saw their lives being on a separate track from any of us. I attempted to bring them along all the time. His board . . . got tired of him saying all this awful stuff about me, and finally after several months they just told him they had heard enough and proceeded to allow us to move ahead.

Current funding sources remain similar to those used in the past, except that workcenter funding has been shifted gradually to fund community-based services. Funding is now used to support staff as they help people to find and maintain paid community jobs. During the period of transition, both the workcenter and supported employment activities needed funding. The executive director explained how she was able to balance the needs of the two:

> We were funded pretty typically. We received a per-hour rate for people in the [workcenter]. So when people went into the community, that money just shifted to the community. At the same time the state received a systems change grant and sent out RFPs to counties to apply for that funding. We received a $60,000 grant on behalf of these two counties for a 2-year period. The goal for the grant was to complete our conversion by placing the last 13 people into the community and to provide ongoing support services for them. The funding helped carry us through the transition period of moving from segregated to community-based services. We also wrote a business plan and created

a business from our most profitable work activity. So that $60,000 helped us both psychologically and financially to make the leap.

CONSTITUENT RESPONSES TO NEW HORIZONS'S CHANGES

Consumer Responses

The executive director described how staff worked with workcenter participants in preparing them to move into community jobs. Staff discussed participants' feelings about 1) how they were viewed and treated by community members, 2) what opportunities were available in the community, and 3) what kinds of activities they might like to pursue in the future.

The decision of whether to look for community jobs was left up to the workcenter participants themselves. Although the idea of working in the community was new to many people, their enthusiasm for trying it was never an issue, especially after they saw their peers doing it:

> When some people who worked in the community came back to the workcenter for part of the day, they often still had their uniforms on. Others would see them and get very excited, asking us, "When am I going to get a chance to do that?" Some staff didn't want to face the workcenter participants because they . . . always . . . asked when [they] would . . . be getting [jobs]. And staff couldn't answer them. So it just was infectious.

Family Responses

The executive director said that although individual families had particular concerns, most always dreamed of their offspring or siblings working in the community. They just never thought it was possible. Thus, community employment seemed to be such an unlikely prospect that many families did not become overly excited about it.

In addressing specific family issues, the executive director met with families individually and focused on their concerns. She described her approach:

> I never met with families as a group and said, "This is what we are going to do" for several reasons. One of them was that I wasn't always sure exactly where we were heading. But I did meet individually with them at their request and when I did, they would ask me, "What is going on with this organization? Are you closing up?" That was always the issue. I would tell them what I thought was possible for their son or daughter and how we would like a chance to try and find a job in the community for him or her. Several parents believed that, because of the severity of their adult child's disability, the staff would never

find a job for him or her. And, although I wasn't always sure myself, I would say we think we can do it and ask that they let us try. And most parents allowed us to try as long as their son or daughter had something to do during the day.

The executive director described some instances of working with people whose families were initially opposed to the idea of community employment. They described her approach as "somewhat sneaky" but effective. In several instances, the resistance of families dissipated after observing their offspring or siblings working in community jobs:

> One mother we knew would be very hesitant about allowing us to place her daughter in the community. The daughter regularly came into the center to work. We placed her in a job washing dishes at a local restaurant for a few hours a day, and we did not tell her mother about it until she had worked there for a couple of weeks. We then called her mother and said that we have been letting her daughter wash dishes down at this restaurant and did she want to come and see how she was doing. She came down and was surprised and impressed. That was 6 years ago. Now the family is very proud of her community job and [they] like the fact that there is more income coming into their home.

In another instance, a parent opposed her son's being placed in the community because she felt that he was incapable of competitive work. After New Horizons placed him in a job in a library, she came to the executive director in tears. She said, "You know he never even graduated from first grade, and now he is working in a college library. I can't believe it's so. I'm so proud."

Of course, not all families were convinced, and some remained opposed to New Horizons's changes even after their offspring or siblings found and retained community jobs successfully. With regard to one parent, the executive director noted that,

> His son was one of the most highly skilled people in our agency. We would have liked for him to be one of the first people placed in community employment, but unfortunately, due to his father's resistance, he was one of our last placements. He is now working 30 hours a week at a pizza place and he loves it.

Due to their disagreement with New Horizons's direction, one family pulled their daughter out of the workcenter. She remains at home because there are no other workcenter services available in the area.

Staff Responses

Some staff were not sure about the parts they wanted to play in New Horizons's future and were threatened by the agency's changes. Many staff were worried about losing their jobs. Initially there was a sharp division between those who felt that advocates of New Horizons's changes were being unrealistic and those who characterized opponents of the changes as overly negative. Staff tensions were reflected during meetings and often caused debates about consumer choice and how staff should deal with people's choices concerning where they lived and worked and even what they wore.

The executive director admitted that staff did not accept the changes smoothly. She believed this was so in part because the proposed changes caused anxiety among staff and in part because she could offer no reassuring vision of New Horizons's future structure. That vision evolved over time.

Workcenter staff had several major concerns of their own. First, they objected to losing their best workers to community jobs because they were under pressure to complete contract work for area businesses. Second, they were unhappy about accepting new workers whom they described as less productive and in need of more supervision than those they lost. As a result of these circumstances, many of the participants remaining in the workcenter were not capable of doing the amount of work necessary to fulfill contract obligations. Therefore, staff not only had to do more of the contract work themselves in order to keep up with production, but they had to provide more intensive supervision as well.

The executive director mentioned that during this period, she experienced a particularly turbulent relationship with her work director. Upon reflection, she realized that although she was looking at change in terms of agency growth and progress, he viewed it as a personal loss. She described the situation:

> It is important to recognize that significant change means difficult times and often results in loss and anger. That was something my work director and I had a real difficult time with. Here we were looking at disassembling the whole work program that he had spent the last 10 years building up. And it wasn't that he didn't believe in what we were doing, but it was just the pain of letting go of something in which he had invested so much of himself.

Although problems persisted, some things stood out that really propelled the staff forward. One positive consequence of productive workers leaving the workcenter was the emergence of other workers who were not previously considered to be very capable. The executive director cited one example that illustrated dramatically how grossly staff could devalue and underestimate the abilities of workers:

When we needed someone in the wood shop to cut boards and couldn't find anyone, someone, just as a joke, said, "Let's put Marv in there." Marv is this old guy who could hardly see. And one of the staff said, "I'm going to do that. I'm just going to try him." Well, with some jigs, he worked out beautifully . . . and we thought, "Man, we have been limiting these people all along just by our limited vision of what they can do."

The executive director felt that the time she spent acknowledging and trying to address their concerns also helped staff to accept the changes:

In our staff meetings I would want to get everyone's concerns up on the wall and say, "Yes, this is a real concern." I talked to people and said that if you couldn't bring yourself to say, "I am afraid of losing my job" in the meetings, I'll identify it for you. Then we will systematically try to address each issue. Some turned out not to be significant concerns in the end, but at the time they were important for those individuals and needed to be acknowledged.

I also tried to figure out ways to get staff to come to some consensus on what we finally decided to do. They did not have to agree with or 100% support what we were trying to do, but just agree to try it. I asked for that commitment at a large staff meeting by a show of hands. It was pretty tense. Some hands went up reluctantly, but they all did go up. And I said I understand that not everyone is 100% behind this, but I just want your willingness to try it. And I did get that commitment.

Another thing I did was try to identify for staff what I call *responsibilities for success*. I said, "If this is going to work, then what you are responsible for is this portion of it." I would then identify specific activities or areas each person had responsibility for. And we worked hard to develop a team approach to services. The organization now is completely organized around teams.

The executive director believed that her efforts to acknowledge staff concerns and to encourage continuing discussion and mutual cooperation ultimately helped to minimize attrition. She also believed that she was successful in getting staff to at least give the changes a chance so that everyone could come together as a team to address any problems that were identified.

Three of 11 staff members eventually left New Horizons. They left for a variety of reasons, ranging from impatience with the slow rate of change to a lack of skills to perform new job duties. In some cases, staff members were identified as having skills that, although useful in the old system, were especially valuable given the agency's new focus. For example, the resource room teacher, who taught individuals with the most severe disabilities, was moved to the workcenter initially to teach work skills and practical reading and writing skills. Her ability to break down tasks while teaching, however, made her particularly valuable as a vocational trainer. Eventually, she became the director of the supported employment program.

Responses of Community Members

When members of the community heard that New Horizons was moving people into community jobs, they expressed serious concerns. The mayor and some city council members met with New Horizons's executive director to discuss the situation. The executive director remembered telling them that, "We're a service. We're not a building. Our services are just being provided in a different location, but we are not going to close up." They did not believe this, however, until the executive director drew for the group a schema that illustrated how people were spending their days. The visual depiction apparently demonstrated successfully that New Horizons was doing the same thing it always did, except that its base of operations was now the community instead of the sheltered workcenter.

Other community members were slower in getting this message. As the executive director noted, "About a year ago, we moved out of the building that had housed our sheltered services for years into these offices. Recently, someone asked me, 'Well where do you work now that [New Horizons] is closed?' So, it is still a mystery to some people out there."

THE EXECUTIVE DIRECTOR'S PERSONAL REFLECTIONS

In reflecting on her experiences, the executive director listed several factors that she thought were instrumental to New Horizons's successful conversion. These included the following: 1) the staff's ability to truly change their thinking about the people receiving services; 2) the willingness of staff to put this new thinking into practice; 3) the decision to start small and build on whatever success was achieved; 4) the effort to begin with people who could succeed and learn from their experiences; and 5) the use of outside assistance for values clarification, technical assistance, and emotional support. The final factor was noted by the executive director when she described what helped her to get through the process:

> Many times [I had] this fear, "Where am I taking this place? Where am I going?" And I honestly got through that with the support of [outside consultants]. I would say to them, "I don't know what I am doing here. I need help." And so I think that is one of the things that I often talk about in this process. . . . I remember [one of the consultants] coming

up here and saying, "Look, you guys are your own worst enemies. You stand here looking at your feet. Look where you've come from and where you are headed. And you just continue on that path." And that did it for me. Look at the significant progress we made here.

You have to be willing to take risks and you have to learn to live with uncertainty. You have to believe strongly in what you are doing. And you can't wait for all the pieces to fit together before you take action because if you do, nothing will ever happen.

SUMMARY

New Horizons's conversion was similar in many respects to that of Kaposia. But New Horizons began as a small day activities program rather than as a sheltered workcenter. The impetus for change came from influential leaders in the field who presented a new vision regarding employment services for people with disabilities. This resulted in New Horizons's staff reevaluating their services. Like Kaposia, New Horizons's initial plan for change did not speak of conversion; that may have been the reason for the board's receptiveness from the start.

After a new mission statement was developed, a task force was formed to develop and implement a plan for change. This task force was made up of many key people, including community members, in order to solicit their involvement and support from the outset.

The executive director spoke of her uncertainty about how to go about making the desired changes and of the importance of using outside consultants. These consultants helped to 1) keep the process moving smoothly, and 2) bolster the confidence and spirits of the executive director and staff during difficult times.

Efforts were made to normalize the workcenter environment (i.e., to make the workcenter's environment more like a community work setting) as well as to change the agency's image in the community. As the focus on community employment grew, in-house tension with staff increased. It was clear that New Horizons could not provide both sheltered employment and integrated employment services, nor could it support its segregated recreation and group home services. Much upheaval occurred, which in turn caused some staff turnover.

A key strategy of both Kaposia and New Horizons was to work initially with people who wanted to leave sheltered employment settings. Staff received training and technical assistance, and attempts were made to cater to staff preferences regarding their roles.

Constituent responses were similar to those reported by Kaposia. Individuals with disabilities who had community jobs influenced others who were still in-house to try employment in the community. There seemed to be little resistance among these people. Nonetheless, some families were resistant. By addressing concerns individually rather than meeting as a large group, however, the executive director diffused much of this resistance.

Staff initially resisted the changes as well, and this caused sharp divisions among staff. A team structure was beneficial to both staff and consumers, however, and successes were celebrated.

Some community members reacted negatively when informed of New Horizons's plan to close its workcenter. It was difficult for many to understand that a building was not essential to providing the services that people needed to be successful. New Horizons has separated itself completely from the physical remnants of its workcenter. The facility was sold 5 years after the workcenter closed officially.

New Horizons currently provides services for 65 people with developmental disabilities and 20 individuals classified as having mental illness in supported work settings. The majority are served on individual sites. In some instances, however, two people are paired at one site and paid subminimum wages based on performance.

The agency recently reorganized internally, and teams were created that comprise both supported employment and supported living staff. Reportedly, the result is less fragmented, more wholistic services. Staff on these teams may eventually become more generic in that they could provide supports to individuals on their jobsites, in their homes, or in the community as need and availability dictate.

8

Avatrac

Avatrac, a division of Developmental Pathways located in Denver, Colorado, provides services for a largely urban population in the western United States. It offers vocational, residential, transportation, and service coordination services. In 1985, the employment division of Avatrac was providing services at two different workshop sites for about 248 people classified as having mental retardation. Avatrac emphasized production, generating about $500,000 worth of contracts annually. Reportedly, downtime was being virtually eliminated through effective and aggressive marketing.

The agency operated like a traditional sheltered workshop. People entered through the vocational evaluation system and were assigned to the in-house program that was determined to best meet their vocational needs. Those assigned to the prevocational program learned activities of daily living until they were promoted to the work activities program, wherein work was offered as a therapeutic activity. Those progressing through the work activities program, which developed participants' employability, eventually could move to work adjustment training (to enhance employability) and finally to competitive job placement services (i.e., job acquisition) if they were deemed ready. Those individuals who found community jobs were offered follow-up services through periodic visits to their worksites. About 95% of those placed were unemployed within 6 months, however, and returned to the workshop.

INITIAL IMPETUS FOR CHANGE

Until 1985, Avatrac was considered to be a very successful sheltered workshop and in fact was looking to expand its sheltered employment operations. The agency bought 5 acres of land on which to build a plant to pursue its major ambition—to become a respected and efficient subcontractor within the business community. The opposition of two local human services agencies to the expansion of segregated services coupled with several other events, however, led to Avatrac reconsidering its plans and eventually to the development of an entirely new agency focus.

In addition to the opposition of these local agencies, Avatrac's director of adult services pointed to several other events that facilitated Avatrac's change in focus. These included the following: 1) several presentations about supported employment that formed the basis for developing alternative employment services, 2) a staff gripe session about the workshop that led to the identification of eight problems that would remain unsolvable for as long as the workshop remained in operation (these problems were used ultimately as justification for converting the workshop), and 3) the staff's trip to another state to observe a new supported employment program that had converted virtually its entire sheltered workshop.

Although this trip was intended originally to gather information to fight for workshop expansion at home, it helped to educate staff about the integrated vocational options that could be available to those in their sheltered workshop and served ultimately as a major impetus for abandoning the expansion effort. Staff returned believing that integrated employment was "real doable." Nevertheless, the thought of converting the workshop was not considered until they hired a consultant who encouraged them to move in that direction. As the director of adult services noted, "Until [the consultant] came, we had no thought about converting. We just thought, 'Yes, supported work looks like a good thing, and we need to be looking at it.' "

Preliminary Planning

Staff eventually held a strategic planning meeting in which they asked an outside consultant to help them analyze their entire operation, including demographics, employment costs, service alternatives, and so forth. The director of adult services believed that this meeting was instrumental in moving Avatrac toward radical change:

> I mean it came down to if we were in business to create employment, [then] what could [we] lose to look at [supported employment]. We had the traditional placement model, and I guess the question in the end we had to ask [was], "Why would we continue to do what we are doing when we can skip that and go right to the punch line?"

Creating a Vision

During the 2-day meeting, staff determined that their major objective should be community placement—a goal that was seen as incompatible with Avatrac's workshop operations. As the director of adult services noted, "The outcome of the meeting was, 'Yes, we were going to convert. . .' And part of our rationale was we believed in [supported employment], and . . . we knew we couldn't do both. We couldn't run workshops and do supported employment."

After the planning was complete, agency staff submitted a 3-year plan to the board of directors. The plan outlined their intentions to eliminate all sheltered employment services and to develop an integrated employment model.

TRANSITIONAL FUNDING

One problem faced immediately by Avatrac was that its funding was contingent on people being served within its workshop. Once a person left the workshop for a community job, for example, the financial assistance received for that individual from Colorado's Division for Developmental Disabilities (DDD) was cut off. This was a major problem when Avatrac's proposal for conversion was presented to agency constituents such as service recipients, staff, board members, and state representatives. Staff and others said that such conversion could not be done. The director of adult services described this negative thinking and how she fought against it: "Initially we started saying, 'Well we can't do this, and we can't do that.' And it started to get so frustrating that finally we said, 'Look, if we base this plan on all the what ifs, we aren't going to do anything.' "

The most pressing issue for Avatrac was to analyze the restrictions that the DDD imposed on its funding so that it could find a way to fund the proposed conversion. One thing working in Avatrac's favor was that the state had been encouraging agencies to provide more integrated employment services. No new funding was available to aid in such endeavors, however, and agencies such as Avatrac had to implement changes within budgetary constraints.

Avatrac decided to ask the state to waive the restrictions that limited funding to specific transportation and adult services in favor of allocating yearly funding through a 3-year block grant whose amount would be determined by multiplying the number of people to be served annually by their projected hours of service and their hourly pay rates. In addition, Avatrac promised to carry out specific tasks such as developing accounting and tracking systems, providing a marketing plan, and maintaining outcome data.

Interestingly, staff felt that their plan was too radical and would not be accepted by DDD representatives. Their conclusion seemed correct when the DDD replied with a memo of understanding that was very different from the staff's original proposal. But Avatrac staff persisted. They resubmitted their original proposal with only minor modifications and prepared for some hard bargaining. When they met with DDD officials, however, staff were amazed to discover that they signed the resubmitted document with no changes.

Three years later, when the block grant was about to expire, the state announced that it was reestablishing its previous funding procedures and that no individually negotiated deals would be approved. Nevertheless, Avatrac was successful in persuading the state to renew the previous arrangement.

In addition to redesigning its funding arrangements with the state, Avatrac began to search for new sources of financial assistance. One source that staff had never used was Colorado's Division of Vocational Rehabilitation (DVR). The DVR proved to be fertile ground because Avatrac purportedly received about $500,000 through the DVR. This funding came through allocations for case services and demonstration grants. Again, as it did with DDD funding, Avatrac used DVR funding creatively. Although staff were told that DVR funding had to be allocated in a certain way, they negotiated a special arrangement by which case services funding was provided through a block grant. In this way, Avatrac was able to use the funding to hire a job coach.

The state's funding did not, however, offset the agency's expenses dollar for dollar. In order to cover those expenses, Avatrac had to negotiate an average funding allocation for each individual receiving services and hope that some of those individuals would not require the full allocation. As the director of adult services said,

> To be honest, the only way that [individual funding] works is when people are paying what [services] cost. And that is clearly not the case in [this state]. The only way we can do what we are doing is if we have a block of money that we can shift around. Like if we get $5,000 per person, but only spend $500. We can shift that $4,500 to someone else who requires more support to be successful in community employment.

AGENCY PLANNING

Initially, Avatrac decided to adopt an enclave model as well as an individual placement model of employment services. Under these models, everyone attending the workshop eventually would be assisted in finding an enclave or individual job in which to work, and it was estimated that the workshop would be maintained for about

3 years. This was due in part to staff assurances that if a workshop participant lost his or her job, he or she could return to the workshop for as long as it existed. The director of adult services believed that this was a critical element in the agency's strategy for marketing to its constituents.

Staff Reorganization

There was a need to reorganize the agency to make its structure and functions more consistent with its new mission. Avatrac needed to become less bureaucratic and more businesslike. The director of adult services developed a schema that was consistent with the agency's new organizational goals. This schema consisted of a career ladder that led to increasing responsibility and salary. The director of adult services asked people to identify their first, second, and third job choices. They then were interviewed and hired into one of their job choices in most cases. Eventually, the director of adult services ended up with 12 job coaches, pared down the number of workshop supervisors as people found community employment, and hired a marketing manager. Initially, staff were given assigned readings to help them learn about supported employment, and time was set aside to discuss Avatrac's changing structure and functions.

From Workshop to Storefronts

Soon after deciding to change, Avatrac staff projected less need for a large workshop and began planning alternative ways in which to use the workshop facility. Based on first-year placement projections, they leased space in the facility. In each succeeding year, less space was to be allocated for the workshop.

The most well-behaved and competent workers left the workshop. Remaining in the smaller workshop were the participants who had fewer work skills and more behavior difficulties. This situation reportedly created a supervision problem for staff. To address the problem, they proposed to replace the workshop with several smaller storefronts. In describing the problem, the director of adult services implied that it was primarily a workshop management dilemma:

> Part of [the problem] may have been that the space was small, but I don't think so because people had plenty of room. But it was like people were vying for attention. If one person went off, everybody went off. It was just unmanageable.
> I think our real motivation in moving [from the workshop] to the storefronts was to give people some space, particularly because half of

the individuals lived in the same residences. When we had the bigger facility, it was easier for us to separate some of those folks and give them some time away from one another. But when we had the smaller site, half of them who also lived together were saying, "This is not where we want to be."

Thus, about 4 years after the conversion began, Avatrac shut down its two large sheltered workshops and created eight rented storefronts in the community. Initially, each storefront had between 8 and 15 participants in attendance and one or two supervisors. More recently, at least one storefront has taken on the appearance of a sheltered workshop. It has become quite large, with 45 people in attendance, and is beginning to do subcontract work. The director of adult services described how this occurred:

> We sort of went backwards for a variety of reasons. Part of our rationale was that it didn't matter what it looks like. A workshop is a workshop. Let's just call a spade a spade. What was happening was that people on the east side of town really wanted to work while they were waiting for employment. But the storefronts weren't conducive to us doing subcontract work.
>
> We had also gotten into some problems with single coverage [at the same sites] where people weren't safe. . . . We heard from our families and advocates that they had real concerns about single coverage. So when we looked at the east side, we made the decision to get bigger again. . . . We did not make that decision on the west side of town. Even though the eastside site was established, it has not changed the employment-for-all goal.

STAFF FOCUS AND TRAINING

According to the director of adult services, the big issues confronting Avatrac were how to motivate staff to embrace change and how to give staff the training they needed to participate in the conversion process. She believed that dealing with these issues was the key to overcoming initial staff anxieties:

> These were not stupid people. They understood real quickly that what we were suggesting did not include some of their options. . . . I really believed that the degree to which staff believed in [change] was a real good indication of how much technology they knew and felt comfortable with. . . . If someone [was] a nonbeliever, you [could] almost bet that they [didn't have] a lot of training and [didn't] feel comfortable or understand the technology.
>
> The other thing we did [was] allow staff very quickly, even though they did not have the technology, to get out there and do some job coaching so they could see the change in the consumer. That worked so well.

Agency administrators were encouraged to put forth a lot of effort indicating to staff that they believed in them, and staff were encouraged "to hang with the agency and come through the changes together." Administrators also invested considerable agency resources in staff development, allocating about $30,000 for staff training and travel to supported employment conferences. This money came from the savings that resulted from the agency's reorganization.

Training Alterations

As Avatrac staff learned more about and developed experience with supported employment, they altered their training significantly. Over the course of several years, they developed a team approach to job placement. They did this because some of the 90 people awaiting vocational services had been waiting for a considerable period of time and had gotten a little frustrated and angry. As the director of adult services explained,

> The team method consisted of three teams of four job coaches. Each team was assigned [five or six] people for whom they were solely responsible. It was each team's task to find community employment for each person on their list and arrange for and/or provide the ancillary services required to support those individuals served.

Staff Attrition

Not all staff made the adjustments necessary to remain with the agency. Although no one was laid off, several individuals were "out counseled" (i.e., persuaded and assisted to leave Avatrac due to poor job performance). With other reductions in personnel occurring as part of the typical attrition rate, remaining staff were given raises of between 5% and 22%, and Avatrac reportedly still saved a total of $30,000 after reorganization. Apparently, much of the savings went toward staff development.

CONSTITUENT RESPONSES

Responses of Service Recipients

The director of adult services indicated that there was little initial desire on the parts of participants to leave the workshop. The impetus for change came from people outside the agency; it later came from staff who saw the kinds of community employment options that could be offered to people with disabilities. The director of adult services said that as workshop participants obtained community jobs, they began to express more explicit preferences:

> In the beginning, if you asked these folks, which we did, 99% of them
> said they wanted to stay here [in the workshop] . . . because they didn't
> know what community work meant. . . . When we took that [first]
> group down there [to a local company] for the 6 weeks of work, we
> didn't have to convince them anymore. We put yard crews together to
> cut lawns . . . and the more we did, the more we started to hear people
> say, "I don't want [the workshop] anymore."

Staff decided to develop the storefronts as the number of participants remaining in the workshop decreased. Reportedly, the change
to small storefronts was initially unpopular, but it was accepted
eventually by the workshop participants. They became very unhappy, however, when the small storefronts were shut down to create one large storefront. As the director of adult services said,

> [When] we went to storefronts, that was tough on [the people in the
> workshop] initially, although that was short-lived. People really liked
> [the small storefronts] because there [were fewer] people. There was
> more a sense of ownership. . . . It was a lot more intimate. When we
> went from the smaller storefronts to the bigger one on the east side of
> town, people just came unglued. They were angry at us, and it was real
> interesting. Talk about not listening to your customers. We thought,
> "Boy they are really going to like this because they missed the plant"
> and all that good stuff. They hated it, and they hate it today.

Family Responses

Apparently, families gave little opposition to Avatrac's conversion.
There was, however, a group of families who were initially
skeptical:

> The hardest to bring along were families of people who had more sig
> nificant needs even though they said things like, "This sounds great,"
> "I'd really like this for my kid," and "I don't know how you are going
> to do it." But they weren't fighting us. They had a really hard time un
> derstanding it. It took several years, and now they are upset because
> we haven't made it happen.

Staff Responses

In the beginning, staff were very nervous about the proposed conversion and feared for their jobs. As the director of adult services
said, "The big question was, 'What happens to me?' That's where
[staff] were." For years they came to work knowing what their jobs
and responsibilities were, and now that certainty was in limbo.

Some staff were devastated by the proposed conversion not
only because it was an implied criticism of previous work of which

they were proud, but also because it seemed so necessary after it was fully explained. The director of adult services described her reactions:

> It wasn't comfortable. I mean when [the consultant] left, I was in such a state I wouldn't even give him a ride to the airport. You kind of see your world crumble. . . . I'm not going to say that I was 100% [for the conversion] because it was pretty painful. We were pretty proud of what we were doing, and now all of a sudden the writing was on the wall that we weren't doing anything. . . . I think it was a hard pill to swallow because it was pretty simple. When you looked at it . . . it doesn't take a mental giant to figure it out. How did we miss it?

As noted above, several important factors seemed to help staff adjust to and participate in the conversion. Among these were the provision of training and direct experience in supported employment, encouragement regarding staff abilities, assurances of support, and the fostering of a team effort.

Responses of Other Professionals

Service coordinators, especially those who worked with people at their residences and during and after their shifts in the workshop, were the most resistant to Avatrac's proposed conversion. The director of adult services believed that problems with service coordinators could have been worked out if Avatrac's staff had done a better job of involving them in the initial planning:

> [Residential] was the toughest to sell and the last to become a part of [the conversion]. Part of that [was] we didn't do a very good job with them. . . . The thing that we did really poorly was to not involve residential [service coordinators] in our initial planning. We did a lot of informing . . . and if we had to do it again, they would have been involved in the process from the very beginning.

AVATRAC'S CURRENT SITUATION

As of 1995, Avatrac is providing services for about 300 people with approximately 51 staff. In addition, it is running several different programs, including a supported work program, a partial employment program for people considered to have challenging behaviors, an adult day program, and a social/vocational program for people who have been classified as having both emotional and developmental disabilities.

About 60% of those receiving services have community jobs. Eighty-four percent of those are individual placements, and 16% are group situations. About 100 people are still in the workshop.

A RETROSPECTIVE ANALYSIS OF AVATRAC'S CONVERSION

Enclaves

The director of adult services and the staff decided that enclaves were not a desirable form of employment and abolished them all. It was found that they duplicate many of the same problems that exist in sheltered workshops. For example, people served by enclaves remain in those enclaves for as long as they would work in workshops, even if they are good workers.

Backfilling with New Referrals

The question arose about what to do with people while they were awaiting services or when they lost their jobs: Should they be allowed to return to the workshop? The director of adult services indicated that, in retrospect, she would still give the people who lost their jobs the option of returning to the workshop so long as the facility was still available. She would not, however, replace individuals who found community employment with new referrals. She further indicated that if she were given families' permission, she would search more actively for other workshops for those at Avatrac who wanted to continue in workshop programs.

According to the director of adult services, the workshop would have closed 2.8 times if people were not allowed to return after placement. On average, however, 3.13 jobs were found for each person over a 5-year period. This, in her opinion, necessitated the continuation of some day services.

Promising Too Much to Employers

According to the director of adult services, the agency's initial relations with employers were not satisfactory and should have been modified more quickly. Initially, Avatrac marketed its services by promising prospective employers too many services. In a short time, staff realized that they were providing a "no risk, no investment" situation for employers and that they had to rearrange the way in which they described their services so that employers would be motivated to invest in people's success.

Communicating with Residential Service Coordinators

The director of adult services believed that relations with residential service coordinators were handled poorly. Residential service coordinators were informed but not involved in Avatrac's initial planning. As the director of adult services noted, "We did a lot of informing. . . and if we had to do it again, they would have been involved in the process from the very beginning."

Inaccurate Service Projections

Because of her initial projections, the director of adult services allocated too much agency funding and time for traditional facility-based services. Thus, Avatrac was committed to providing facility-based services for a specified period. This precluded total agency conversion until the service contract ended. The director of adult services wished that she would have estimated more accurately both the costs of providing and the time frame for phasing out facility-based services so that the break might have been effected more quickly and easily.

SUMMARY

Unlike Kaposia and New Horizons, Avatrac was a large, urban agency that wanted to expand its workshop program. It ultimately decided to focus on supported employment because of external pressure not to expand the workshop, staff identifications of problems with services, and information gathered from outside presentations on supported employment and a visit to a supported employment agency.

An outside consultant assisted in the development of a strategic plan that had conversion as its desired outcome. It was clear from the start that Avatrac could not provide both sheltered and integrated employment services.

Because funding was tied to the workshop program, it was necessary to negotiate block grant funding through state agencies. As people moved into community jobs, facility space was leased to area businesses. Storefronts were used as a way of getting people out of the workshop. It was realized, however, that this was not ideal.

Organizationally, Avatrac streamlined its hierarchical structure and developed a career ladder for staff. A big investment was made in staff development. A team structure like the one developed by New Horizons proved very effective.

Although the workshop participants were not eager to leave initially, they became more enthusiastic as peers obtained community employment. Families were generally supportive of Avatrac's changes. Staff and service coordinators were the most resistant.

A key factor in Avatrac's slow pace was the fact that people were allowed to return to the workshop after being placed in community jobs. Although enclaves helped to move participants out of the workshop more quickly, the agency since has decided that enclaves are not desirable and has therefore eliminated them.

Avatrac has been in the process of conversion for 8 years now, and it continues to work toward providing desired lifestyles for people with disabilities.

III

WHERE DO WE
GO FROM HERE?—
IMPLICATIONS FOR
SYSTEMS CHANGE

9

Critical Issues in Conversion

Lessons Learned

Each of the agencies described in this book was unique in history, personnel, leadership, politics, and structure, and each pursued conversion in ways that reflected such uniqueness. Based on their reported experiences, there is clearly no uniform *best* way to effect organizational change or to move from segregated to integrated services. These agencies, however, experienced the most practical kinds of trials and triumphs and, over the course of years, acquired valuable, detailed knowledge of change that is not described elsewhere in the field's literature.

Existing business and human services literature provides a wealth of information about organizational change in general and a more limited but emerging body of information on agency conversion from segregated to integrated services for people with disabilities (Albin, 1992). Still missing from both bodies of information, however, is an in-depth description of the process and effects of conversion from the perspectives of its various participants. This kind of information, although certainly not an exact formula for agency action and success, can offer some suggestions to agencies contemplating significant changes. This chapter presents wisdom regarding the conversion process that was gleaned from the agencies and people studied.

INGREDIENTS FOR SUCCESSFUL CONVERSION

The readiness approach that pervades traditional day treatment and sheltered workshop services is being deemed by an increasing number of consumers, families, and professionals to be outdated and far removed from the language and intent of the Rehabilitation Act Amendments of 1992, PL102-569. Change within most traditional human services agencies has come slowly or minimally, or has not come at all. The following is a list of essential ingredients for change that was compiled from the case studies in this book and from the human services literature on organizational change (Albin, 1992; Dufresne & Laux, 1994; Hagner & Murphy, 1989; Kiracofe, 1994; Magis-Agosta, 1994; Murphy & Rogan, 1992). Contained in this list are some implied, potential impediments to change as well as concrete suggestions for undertaking a serious conversion effort:

- Build support for change from within the agency.
- Define clearly the values that drive the agency's vision and mission.
- Ensure that internal leadership provides support, encouragement, and guidance throughout the process of change.
- Plan to act, and act on plans.
- Consider the use of outside consultants to plan for and guide change.
- Invest heavily in staff development and support.
- Strive for a flat organization with most staff providing direct services.
- Change the agency's image to match its values, vision, and mission.
- Define, demonstrate, and celebrate large as well as small successes.
- Pursue creative, alternative funding options.
- Involve key stakeholders from the beginning.
- Unload *sunk costs*.
- Terminate facility admissions and backfilling as soon as possible.
- Do not wait for everything to be in place before beginning the process of change.

In the remainder of this chapter, each of the above ingredients is discussed in detail using examples and citations from the field's literature and the agencies studied.

Build Support for Change from within the Agency

In explaining the slow pace of conversion from sheltered to integrated services, Dufresne and Laux (1994) point to an absence of external, strategic pressures for such change and to a lack of sufficient internal dissatisfaction among leaders of agencies providing sheltered services. Understandably, agency leaders might be the last to advocate for such change. Indeed, weighing against their dissatisfactions with existing services are the complex, controversial actions required for conversion and the security, efficiency, and familiarity of existing service arrangements.

External Forces   Each of the agencies studied reported that external forces provided a strong, initial impetus for conversion. These external forces, which varied among agencies, often led to internal discontent and/or review of activities and eventually to significant conversion efforts.

Avatrac was pressured to change its plans for workshop expansion after its intentions were contested hotly by several local agencies. Kaposia began to review its mission and activities when 1) the local citizenry became generally disgruntled with the community's social services programs, and 2) its workcenter participants began to display dissatisfaction. At Pioneer, the need for conversion was precipitated by a financial crisis brought about when local funding sources became disenchanted with the agency's fiscal management. New Horizons's executive director became convinced of the need for conversion after attending presentations by persuasive advocates of integrated employment. In fact, three of the four agencies studied reportedly were influenced by persuasive outside speakers who criticized traditional sheltered services and advocated for competitive employment opportunities.

Internal Forces   Conversion was initiated by staff within each agency reexamining the services they provided and the direction their agency should take in the future. As noted above, the initial sources for such reexamination were most frequently external. Several agency leaders, however, expressed personal dissatisfaction that preceded the pursuit of new ideas and led them to visit other agencies, seek out inspirational speakers who advocated for change, or learn about innovative techniques for organizational change.

Although agency personnel may be stimulated or, in some cases, forced to change because of external pressures, they should, according to Kiracofe (1994), be motivated eventually by internal forces if the change is to be seriously pursued, meaningfully implemented, and vigorously sustained. Kiracofe (1994) discussed three stages of internal awareness that an agency undergoes prior to the onset of real organizational change:

1. Acknowledgment that the present way of doing things does not work very well or needs improvement
2. Awareness of a better way or best practices in the field
3. Commitment to discover or explore new and different ways of doing things

Although these stages reflect a level of organizational dissatisfaction with existing circumstances and an initial commitment to explore change, they may or may not lead to actual agency conversion. According to Dufresne and Laux (1994), for conversion to actually occur, the initial impetus for change must be perceived as being greater than the cost of change and must be followed up by establishing a clearly desired goal and by pursuing specific, practical steps for achieving that goal.

Such a rational formula for conversion sounds good and partially describes the paths of several agencies after the conversion process began to unfold. What actually happened was reportedly less orderly because the impetus for change was often unplanned, goals were described frequently as ambiguous, and steps taken were more experimental and tenuous than they were clear. But once conversion was underway, the agencies described in this book worked informally to build support.

Define Clearly the Values
that Drive the Agency's Vision and Mission

Many of those studying organizational change within the human services field have pointed to the importance of embracing the values, vision, and mission consistent with an agency's shifting ideas and methods (Albin, 1992; Dufresne & Laux, 1994; Kiracofe, 1994; Magis-Agosta, 1994; McGaughey et al., 1993). Bennett (1962) noted, for example, that a change in values and assumptions is essential to effect true change in staff behavior, which can then alter an agency's culture. In order to better investigate the need for change, the staffs of the agencies studied typically examined the services they offered and the outcomes they achieved. Such examinations led invariably to reviews of their underlying values, changing visions, and formal missions. In most cases, new values represented a general set of principles that affirmed the rights of all individuals to participate in typical community activities and settings with other community members.

For example, Pioneer affirmed that 1) people with disabilities have the same human similarities and differences that exist among all individuals; 2) disability should be viewed as being as much a function of setting-related factors as of individual characteristics; 3) people with disabilities have the right to the same community opportunities, risks, relationships, and activities experienced by other members of the community using, if necessary, individualized sources of support to achieve such participation; and 4) having the opportunity for valued, integrated employment and community participation of one's choosing is a right, not a privilege to be earned.

Pioneer's practices, like those of the other agencies studied, did not always flow logically, sequentially, and smoothly from these philosophic principles. In some cases, practices veered from desired principles as outside pressures were exerted. Nevertheless, most agencies attempted to make principles consistent with principles. Problems arose, however, when agencies offered supported employment services but retained sheltered work facilities as well. Although these services were seen as parallel, they operated according to different, conflicting philosophies and methods.

Agencies stimulated discussions about values, visions, and missions through various methods, including retreats and strategic planning sessions. In some cases, these meetings were held before conversion was more than a tentative idea. Conversely, the executive director of New Horizons emphasized the importance of a retreat several years after the conversion process had begun, when the agency was experiencing staff conflicts during the final stage of the transition from the old to the new system.

Some agencies included board members in their planning sessions from the beginning; others involved only staff initially and later presented their proposals to their boards of directors for discussion and approval. Avatrac opened up its planning meetings to a wide constituency that included staff, workshop participants, board members, and state agency representatives. During these meetings, outside consultants sometimes were hired to facilitate discussion and decision making. In fact, Avatrac reportedly was persuaded by a consultant to consider total workshop conversion rather than smaller, incremental changes.

Although Avatrac and Pioneer decided quickly to convert their workshops and to announce their intentions publicly, Kaposia and New Horizons assumed more conservative postures, deciding to close their workcenters after the conversion process was well under way. There are pros and cons to both approaches. By proposing a mere shift in or expansion of services, staff, participants, and constituents may be more agreeable and less resistant to change. Moreover, if the need to convert emerges slowly and gradually, staff can point to a sustained record of experience and success to assuage the concerns of constituent groups. As the executive director of New Horizons noted after pursuing an incremental approach to change for several years, "We didn't plan to close the [workcenter]. It just evolved that way."

Conversely, the incremental approach may only delay conflicts that will emerge eventually as changes take effect. In the process of introducing a vocational philosophy that is different from the existing philosophy, contradictory practices may become apparent, staff disharmony may increase, program participants and community constituents may receive conflicting messages, and planning may become disjointed. Also, agencies may become "caught in conversion"—a perpetual period of transition during which principles and practices never really match, the sense of urgency is lost, and the conversion is never fully realized.

Alternatively, those who commit to conversion up front are more likely to have clear values, offer a clear vision, pursue methods consistent with that vision, and plan a coherent mission. In the process, however, they initially may encounter stronger, more vociferous, and more negative reactions than if they utilize a more covert, incremental approach. Such resistance may overwhelm decision makers, confuse people about the merits of conversion, decrease the resolve of proponents, and make the conversion process very adversarial.

A middle-ground strategy has been used whereby leaders within an agency commit to conversion from the start but conduct the conversion in a quiet fashion, placing more and more people in jobs and never announcing their intentions until the need to close the sheltered work facility becomes apparent.

Pioneer's new director proposed explicitly to close the workshop. He provided a list of specific practices that were intended to mirror Pioneer's philosophic principles and express its intentions clearly. These practices included the following: 1) accepting all referrals (rather than screening on the basis of type or severity of disability or projected level of long-term support); 2) conducting individualized, community-based assessments (rather than using standardized tests, simulated work samples, or preexisting worksite placements to assess individuals' abilities); 3) providing individual placements (rather than placing people in congregate work settings of any kind or size); 4) finding community employment based on individual preferences (rather than basing employment on the availability of existing jobs); 5) facilitating use of natural worksite supports (rather than relying exclusively on the support of a job coach and eventual fading); and 6) providing support for indefinite periods of time if necessary (rather than withdrawing supports because of cost).

Likewise, Avatrac pursued conversion explicitly. Staff thought that the plan was too radical, however, and they reacted very negatively. This in-house opposition caused some serious setbacks for

Avatrac's conversion plan, but it was not defeated. Moreover, because they stuck with their original plan, proponents of conversion were able to present a clear, consistent vision of what they wanted to state officials, who accepted the plan with minimal revision. This was amazing to the opponents of conversion on the staff, and it paved the way for the conversion to proceed as conceived.

**Ensure that Internal Leadership
Provides Support, Encouragement, and
Guidance Throughout the Process of Change**

An essential ingredient for achieving successful agency conversion is a strong commitment to change (Murphy & Rogan, 1992). Although such commitment must be shared and acted on by important agency constituents, it must begin with and/or be well supported by agency leaders. Brunsson (1985) underscored the importance of effective leadership in conversion efforts and pointed to successful management as including "the ability to motivate people, to establish a good organizational climate, to create appropriate social networks, or to develop a powerful organizational ideology" (pp. 207–208). After studying the conversion process in several sheltered workshops, Hagner and Murphy (1989) reiterated the importance of leadership, noting that each agency they studied had one or two individuals in key positions who supported community services strongly and largely orchestrated the conversion process.

Similarly, in each of the agencies studied, a leader assumed an instrumental role in initiating, emphasizing, pursuing, supporting, and/or sustaining change. Leaders do not have to know how to do everything, and they certainly do not have to do everything themselves. A leader's role is to provide a structure through which staff energy may be channeled in working toward a common vision (Bushe & Shani, 1991). The most effective leaders are risk takers, are passionate about their charges, and have a clear vision and strong values. They are able to instill in staff a sense of personal commitment, and they provide guidance and support toward as well as through innovation. Provencal (1987) said that real change takes place only when there is a sense of urgency. The leaders of the agencies studied admitted to being so consumed by the task of conversion that they could not relax until it was complete.

The qualities and activities of the agency leaders described in this book are consistent with those ascribed to leaders in business, education, politics, and other areas of endeavor. Below is a list of activities that the agency leaders reportedly completed as part of the conversion process. The list is not exhaustive, but it highlights at least some of the important contributions made by those who spearheaded agency conversion efforts:

- Articulated a clear service philosophy
- Translated a service philosophy into a clear organizational mission
- Developed concrete steps for pursuing conversion that were consistent with the agency's philosophy and mission
- Initiated, communicated, and defended the idea of conversion to key agency and community constituents such as staff, board members, consumer groups, families, and referring and funding organizations
- Gained the support of key community members
- Identified and attracted competent and committed staff to implement desired changes
- Provided technical training and emotional support to staff
- Weathered setbacks without changing the agency's philosophy or mission
- Managed uncertainty
- Sought help from outside sources
- Evaluated the conversion process from within and outside the agency on an ongoing basis
- Assessed service outcomes quantitatively and qualitatively from the perspectives of involved constituents such as service recipients, family members, staff, funding representatives, and outside consultants.

Plan to Act, and Act on Plans

Agencies approached planning in different ways. Some, such as Avatrac, developed a formal, long-term, strategic plan. Others, such as Kaposia, focused on informal, short-term action plans. Still others, like Pioneer, had an informal, long-term goal in mind (i.e., closing the workshop completely) but tried to maintain a focus on one person at a time, emphasizing the short-term activities of finding a community job for each person in the workshop and building community connections.

Although each of these agencies utilized different strategies and activities, they shared a strong bias for action. Peters and Waterman (1982) described this bias as a prevailing preference among innovative people. A common problem for agencies contemplating change is that they contemplate rather than act. They spend so much time talking, meeting, planning, persuading, and writing that they lose momentum for change and eventually may have trouble actually *doing* the things that they have planned.

A common sentiment expressed by agency leaders who pursued and achieved change actively was the necessity of acting in the face of uncertainty. Because conversion was a very new and dynamic concept, it was difficult to plan far in advance and often impossible to predict even short-term effects. This is not to say that proponents of conversion should reject careful planning, reflection, and discussion. It is only a reminder that real change will 1) involve uncertainties and risks that even the best planning cannot identify or eliminate, 2) include anticipated as well as unanticipated actions and reactions, and 3) have an identifiable starting point but a far less recognizable point of completion.

Albin (1992) made some suggestions for maximizing the chances of plans being translated into actions. She noted that

- Change-related actions should be incorporated consciously and concretely into the staff's everyday jobs.
- Staff should be assisted and supported to integrate proposed changes into their activities.
- Short-term timelines for implementing changes should be developed to reinforce an action orientation.
- Employees who resist taking concrete actions should be replaced after a decent period of training and support has been tried.

Consider the Use of Outside
Consultants to Plan for and Guide Change

Each of the agencies studied reportedly benefited from the expertise of outside consultants. The points at which consultants were used differed from agency to agency. Some agencies relied on outside assistance when they were only contemplating changes or just beginning to take specific actions. Several agency leaders indicated that outside consultants stimulated them to consider conversion seriously in the first place or to make major changes when only small modifications were contemplated. Others used outside consultants only after they were well into the conversion process and encountering difficulties. Several agencies relied on outside consultants periodically over an extended period of time.

Outside expertise was sought regarding values clarification, organizational strategies, best practices, staff development, funding opportunities, and other critical components of conversion. In several cases, outside consultants reportedly provided invaluable emotional support to agency leaders during difficult, demoralizing periods. Outside consultants could raise issues that staff did not feel comfortable raising. Consultants could also redirect negative perspectives among staff and others, thereby relieving agency leaders of some adversarial situations. Overall, it was agreed that good consultants can guide and support an agency by providing perspective, encouragement, and technical assistance at key times.

Invest Heavily in Staff Development and Support

The creation of a positive learning culture has been cited as essential to successful conversion. Two requirements of a positive learning culture are that 1) staff must be treated with respect, and 2) leadership must convey a willingness to learn (Moss-Kanter, 1983).

Ordinarily, a well-entrenched organizational culture is established around old systems and practices. Staff, board members, and families become invested heavily in and responsive to that culture. At the very least, most staff have accepted and followed an agency's methods and assumptions unconsciously. When introduced, change can elicit strong feelings of fear, threat, hurt, and/or devaluation. People's reactions to change have been likened to responses to personal loss that require periods of grieving.

The agencies studied made significant investments in helping existing staff to understand and, through the use of staff retreats, teamwork, and training, to plan for impending changes. The agencies also helped staff to learn the necessary skills to carry out the changes. Proponents of organizational learning believe that those staff who are most resistive to change are often the least well informed, trained, and involved. To instill new organizational learning requires not only instruction in new methods, but, as importantly, the provision of opportunities for staff to share their feelings and viewpoints through group discussions as well (Bushe & Shani, 1991). This is not to say that staff were encouraged to resist or debate the decisions to convert. Rather, staff in the agencies studied reportedly were given frequent opportunities to discuss proposed changes in supportive climates in order to create common understandings, develop varied strategies and solutions, and facilitate ownership of the agencies' new directions.

Despite staff orientation and training sessions, three of the four agencies reported sharp divisions among staff at various points in the conversion process. Some staff were unable or unwilling to participate in conversion efforts and consequently chose or were asked to leave their respective agencies. Pioneer and Kaposia reported that nearly their entire staffs were replaced within 2 years. Such turnover, however, might not have been bad for either departing staff or the agencies. In most cases, staff who could not accept or understand the changes left voluntarily and were either assisted in finding new jobs in other sheltered work facilities, or otherwise left the human services field completely.

From an agency perspective, hiring new staff who had the desired attitudes and skills could have exacerbated existing staff fears and caused upheaval among agency participants. Such new people, however, enhanced staff learning greatly, brought renewed energy and enthusiasm to the agencies, and accelerated the agencies' rates of conversion.

Pioneer, like some of the other agencies studied, had a relatively short amount of time in which to demonstrate success to its staff, workshop participants, and funding organizations. In order to demonstrate progress as rapidly as possible and to stimulate staff to embrace the changes, Pioneer's director immediately hired several skilled people from outside the agency to initiate the conversion effort. Pioneer's workshop participants recalled the disruption they experienced as old staff left and new staff replaced them. The vast majority felt, however, that the conversion was worthwhile. They knew why changes were occurring, and they understood that they benefited from the changes because new staff were friendly and helped them to get jobs.

Several agencies studied used a team structure to facilitate staff learning and support as well as to provide direct services. Teams consisted of small groups of staff who 1) met regularly with a supervisor or senior staff member to discuss their activities, progress, and problems; and 2) worked cooperatively to place and support people in community jobs.

At Pioneer, new personnel were assigned to teams and paired with experienced staff as part of their initial training. While they were given an orientation and didactic instruction by a supervisor, new staff observed and worked closely with experienced staff as they began to provide direct services. Staff then worked interdependently within their team structures.

Regular team meetings were held in which members shared issues, problems, successes, and failures and solicited assistance or support. In addition to facilitating technical assistance among staff, the team approach also was seen as effective in assuaging loneliness and insecurity—two possible causes of resistance (Harvey, 1990).

Strive for a Flat Organization with Most Staff Providing Direct Services

Once a vision was created and key constituents were informed of pending changes, all of the agencies studied moved quickly to change some of their most basic structures and functions. In some cases, these changes were gradual and consensual; in others, they were rapid and directive.

The most common example of agency restructuring was the change in job descriptions to reflect a focus on integrated community employment. The most dramatic example of this occurred at Pioneer when the new director created the CJS position (see Chapter 3) and encouraged all existing staff to apply for it. Other agencies reported similar changes later in the process. Whether these changes occurred in a rapid and directive fashion or in a gradual and consensual manner, all the agency leaders saw them as a means to formalize and hopefully finalize all the desired changes. Hagner and Murphy (1989) pointed out that although the agency leaders might initially have wanted constituents to think that the changes were reversible, eventually they took concrete, formalizing steps, such as creating new job descriptions, to ensure their permanence.

Another example of agency restructuring was the dismantling of settings and the discontinuing of activities that were considered to be inconsistent with the agencies' new directions. At Avatrac, initially this meant breaking up two large, centralized workshops into several smaller storefront units. New Horizons and Kaposia eliminated nonwork activities from their work activities centers. Also, participants at New Horizons who were doing only work activities previously and were considered unqualified for even sheltered work were admitted to the workcenter.

While creating new job descriptions and reorganizing staff functions, several agency leaders saw the need to simplify their agencies by reducing the number of administrative and supervisory positions. This was designed to reduce costs and realign agencies' resources to provide direct community services. In this regard, Avatrac reduced its supervisory staff by 66%, and Pioneer eliminated five positions initially and eventually reduced its workshop staff from eight to zero. Flattening the organizational structure likely kept administrative staff more involved with and informed about day-to-day matters. Staff indicated that they felt more supported and were more likely to take risks if the administration was familiar with them and their activities.

Whether these changes were implemented in a gradual and consensual manner, thereby implying possible reversibility, or in a rapid, directive way, even the most conservative agency leaders recognized the need to rearrange basic agency structures and functions early in the conversion process. Such actions seemed integral to enhancing the success and permanence of desired changes.

Organizational restructuring may also have saved some money. The director of adult services at Avatrac spoke of increasing staff salaries with the money saved by restructuring. By eliminating several positions, Pioneer was able to offer salaries that were higher than those offered by other agencies in the area. This attracted more qualified, experienced people and allowed Pioneer to set high performance standards.

Change the Agency's Image to Match Its Values, Vision, and Mission

Changing agencies that provided primarily segregated employment services into what agency leaders described frequently as community-centered, business-oriented agencies required dramatic changes in the ways in which the agencies and the people they served were viewed by their surrounding communities. The executive director of New Horizons spoke candidly about the stereotypes and negative images of pity and charity that were projected by the agency through its orientation and services. Early in the conversion process, she worked to abolish materials and practices that reinforced these stereotypes and images, and she replaced them with services that reflected status-enhancing roles and activities.

Both New Horizons and Kaposia wanted to have more business-oriented approaches and images. New Horizons renovated its physical plant, initiated a stricter attendance policy, asked workcenter participants to use a time clock, and assisted workcenter participants in dressing appropriately for work. In addition, New Horizons began a media campaign to change its image from one of charity to one of training and production.

Kaposia also adopted more business-like methods, emphasizing the language, procedures, and orientations of local employers. Staff were trained to present themselves and their services in ways that businesspeople could understand and relate to. Additionally, when Kaposia was contemplating a name change, they sought the advice of local employers.

Kiracofe (1994) said that "The best way to spawn change in thinking is to go back to basics and start all over with the people for whom the service exists" (p. 285). Interestingly, as agencies moved toward more community-based approaches, they identified their surrounding business communities and major funding organizations as primary customers. As such, businesses and funding organizations were often the parties for which quality was defined. Although agencies stated that their priority was to adapt services to the needs of participants and their families, these people were seen as the focus of service delivery, not as the judges of service quality. Individuals with disabilities should be able to judge the quality of the services they receive and should therefore be involved in the formal assessment of those services. Assessment of service quality requires recognizing that people with disabilities are competent individuals, not collections of limitations associated with labels (Kiracofe, 1994).

Albin (1992) said that achieving service quality is not synonymous with merely implementing community-based agency change, no matter how well intentioned such change is. Providing quality services requires 1) an intra-agency commitment to ensuring the health, safety, and rights of service recipients; 2) an emphasis on the perspectives of service recipients; and 3) a program evaluation system that has kept pace with emerging service developments. Albin (1992) further noted that having an appropriate program evaluation system has more often been the exception than the rule, especially among government regulatory bodies: "Although developed with an intention of improving services, many of the practices actually used by government agencies to monitor service quality have tended to place barriers in the path of ongoing program enhancement" (p. 329).

Define, Demonstrate, and Celebrate Large as Well as Small Successes

Converting from sheltered to integrated services may be described as a complex, anxiety-provoking, emotionally exhausting undertaking that can be an exhilarating, challenging, and satisfying experience for all involved parties. Change is complex, anxiety provoking, and exhausting because it manifests itself at different levels. At the direct services level, participants and staff are expected to embrace an entirely new set of methods and to define the concept of success as the securement of community jobs of people's choosing. At the level of organizational change, participants and staff are required to operationalize integrated employment services and to implement the new definition of success.

The agency conversion process itself has its own definition of success that is in some ways independent of, but is in other ways intimately intertwined with, the process of service change. For example, although agency conversion may progress at a significant and satisfactory pace, that conversion may not yet be reflected in new community job placements. But the process of conversion to integrated services cannot be successful without eventually achieving community job placements. Thus, the conversion process itself has its own intermediate definitions of success that are very important to recognize and celebrate. They may be very difficult to achieve, however, and sometimes even harder to recognize. For example, as conversion unfolded at Kaposia, the CEO became so discouraged and frustrated that she had to be reminded by an outside consultant that she had made a lot of important progress in a relatively short period of time.

Defining, demonstrating, and celebrating conversion success could be further confounded by the sharp divisions among staff that often are caused by proposing changes. Success to one party might be failure to another. This was especially acute in situations in which integrated services were offered by agencies that had well-established sheltered programs. Even agency leaders who initiated the conversion sometimes felt very torn between old loyalties and new convictions.

Several agencies hit what Dufresne and Laux (1994) called a *critical mass* (p. 275), a situation in which progress and morale seemed to reach low points and the goal seemed far away. As the director of adult services at Avatrac related, reaching this critical mass was among the most frustrating times of the entire conversion process because it felt like "your world is crumbling. . .and you weren't doing anything."

In order to counter the inevitable low points, an agency must continue to celebrate its successes and showcase its efforts both internally and externally. At the direct services level, staff need to recognize things such as successful job placements, promotions of those whom they support, or healthy supported employee relationships on and off the job. At the level of organizational change, celebration might focus on such things as the new image of the agency portrayed in the media or by constituents or the sale or lease of a building.

By showcasing successes, an agency is utilizing several important conversion strategies. It is signaling strongly and explicitly that a new definition of success is 1) dictating its actions and use of resources; 2) defining what constitutes successful (or unsuccessful) actions and outcomes; and 3) addressing staff and participant support needs as staff struggle with new, difficult, and ambiguous situations.

The single most prevalent criterion of successful conversion for the agencies studied was the achievement of community employment for participants. Because many agencies had little experience in finding community jobs, and because agencies had to demonstrate their proficiency in a relatively short amount of time, they tended initially to pursue policies that would demonstrate success most quickly. With Avatrac, this meant providing group placements. In New Horizons's case, it meant 1) selecting workcenter participants who expressed the keenest interest in working competitively and were perceived as having the fewest problems, 2) developing jobs and then placing participants in those jobs, and 3) promising employers almost anything in order to get jobs.

These strategies were effective in that many successes were achieved quickly. Group placements maximized the number of people who received services, and many of the most assertive workcenter participants needed minimal help in finding and keeping community jobs. Moreover, the power of demonstration should not be underestimated. Apparently seeing was believing for all the constituents of the agencies studied. Successes inspired confidence among participants, staff, and funding organizations in the agencies' conversion efforts.

The above strategies did, however, backfire in some cases. Avatrac found that group placements duplicated many of the problems of the workshop and prolonged the conversion process; they eventually were discontinued. In retrospect, Avatrac's staff believed that they should have done it right the first time. But Avatrac was not alone. Many agencies opted to use enclaves and work crews 1) in order to move people into the community quickly, or 2) as a permanent strategy for providing supported employment services. Problems with group models of supported employment have been documented in the literature (Brown et al., 1991; Conte et al., 1989), and many of these problems mirror those described by Avatrac.

Working first with individuals who were perceived as being the most capable workcenter participants, New Horizons encountered problems when it began to provide services for those who presented more challenging issues. Staff found that they lacked confidence and experience in working with such individuals. This created difficulties in effective service provision, caused frustrations among all the parties, and contributed to delays in the provision of services. Realizing that they had a problem, New Horizons's staff selected a person with particularly severe disabilities to be placed in community employment. This situation worked out well for the person with disabilities, who eventually found a community job, as well as for the staff. The staff gained confidence in working with a variety of people and, in the process, clarified important aspects of job development that ultimately benefited everyone receiving services.

If agencies intend to provide integrated employment services for all who apply or are referred, it is important that they adopt specific policies and practices that are consistent with a "zero-reject" philosophy. As the experiences of Avatrac and New Horizons illustrate, by overemphasizing quick and easy placements, agencies run the risk of undermining their guiding philosophies and long-term objectives; delaying the provision of needed staff training and experiential learning; providing less effective services for people with severe disabilities; and/or losing the confidence of staff, funding organizations, family members, and service recipients. By demonstrating proficiency and by assisting people with different abilities to secure community employment and supports, however, staff practice what an agency preaches philosophically and acquire confidence and expertise in working with a cross section of individuals. In addition, people who are skeptical of conversion may be confronted early with a list of successes that includes more than a limited group of people. Finally, by providing services for a range of individuals, integrated employment staff may diffuse some of the criticisms of sheltered facility staff who often complain that they lose their best workers to community employment.

Another consideration in demonstrating success is to initially make the conversion effort small in scale. Kiracofe (1994) advocated making conversion more manageable by beginning with just a few people who "become the pioneers who guide the rest of the organization through the change process" (p. 286). The decision to start small seemed to be a recurring theme with the agencies studied. In assessing the factors that they thought were instrumental to their agencies' successful conversions, staff of both New Horizons and Kaposia mentioned prominently their decisions to start small and selectively and to use a "one person at a time" approach.

Pursue Creative, Alternative Funding Options

For most agencies, funding drives services. In a survey of MR/DD agencies across the United States, McGaughey et al. (1993) found that 80% mentioned funding difficulties as a major barrier to expansion of integrated employment services. In fact, the bulk of existing funding for individuals with severe disabilities continues to be directed primarily toward segregated services.

Another problem is that the relatively few supported employment programs that do exist are often grossly underfunded. This leaves agencies that provide such services with the financial burden of supplementing existing funding with their own scarce resources.

(See Chapter 10 for a more thorough discussion of funding.) Providers of integrated services may be covering some costs for at least 25% of all the people receiving services in their supported employment programs (McGaughey et al., 1993).

Certainly, current funding patterns and policies are a major disincentive to the expansion of integrated employment services for people with severe disabilities. Until adequate and equitable funding policies are implemented at all levels, agencies contemplating conversion must seek creative solutions to these funding dilemmas. There are, however, some sources of funding for integrated services. Some of these sources are designed exclusively for integrated services; others must be redirected toward those services.

New Horizons successfully negotiated a direct shift in funding from sheltered to integrated employment services. In effect, funding streams that financed people's entry into and maintenance in the workcenter were changed to assist people in finding and retaining community employment. Similarly, Avatrac took advantage of Colorado's desire to expand integrated employment by asking that restrictive funding policies be waived in order for its usual budget allocation to be offered in the form of a flexible block grant. Much to the staff's surprise, the state agreed, which gave the agency the flexibility to offer integrated employment services.

Pioneer and Kaposia sought and received new federal, state, and/or local funds that were targeted specifically for their supported employment programs and/or their conversion efforts. Of these funding sources, local funding was reportedly the most flexible in covering the transition and administrative costs not covered by other types of assistance. The following sources could also be used to support conversion efforts: the United Way, Medicaid waivers, MR/DD councils, Social Security work incentives (e.g., Plans for Achieving Self Support [PASSs] and Impairment Related Work Expenses [IRWEs]), fund-raising, and private foundations.

No funding source should be dismissed or overlooked unless it is inconsistent with an agency's philosophy or policies. Several of the agencies studied expressed amazement at the unexpected receptiveness of funding organizations regarding requests for redirected funding. Apparently, many funding organizations had been reconsidering the ways in which they viewed, prioritized, and funded vocational services. Both Avatrac and Kaposia found that their respective state agencies of vocational rehabilitation, agencies with which they had minimal contact previously, were very committed to nurturing new supported employment efforts as part of their own redirection toward serving more individuals with severe disabilities.

Avatrac also was surprised to discover that its state MR/DD agency agreed to renegotiate a contract that facilitated its plans for conversion. From these examples, it may be seen how important it is not to assume that a funding organization's response to new and innovative proposals will be negative.

Financial disincentives continue to be a primary barrier to conversion, and funding issues are certainly a critical factor in many conversion efforts. Although they require persistence to find and creativity to secure, it seems that there are indeed sources, however limited, of financial assistance for integrated employment programs.

A caveat about funding is in order at this time. Although important, funding alone should not determine an agency's actions. In other words, an agency should not develop a vision of change based exclusively on existing funding definitions, activities, and/or priorities unless they conform to the agency's primary service principles. Based upon the agencies studied, an agency should first have a service philosophy and a direction and then should creatively and persistently seek sources of funding, no matter how scarce those sources may seem to be.

Involve Key Stakeholders from the Beginning

Traditional sheltered services are relatively insulated, self-contained programs in which environments, activities, and people are controlled tightly by professionals within the human services system. Supported employment, by contrast, is a less orderly, more unpredictable enterprise that requires support from outside sources (e.g., businesses, community members, residential staff) to be successful. Consequently, it is imperative that agencies in conversion involve key stakeholders in planning and implementing proposed conversion activities.

Internal as well as external planning teams are viable mechanisms used by agencies to involve constituents. Internally, a leadership team that comprises agency leaders and other key personnel (e.g., workshop participants, workshop supervisors, directors of day activities, supported employment leaders) can be used to plan and oversee the conversion process. Although a small core team of committed individuals may meet to "mastermind" the conversion plan, all stakeholders must ultimately be involved and informed.

New Horizons established an external task force of community constituents in order to help implement its new mission and educate the community about its conversion. Such a task force might include family members, school personnel, funding organizations, employers, and residential staff. Pioneer included community constituents on the planning team that developed new job descriptions, organized proposals for agency change, and interviewed job applicants. This planning team was composed of many representatives, including workshop participants, staff, family members, funding organizations, and faculty from a local university.

It is important to understand support and opposition from within and outside of an agency in order to build allies and deal with resistance. Not surprisingly, agency staff and community professionals often resist change the most. Three of the four agencies studied reported that community professionals offered major opposition to their conversion efforts. Pioneer and Avatrac reported a lack of cooperation from residential service coordinators. Pioneer also described difficulties with professional specialists, such as mobility instructors and rehabilitation teachers, who felt that the agency was putting service recipients at great emotional and physical risk. New Horizons reported receiving the most resistance from service coordinators who believed that many workcenter participants were not ready for such changes and that individuals receiving services needed to be taken care of in a specific human services setting.

Significant changes within one agency can affect the routines, schedules, and activities of other agencies appreciably. For example, residential service providers who are used to a daily, predictable workshop schedule might resent the fact that residents working in various community jobs may have different schedules, more complex transportation needs, and expanded financial resources. Such resentments are usually exacerbated when agencies begin conversion unilaterally without consulting the surrounding service providers upon whom they rely for assistance and support. Avatrac's director of adult services concluded that she and her staff did not work hard enough to educate residential service coordinators regarding what was planned or to include them in their initial planning. Several of the agencies studied also thought that their own sustained, self-contained histories contributed to their ignorance regarding how other professionals and organizations functioned.

Unload Sunk Costs

Kaufman (1971) refers to organizational investments in capital equipment or buildings as sunk costs. Commitments to equipment and buildings often result in an agency's resistance to change due to what Colleen Wieck, executive director of the Minnesota Governor's Planning Council, calls the "edifice complex." In many cases, agencies are tied financially to their equipment and buildings because of long-term loans taken out to pay for them. Agency leaders often are wed professionally and psychologically to such commitments because of the time and energy spent persuading their boards and local banks to approve necessary loans. In contemplating a conversion to integrated services, agency leaders may risk their credibility with constituent groups by requesting changes in agency priorities. For agencies that must address sunk costs as a serious impediment to conversion, some alternative uses must be found for capital expenses.

The agencies studied pursued several solutions to this problem. Some worked better than others. Several decided to maintain their sheltered work facilities while simultaneously increasing their integrated services. Kaposia used this strategy at first but later pursued a different course as referrals increased to the point at which Kaposia's CEO feared that the workcenter would only increase in size. Avatrac replaced its two large workshops with community storefronts. The director of adult services noted, however, that the storefronts became increasingly large and began to take on the appearance of the old sheltered facilities.

Pursuing different courses, Pioneer and New Horizons saw their new directions as incompatible with any sort of segregated businesses, however profitable those businesses might have been. Pioneer made the decision to close its workshop completely and not to admit new referrals. As workshop space became available, the agency first reallocated it for staff offices and later began leasing space to community businesses. New Horizons did not initially and overtly commit to closing its workcenter. As jobs were found for the participants, there was less need for the workcenter. Although Pioneer's participants could return to the workshop if they lost their jobs, few did. Eventually there were so few people attending the workshop that the decision was made to close it completely. In time, New Horizons also sold its lucrative recycling business in which three of its employees with disabilities had jobs. All three were retained after the sale.

Agencies rented or leased space, sold their building(s), or used their building(s) for their own offices as their sheltered work facilities got smaller. The lesson here is that agencies pursuing conversion need to confront their own philosophic, financial, professional, and emotional commitments to sunk costs. This consideration is far from trivial because such commitments serve frequently as a screen through which arguments for conversion are sifted and function as the major filter for ultimately determining what an agency is and what it does.

Terminate Facility Admissions and Backfilling as Soon as Possible

Recurring dilemmas for the agencies studied were how to 1) manage new workshop referrals, 2) handle conflicting sheltered and integrated programs, and 3) serve participants who lost their jobs. Regarding the latter issue, some families and professionals wanted to retain a sheltered work facility as a safety net so that former participants would have somewhere to go in case they lost jobs or had spare time during the day. One solution was to maintain a viable sheltered facility by continuing to allow new admissions as community jobs were found for participants.

Solving one problem, however, may have precipitated others. Pursuing such a course of action often led to difficulties in solidifying agencies' new identities internally as well as externally and in finalizing the conversion process. Avatrac's director of adult services articulated this dilemma when she concluded that by admitting new people into the workshop, the agency gave mixed messages to the community and slowed its conversion process greatly.

Another approach was to terminate all new admissions and try to reduce the size of the sheltered work facility gradually while simultaneously enlarging the community employment program. Three of the four agencies studied used variations of this strategy, which saw supported employment as the primary instrument for agency conversion. The logic of this strategy was that as supported employment placements increased, participation in the sheltered work facility would decrease proportionately to the point at which the facility would no longer be viable.

From the beginning, Pioneer declared its intention to close its sheltered workshop completely in order to provide integrated employment services exclusively. New admissions to the workshop were not accepted. Admissions were limited to former participants who lost their jobs and wanted to return until they could find new jobs.

Unlike Pioneer, New Horizons did not initially declare its intention to close its workcenter. Like Pioneer, however, it stopped accepting new referrals and began to find community jobs for its workcenter participants. When only five people remained, New Horizons decided to close its workcenter completely and to lease and eventually sell the building. Initially, it retained its profitable recycling program, which operated as a free-standing business, but it eventually sold this business to a local recycling company.

New Horizons staff also developed options for individuals who were out of work. Each situation was addressed according to the needs and preferences of the individual and his or her significant others. People could join existing worksites temporarily, participate in volunteer work, stay home, or engage in job searches.

Although Kaposia wanted eventually to reduce the number of participants in its workcenter to zero, it began by offering supported employment to workcenter participants and providing admission to new applicants as community jobs were found for people already in the workcenter. At the same time, workcenter staff, seeing the need to fight for their jobs and improve their operations because of the loss of good workers, proposed to transform the workcenter into an affirmative business. This entailed focusing on the production of prime products and employing workers with as well as without disabilities. Eventually, the CEO concluded that this policy would at best lead to a retention of the workcenter in a different form and to an actual increase in the workcenter's size at worst. She decided that pursuing supported employment was incompatible with operating a sheltered business and workcenter and elected to accept only referrals for community employment.

Changing to integrated employment required both an ideological leap and a financial leap of faith. At some critical point, all of the agencies studied had to decide whether they were going to perpetuate their sheltered facilities and accept new admissions. Although this decision reportedly was among the most contentious issues faced by the agency leaders, all of them in various ways eventually decided to discontinue their sheltered work programs because of what they saw as the ideological dissonance between sheltered and integrated services.

Eliminating or even reducing admissions, however, was like shutting off the lifeblood of most agencies. This greatly threatened staff, angered referring and residential agencies, and worried boards of directors. Moreover, during periods of transition when old funding sources were being depleted, agencies' costs could not be reduced quickly enough and new sources of revenue had not risen to adequate levels. Therefore, agencies required flexible funding assistance. As noted earlier, all of the agencies studied received such assistance through federal, state, and/or local allocations, but these resources often were temporary and had to be supplanted eventually with long-term funding secured through creative proposals. Despite the conflicts and uncertainties that surrounded their decisions to eliminate or reduce admissions to their sheltered work facilities, however, all the agency leaders and boards eventually came to the same conclusion. Perhaps as much as any other finding, this result seems to reveal dramatically the most basic intra-agency incongruities regarding sheltered and integrated services.

Do Not Wait for Everything to Be in Place Before Beginning the Process of Change

A list of strategies for organizational change may imply that plans for conversion can be implemented like recipes. Nothing could be further from the truth, as illustrated clearly by the four agencies studied. At some critical juncture, conversion required a leap of faith. Ambiguity, risk, and conflict were integral elements of that leap. Such elements were not eliminated by careful planning and/or the consultations that often accompanied the agencies' conversion efforts. All the elements of the conversion process will not come together at the beginning, and they may become even less orderly as the process unfolds. If people always waited for certitude, however, they would never begin anything.

Although all of the agencies studied pursued change in their own ways, at their own speeds, and to differing degrees, they had philosophic visions and directions in common. Despite the fact that these visions and directions were not always articulated clearly and consistently at the very beginning, their development seemed necessary if the agencies' conversion efforts were to persevere.

All of the agencies studied encountered some opposition to their plans from important agency constituents sometime during the conversion process. Much of this opposition was based upon legitimate issues, realities, and uncertainties. What seemed to override such opposition was not a lack of validity but rather its subjugation to the strong conviction in the need for change. What contributed to eventually overcoming many of the objections to conversion were the often misunderstood and unanticipated effects of change itself. Murphy and Rogan (1992) pointed out that opponents of conversion failed to understand that change begets change through the ways in which an agency is perceived by others and perceives itself. In Pioneer's case, agency conversion led to new opportunities and actions and to a new receptivity on the parts of community professionals, individuals with disabilities and their families, and funding organization representatives who had not supported the agency previously. Also, the conversion changed staff and forced them to seek community, professional, and financial resources that were previously untapped.

SUMMARY

As of 1995, vocational opportunities for individuals with severe disabilities across the United States remain limited and restrictive. Supported employment has been offered as an important, viable means of expanding these opportunities.

As a credible replacement for sheltered workshops and day activities programs, supported employment represents a rebellion against the prevailing conceptions of people with severe disabilities and the vocational services they receive. The current system is neither designed for nor sympathetic to supported employment as an alternative of equal standing to segregated employment services. Thus, it is most often assigned as an addition to the continuum of services offered predominantly by sheltered programs.

The arguments for considering supported employment as an option independent of segregated services, however, are strong and loud and are coming from a growing array of important parties. It is hoped that the examples summarized in this chapter not only add to these arguments for change but also demonstrate through concrete actions how traditional thinking, services, and outcomes can be reversed and significant agency change can be accomplished for the benefit of people with severe disabilities.

The question is no longer *whether* segregated vocational programs should change, but rather *how* such change should occur. The next chapter attempts to address this issue by discussing some specific strategies to 1) eliminate the barriers to integrated employment practices; and 2) achieve the intents of the Rehabilitation Act Amendments of 1992, PL 102-569, the Americans with Disabilities Act of 1990 (ADA), PL 101-336, and the Developmental Disabilities Assistance and Bill of Rights Act Amendments of 1987, PL 100-146.

10

Toward Full Citizenship

A National Agenda for Change

$\mathbf{T}$his chapter begins with a brief overview of the development of supported employment initiatives and a review of the current status of employment for people with disabilities in the United States. Following this is a discussion of national conversion efforts to date. The remainder of the chapter focuses on a national agenda for change not only with regard to employment, but also with regard to the broader issue of full citizenship for all people with disabilities.

SUPPORTED EMPLOYMENT, THEN AND NOW

Demonstrations of the abilities of people with severe disabilities to work in the community emerged in the United States in the late 1970s and early 1980s (Gold, 1976). During the same period, a growing dissatisfaction with segregation in the forms of institutions, separate schools, and sheltered adult day programs spread among families, professionals, and advocates. As Mank (1994) wrote, "What emerged was an initiative on a nationwide scale with the ambitious objective of changing the entire system of day services—of virtually replacing unemployment and segregation with real jobs, for real money, in real businesses in the community" (p. 4).

The supported employment initiative is considered to have begun in 1984. Since then, it is estimated that between 90,000 (Wehman, 1994) and more than 110,000 people (Mank, 1994) have taken part in supported employment programs in the United States, and approximately $100 million has been directed toward statewide supported employment systems change projects (U.S. Department of Education, 1993). Additional federal funds totaling more than

$40 million per year have been funneled through state MR/DD or mental health agencies to over 2,600 community programs (The Association for Persons with Severe Handicaps, 1993).

The Rehabilitation Act Amendments of 1986 and 1992, PL 99-506 and PL 102-569

Supported employment was originally defined in the Rehabilitation Act Amendments of 1986, PL 99-506, as

> competitive work in integrated work settings for individuals with severe handicaps for whom competitive employment has not traditionally occurred, or for individuals for whom competitive employment has been interrupted or intermittent as a result of a severe disability, and who, because of their handicap, need ongoing support services to perform such work. (p. 3520)

House Report 99-571 included the following language in reference to PL 99-506:

> [The] Assistant Secretary for Special Education and Rehabilitation Services is currently pursuing a major initiative referred to as "supported employment." Ms. Will, in a position paper developed several years ago, described the four characteristics of supported employment:
> 1. *Service recipients:* Supported employment is designed for individuals who are served in day activity programs because they appear to lack the potential for unassisted competitive employment.
> 2. *Ongoing support:* Supported employment involves the continuing provision of training, supervision, and support services that would be available in a traditional day activity program. Supported employment is not designed to lead to unassisted competitive employment.
> 3. *Employment focus:* Supported employment is designed to produce the same benefits for participants that other people receive from work and these can be assessed by normal measures of employment quality (e.g., income level, quality of working life, security, mobility, advancement opportunity).
> 4. *Flexibility of support strategies:* Supported employment incorporates a variety of techniques and services to assist individuals [to] obtain and perform work. Examples include assistance to a service agency that provides training and supervision at an individual's worksite, support to an employer to offset the excess costs of equipment or training, supervision of individuals with severe disabilities, and salary supplements to a coworker. (p. 3501)

Initial supported employment language encouraged an average of 20 hours per week of work, but this was not mandated. Placements of up to eight people in groups in the forms of enclaves or work crews were considered to be acceptable. Along with individual placements, these soon became touted as models for supported employment.

It is interesting to examine this early language in light of current practices. The majority of recipients of supported employment services are clearly not those once served in day activities programs, as was initially envisioned. Ongoing support services comparable in scope and intensity to those provided in day activities programs are often not available because of restricted funding. Nevertheless, a growing number of people in supported employment programs receive the same benefits from their jobs as typical people, including positive and significant personal and employment outcomes and community integration. Nearly 75% of all supported employees experience significant interactions with co-workers on the job (National Institute on Disability and Rehabilitation Research, 1993). Still, many lack comparable benefits and opportunities for career growth. Only about one third of all supported employees receive some kind of company sick leave or vacation time (National Institute on Disability and Rehabilitation Research, 1993). Although flexibility of support services was originally intended, support in reality has become quite rigid and inflexible due to funding constraints and regulations.

The Rehabilitation Act Amendments of 1992, PL 102-569, made significant changes in the overall tone of PL 99-506 as well as in the language specific to supported employment. They reiterated that supported employment is "for individuals with the most severe disabilities" (PL 102-569, Subtitle C, Section 631). PL 102-569 includes

- Language that promotes empowerment of individuals with disabilities through respect for individual dignity, self-determination, choice, inclusion, integration, and full participation (e.g., the individualized written rehabilitation program [IWRP] requires a joint sign-off between the consumer and the counselor)
- A presumption that people with disabilities, including those with the most severe disabilities, are capable of benefiting from vocational rehabilitation services unless the state agency can demonstrate by clear and convincing evidence that they cannot benefit
- A requirement that appropriate existing data be used in assessments of eligibility and determinations of rehabilitation needs (rather than requiring a series of new tests)
- A 60-day limitation for eligibility determinations

- A choice demonstration project giving states broad authority to implement consumer choice programs
- A shift from facility-based to community-based service delivery with the term *rehabilitation facility* being replaced with the term *community rehabilitation program*
- The recognition of natural supports as a possible source of ongoing support

If states fully implement the intent of PL 102-569, the implications for systems change could be quite significant, especially if consumer choice includes individual control of resources.

Employment Outcomes

Data indicate that the average wage for people in sheltered workshops is about $225 per month, and they spend about 30 hours a week at the workshops. By contrast, people in supported employment programs work an average of 22 hours per week and earn about $400 per month (Albin & Rhodes, 1993). Thus, supported employment outcomes are superior to those associated with segregated services. Still, much improvement is needed.

Many of those who have community jobs are poor and work fewer hours than they desire at jobs far beneath their capabilities. Of all people with disabilities of working age in the United States, two thirds are not working (Harris & Associates, 1994). This number has not improved since 1986. The overwhelming majority of people with disabilities of working age who are unemployed want to work, and the majority of those who have jobs are underemployed (Harris & Associates, 1994).

Wehman (1994) reported that over 1 million people in the United States continue to be served in segregated programs. A mere 16% of people with developmental disabilities are served in supported employment programs. This figure is up from 10% in 1988. People with severe mental retardation comprise only 12.2% of those in supported employment programs. Forty-four percent of all people receiving supported employment services in 1990 were considered to have mild disabilities. They continue to be the largest population served in supported employment programs. It is estimated that less than 1 in 10 people are getting a fair chance to participate in supported employment programs (Wehman, 1994). These data have spurred a growing awareness that much more needs to be done to improve the system. In calling for a reinvestment in supported employment, Mank (1994) highlighted the following areas of underachievement in supported employment programs:

1. Questionable quality of integration and employment outcomes
2. Self-advocate and advocate dissatisfaction with supported employment
3. Limited access for those with the most severe disabilities
4. Barriers to replacing segregated programs and workshops
5. Continuation versus replacement of the continuum of segregated services
6. Few incentives to change
7. Conflicting policies
8. Slowing pace of expansion in supported employment

Innovations in supported employment, such as internal business supports, choice vouchers, and the use of technology, serve to exacerbate the discrepancy between what is available and what is possible (Mank, 1994). Both supported employment and its implications for systems change, including conversion, have fallen short of initial hopes and expectations. The following section focuses on efforts to date in the United States to convert facilities from segregated to integrated employment services provision.

AN ANALYSIS OF CONVERSION
EFFORTS IN THE UNITED STATES

Examples of full agency conversion show that conversion can happen despite the systemic barriers currently in place. However, few calls for full conversion have been heard at the local, state, or national levels. Therefore, minimal effort has been made to shift resources and regulations to actively initiate the monumental changes envisioned when supported employment was introduced. Since the mid-1980s, little has occurred to change the entrenched system of rehabilitation services for people with disabilities aside from adding supported employment to the continuum of services (Rogan & Murphy, 1991; Taylor, 1988). Unemployment and segregation are still the norms, and integrated employment and conversion are the exceptions. In fact, of all people with developmental disabilities being served, 81% remain in segregated settings. Forty-four percent are in sheltered workshops and 37% are in day activities programs (McGaughey et al., 1993). In a survey of 138 rehabilitation facilities in five states, McAllister and Mank (1992) found that 78% indicated that supported employment was one of an array of services they provided. Only 10% were committed to total conversion.

Revell, Wehman, Kregel, West, and Rayfield (1994) reported that only 15.2% of all employment agencies were downsizing or terminating facility-based services. Sixty-two percent were adding supported employment as an option but without reducing segregated services. In a 1991 study of service trends for people with developmental disabilities, McGaughey, Kiernan, McNally, Gilmore, and Keith (1994) indicated that 77.3% of 632 responding agencies offered both integrated and segregated employment services. Few agencies reduced resources allocated for segregated services in order to provide supported employment services (Revell, Wehman, et al., 1994). In fact, the majority of those that provided supported employment services maintained segregated services as their primary focus. Only 14% of the agencies surveyed provided only supported employment services (West, Revell, & Wehman, 1992). Even these statistics mask the enormous number of people served in group employment models.

McGaughey et al. (1993) reported that $.93 of every federal dollar allocated to MR/DD day and employment programs went to fund segregated services. McGaughey et al. (1993) also found that although more rehabilitation agencies are offering integrated employment options (90% in 1990 as opposed to 42% in 1986), they are serving 82% of their program participants in segregated day programs.

In a survey of service providers, McGaughey et al. (1994) found that although the number of people receiving supported employment services is increasing, so too is the number of those receiving facility-based services. These survey results indicated that more people receive segregated services than either group or individual supported employment placements. Agencies' future projections indicate that 70% of the people served in the United States will continue to receive services in facility-based programs (McGaughey et al., 1994). Since 1989, a mere 2% of those agencies have stopped providing facility-based services; as few plan to do so before 1999.

Few published reports describing total conversion from sheltered to integrated services exist (Albin, Rhodes, & Mank, 1994; Murphy & Rogan, 1992), although a growing number of agencies in the United States claim to be working toward conversion (Indiana Employment Initiative, 1995). States that are reportedly leading the way in terms of allocating resources to supported employment include Michigan (42.7% of all agencies), Vermont (32.6% of all agencies), and New Hampshire (27.5% of all agencies) (Revell, Wehman, et al., 1994). Various incentives are being used by states to entice agencies to move toward integrated employment, including mandating shifts in funding from segregated to integrated services, providing "carrots" in the forms of short-term grant funding, allowing flexibility in the ways in which existing funding is used (e.g., block grants), and directing federal systems change funding to agencies committed to conversion. Leaders within and outside of agencies interested in conversion have been urging the human services system to provide flexible supports during the conversion process.

Agencies that have begun the shift toward integrated employment often get stuck in conversion (i.e., the conversion process slows and momentum toward total conversion is lost). Such agencies may believe that the cost of conversion is too high. In addition to such organizational barriers, McGaughey et al. (1994) offered other reasons why large-scale systems change has not occurred: policy and funding disincentives, investments in buildings and equipment, the continuation of the readiness approach, and the need to keep people in workshops to complete contract work. In the following section, major impediments to conversion are discussed and recommendations for systems change are offered.

AN AGENDA FOR CHANGE

Despite relatively progressive federal legislation (i.e., the Individuals with Disabilities Education Act of 1990 [IDEA], PL 101-476; the Americans with Disabilities Act of 1990 [ADA], PL 101-336; the Rehabilitation Act Amendments of 1992, PL 102-569; the Developmental Disabilities Assistance and Bill of Rights Act Amendments of 1987, PL 100-146), numerous barriers exist at federal, state, and local levels to the full inclusion of people with disabilities in the community. This federal legislation affirms the rights of people with disabilities to experience full participation in community work and living. Unfortunately, it has yet to have a significant impact on the total system of segregated services in the United States. Despite rapid advancements of integrated employment in the 1980s, there has been little growth in the 1990s.

This section utilizes a person-centered focus, as illustrated in Figure 3. Suggestions for change at each level of the human services system were culled from the barriers to employment and community living experienced by people with disabilities. Thus, this section explores the relationship between personal quality of life issues and the larger systemic and societal changes that must come about to support integrated lifestyles for people with disabilities.

Toward Individual Choice and Control

Many, if not most, people with disabilities have very little choice and control of the services and supports they desire and receive.

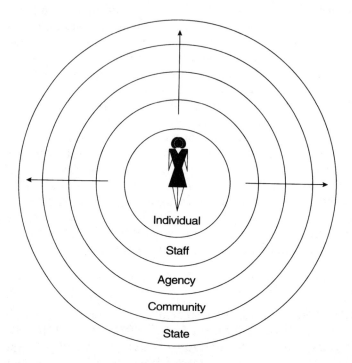

Figure 3.   A person-centered approach to systems change.

Human services professionals and programs dictate the who, what, when, where, and how of people's daily existence, thereby totally dominating most aspects of their lives. The power structure of this system weighs heavily in favor of professionals and the programs they run. To convert from a system-centered to a person-centered approach to service provision requires significant changes in the ways in which things now work. Such a conversion process is like pulling weeds. If you simply pluck off the tops (i.e., make cosmetic changes), nothing is done to get at the roots, and the weeds continue to grow and flourish. In the case of the current human services system, the roots of many problems stem from a one-sided power structure in which people with disabilities are powerless.

The National Institute on Disability and Rehabilitation Research (1993) recommended placing "resources in the hands of consumers, allowing them to seek and purchase the services of their choice; and [making] resources available to consumers as they move from service to service or provider to provider" (p. 21). PL 102-569 called for consumer vouchers and other practices that facilitate consumer-controlled services and supports. There are currently seven federally funded national demonstration projects underway, and each approaches the issues of choice and funding differently. The intent of these projects is to outline examples of how to provide funding for people, not places or agencies. When given a choice, consumers seldom choose segregated services. A more market-driven service structure will result in an array of support options that reflect consumer wishes directly. Thus, the roles of direct services personnel will need to be altered, as discussed in the next section.

Along with a shift toward vouchers (i.e., money allocated to consumers to purchase desired services), there is a need for grass roots leadership to strengthen individual efforts with collective efforts and organizational advocacy. Through self-advocacy and self-determination, people with disabilities can articulate needs and preferences and influence what services are provided, by whom, and how. The next section describes issues related to and recommendations for enabling those who work most closely with people with disabilities to provide supports for integrated employment.

Toward Flexible and Responsive Services and Supports

Human services personnel, in attempts to help people, sometimes impede the inclusion of those they serve because of their attitudes and practices, some of which are influenced heavily by the nature of the system within which they work. Many personnel who provide direct services and support are oriented toward maintaining control of the rehabilitation process, identifying deficits to be fixed, setting low expectations, focusing on a continuum of services, and so forth. Most of the people providing supports for people in integrated employment settings received training and orientation within segregated settings. Given their human services perspectives, they view the community as yet another system. Thus, their actions may not correspond to the cultures of workplaces and other community settings (Hagner, 1992; Murphy et al., 1994). Because job coaches and/or employment specialists have been identified as key to the success of individuals in supported employment, it is important to examine the characteristics and practices of the people in these roles.

Some of the reasons for problems in the support provided by job coaches and/or employment specialists were discussed in a national study of job coaching in supported employment (Human Services Research Institute, 1993). Fifty-one percent of the job coaches in the study received fewer than 8 hours of training before beginning work. At the time of the study, almost one third (31%) had worked as job coaches for less than a year, and about 40% earned less than $16,000 per year. A little over one third (37%) listed high school as their highest level of education. The majority of those who did gain access to postsecondary education did not receive any preparation before assuming their responsibilities as job coaches.

Responsibilities of job coaches are increasing "to create innovative support networks for individuals with complex needs [and] to do more to strengthen the employer as the primary support giver" (Human Services Research Institute, 1993). Although consumers may purchase supports outside of the human services system if they are given the option, it is likely that job coaches and other direct services personnel will continue to be called upon to provide such supports, as least for the time being. Therefore, the success or failure of community inclusion efforts rests heavily on people in their role as job coaches and/or employment specialists.

Shifting Roles of Supported Employment Personnel Agency staff must believe in the capacity of service recipients to participate fully in the community before they can persuade employers, coworkers, and other citizens to develop relationships and provide support. In addition to such attitudinal changes, support staff need adequate training to alter their roles as direct services providers and to become consultants, facilitators, and bridge builders (Mount, Beeman, & Ducharme, 1988).

The body of literature on natural or internal workplace supports highlights the differences between traditional job coaching practices and strategies for facilitating the involvement of workplace personnel (Callahan, 1992; Fabian, Luecking, & Tilson, 1994; Nisbet, 1992; Murphy & Rogan, 1994). Facilitating the involvement of workplace personnel requires that professionals relinquish control, be better listeners, build upon individual interests and abilities, and develop and pursue alliances with typical citizens. To do this will require that support personnel eliminate the separation between their community ties and their professional functions.

Human services personnel may view their community activities, social relationships, and organizational memberships as separate from their daily work. Their typical activities, contacts, and associations, however, can facilitate vital links between the surrounding community and people with disabilities. Just as friends help one another in gaining access to new interests, people, clubs, and jobs and assist with new undertakings and roles, human services professionals can help people with disabilities to engage in opportunities from which they typically have been excluded.

Training personnel in such roles is necessary and will require that a bridge-building function be built into their professional identities, education, and work. Restrictive job descriptions and work and narrowly defined professional roles and partnerships need to be rejected. Using their own community memberships and resources as tools, human services personnel must learn how to use inclusive resources and strategies. This may entail helping people with disabilities to expand their circles of friends, reduce their reliance on professional relationships, and/or expand the restrictive housing, employment, and leisure options available to them.

Ongoing training for job coaches is critical for helping to guide the process of redefining roles and for infusing innovative practices into supported employment. As a public policy strategy designed to expand implementation of supported employment services, Wehman (1994) proposed the establishment of "at least one supported employment training institute in each of the 10 RSA [Rehabilitation Services Administration] regions over the next 5 years as an ongoing resource for training supported employment staff" (p. 3). Certainly, continuing federal leadership and a national training agenda are needed to advance the adoption and practice of supported employment. In these times of shrinking state and federal budgets and given the decreasing availability of other training resources, it is doubtful that a new series of institutes would be feasible or even desirable. Thus, it may be more fruitful to examine existing state and federal resources.

For example, there already exists in each state a university affiliated program (UAP) and in each region a regional rehabilitation continuing education program (RRCEP). Among other reasons these were designed to provide professionals working with people with disabilities with state-of-the-art training in vocational rehabilitation. Current priorities and capacities of these programs should be examined and, if necessary, modified to meet the growing need for supported employment training and services. State MR/DD, VR, and other agencies serving people with disabilities also have training units that could be used to provide supported employment training. Local chapters of The Association for Persons with Severe Handicaps (TASH) and the Association for People in Supported Employment (APSE) could also be enlisted to join with state agencies in developing cooperative training initiatives that offer technical assistance regarding supported employment on a regional basis.

Organizational Change Although realignment of human resources (e.g., rewriting job descriptions) is critical to the provision of individualized and flexible supports, other aspects of agency structures and practices must also change. Figure 4 illustrates the three primary facets of organizational change, all of which must be addressed simultaneously in the context of external local, state, and national influences (Tichy, Fombrun, & Devanna, 1982). Agency structures involve the internal organization of people and programs. Most agencies are hierarchical in nature, with decisions being made by the people furthest from service recipients. The movements toward total quality management, team-based decision making, and flattened organizational structures are intended to make services more responsive to individuals and to empower both service recipients and the staff who work most closely with them.

Many adult services programs serve large numbers of people (i.e., over 100 at a time) and offer programs that serve people of all ages or *birth-to-death* services. McGaughey et al. (1994) reported that smaller agencies are more likely to offer only integrated employment. Bigger usually is not better in terms of the quality of services provided. Thus, the goal of individualized employment would be better met if agencies spin off sister organizations instead of becoming large bureaucracies.

Some agencies are involved in all aspects of a person's life, including work, community involvement, and recreation. Ironically, although one agency may oversee the program, the services are typically offered categorically, with different staff addressing each category. When one agency has too great a level of involvement in a per-

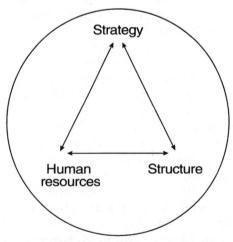

Figure 4. A model of conversion. (From Tichy, N., Fombrun, C., & Devanna, M.A. [1982]. Strategic human resource management. *The Sloan Management Review, 23*[2], p. 48; reprinted with permission of John Wiley & Sons.)

son's life, it is inevitable that the agency will begin to exercise an undue amount of control over that person's life. Human services in general should not provide everything that people want and need. When people with disabilities rely exclusively on service systems, they cannot be part of their communities (Racino, 1994).

Organizational change also involves the different strategies that must be implemented to move people from sheltered to integrated work. Strategies include refusing new admissions to workshops and day activities programs, using person-centered planning processes, facilitating natural support networks, developing partnerships with businesses, and so forth (see Chapter 9).

Ultimately, conversion and the provision of person-centered, person-directed services will depend on the strength of agency leaders and other management-level personnel. There is a dire need for leadership at the agency level to assist executive directors and program managers to understand and initiate the process of organizational change. These people must understand individualized supports from the perspectives of service recipients (Racino, 1994), constantly striving to keep their wishes at the forefront of the decision-making process.

Toward a Unified State and Federal Agenda for Change

As stated above, several fairly progressive pieces of federal legislation have provided a framework for supporting the inclusion of people with disabilities in their communities: PL 100-146, PL 101-336, PL 101-476, and PL 102-569. There is a need, however, to align the language of this legislation with state and local practices, which vary significantly across and within states. State and local regulations and policies often are inconsistent with the language of this legislation.

Most states currently operate three types of support systems: institutional, traditional facility-based, and an emerging individualized support system. Widely discrepant and conflicting practices are characteristic of each. Such disparate support systems send mixed messages to service recipients, family members, service providers, and the community at large regarding values, priorities, and directions.

Federal and State Leadership for Systems Change In order to shift from the segregated service system that currently dominates, there must be leadership at the federal and state levels and a commitment to continue the push toward systems change. Leaders involved in vocational rehabilitation, MR/DD, and mental health systems must convey a unified message, coordinate fragmented and counterproductive policies and practices, and reduce barriers to integrated services and supports (Albin et al., 1994). For example, despite the federal government's emphasis on community inclusion and integrated employment, it continues to assist programs that perpetuate segregation. Federally funded VR agencies "count" sheltered work as a legitimate rehabilitation outcome. Another such program is the National Industries for the Severely Handicapped (NISH) program. It requires that 75% of set-aside federal contract work be performed by people with disabilities. This work is done almost exclusively in sheltered workshops and large group enclaves.

Federal and state personnel must continually review their own employment policies and practices looking for inconsistencies that negate or minimize legislative initiatives toward change. Federal and state personnel also should assess how policies and practices are implemented, identify barriers to successful implementation, and offer technical assistance to ensure that desired outcomes are defined and achieved correctly.

Funding Issues   In many ways, funding drives supported employment and human services in general. Traditional modes of service delivery are intertwined with traditional funding structures. Funding is tied primarily to segregated programs, and there is a weak relationship between funding and individual planning and services (Taylor, Racino, & Rothenberg, 1988). As Taylor (1988) noted, most funding is tied to the most restrictive programs. Conversely, little funding is allocated for the most inclusive environments and activities. Thus, people with the most intensive support needs are relegated to congregate, segregated settings because the funding structure typically allows minimal supports for people in integrated settings.

PL 99-506 established Title VI-C funding for time-limited supported employment services. Many supported employment agencies face per-person caps on these time-limited services that are often less than the actual cost of the services. For example, if VR allocates a total of $3,200 per person for time-limited supported employment services and the actual cost of these services exceeds that amount, agencies are forced to either make up the deficit or otherwise serve only those people with less intensive support needs. In fact, over three fourths of the providers in the McGaughey et al. (1994) study indicated that "Their agencies sometimes covered the cost for on-the-job supports (78%) and job development/placement assistance (76%)" (p. 38). Funding caps nevertheless have served to preclude people with severe disabilities who may require extensive supports from participating in supported employment. Such rigid funding structures do not allow for flexibility and creativity in service provision, and they certainly eliminate the possibility for individualization.

In addition, the lack of sufficient follow-along funding also has restricted the provision of supported employment services. Follow-along funding has been nonexistent in some cases and seriously limited in others. Once again, funding constraints often serve to exclude people with severe disabilities from supported employment programs if it is anticipated that they will need more than a minimal amount of ongoing support.

In relation to the total amount spent on all day and employment services, the amount of federal funding allocated for supported employment in 1990 amounted to 5% of all Title XX funding, 2% of all Title XIX funding, and 17% of all MR/DD funding. Clearly, federal resources continue to be directed toward funding segregated services. Thus, what incentives exist for service providers to shift to integrated service provision if they receive less funding to do so?

Funding that Drives Movement Toward Integrated Employment The most effective federal incentives influencing states' expansion of integrated employment services seem to be 1) the provision of funding that is tied to states' commitments to expand integrated employment services, 2) the requirement that new participants enter integrated work, and 3) the awarding of bonuses for moving participants from sheltered to integrated settings (McGaughey et al., 1994). States must increasingly shift funding from sheltered to integrated employment. Propelling such a shift would be a moratorium on the use of sheltered employment as a legitimate vocational outcome. As a minimum commitment, states should require that all funds for new consumers receiving day services be directed toward integrated employment.

Sufficient and Flexible Funding Funding must be both sufficient and flexible to cover the true costs of services. Given the dynamic and lifelong nature of support needs, flexibility is necessary. Funding should be based on actual costs and driven by outcomes. That is, agencies should be rewarded financially for achieving integrated employment outcomes that are based on individual goals and on recipients' satisfaction with services. Wehman (1994) made the following funding-related recommendations for expanding supported employment services:

- Provide higher levels of funding for supported employment outcomes as opposed to day program activities
- Put a limit on the funding levels for day programs which provide primarily segregated services
- Increase the amount of Title VI-C funds authorized through the Rehabilitation Act by 100% over the next 5 years
- Expand the use of Medicaid Waiver, education, and JTPA [Job Training Partnership Act] funds for supported employment outcomes
- Expand the use of tax credits to corporations who use co-workers to provide ongoing support to supported employees. (pp. 2–3)

Increased Incentives to Work Almost 6 in 10 adults between the ages of 16 and 64 who are not working and are not looking for work reported that they would lose income, health insurance, or other benefits that they receive from private insurance or the government if they worked full time (Harris & Associates, 1994). The complexities of Social Security work incentives and disincentives are largely misunderstood. There is a need to educate consumers and family members about work incentives such as Plans for Achieving Self Support (PASSs) and Impairment Related Work Expenses (IRWEs). Entitlement programs must be modified so they do not create dependency (Green, 1993). Furthermore, if consumers control financial resources allocated for disability supports, there must be assurances that Social Security, Medicaid, and other entitlement programs will not be affected adversely.

SUMMARY

The current human services system continues to use models and practices that are between 30 and 40 years old. This system, which was originally developed to offer specialized assistance to people with disabilities, has had the contradictory effect of perpetuating social isolation, lowering expectations, and exaggerating the perceived differences of people with disabilities. This has hurt people with disabilities as well as businesses and society.

Change is always complex. Even under the best of circumstances, when significant agreement among involved parties is achieved and new initiatives are begun, good ideas can be diluted quickly during implementation. At a time when citizens are calling for reductions in the federal government's size, budget, and focus, the national heart seems to be hardened against those among us who are most in need. Thus, good ideas are often easily dismissed because they are too expensive and out of step.

Ultimately, the success of the changes proposed in this book must be judged in light of whether they improve the ways in which people with disabilities see and live their lives. The next decade, perhaps as much as any in recent memory, will challenge those concerned with heightened justice, opportunity, and inclusion not only to retain their commitments to these social goals, but also to honestly review society's reliance on governmental solutions and resources to solve its problems.

In addressing the continuing commitment to social change, people may have to change as well, expanding their focus to include more creative and effective uses of nongovernmental resources to achieve goals. This is not to say that local, state, and federal governments should be held less accountable for their support of such efforts. Clearly, since the early-1900s, the leadership and activism of the federal government in promoting supported work across the United States has been instrumental to improving community employment success for people with severe disabilities. As shown by many of the stories in this book, however, effective changes can also result from people working together to 1) gain political power and attention, 2) realign community and professional values, and 3) reallocate existing resources to secure more funding.

Interestingly, the political and legal groundwork for heightened community employment is already quite solid. What remains is the really hard work of reallocating existing resources and demonstrating, individual by individual and community by community, that providing integrated employment options for every person is possible. Indeed, providing such options would be an effective, productive, and integral means to achieving the national ideal of full citizenship for all.

References

Americans with Disabilities Act of 1990 (ADA), PL 101-336. (July 26, 1990). Title 42, U.S.C. 12101 et seq: *U.S. Statutes at Large, 104,* 327–378.

Albin, J. (1992). *Quality improvement in employment and other human services.* Baltimore: Paul H. Brookes Publishing Co.

Albin, J., & Rhodes, L. (1993). *Changeover to community employment: The problem of realigning organizational culture, resources, and community roles.* Eugene: University of Oregon, Specialized Training Program.

Albin, J., Rhodes, L., & Mank, D. (1994). Realigning organizational culture, resources, and community roles: Changeover to community employment. *Journal of The Association for Persons with Severe Handicaps, 19*(2), 105–115.

American Psychiatric Association. (1994). *Diagnostic and statistical manual of mental disorders* (4th ed.). Washington, DC: Author.

Association of Independent Living Centers in New York. (1993). *1993 disability rights agenda.* Albany: Author.

Association of Independent Living Centers in New York. (1994). *1994 disability rights agenda.* Albany: Author.

Bellamy, G.T., Peterson, L., & Close, D. (1975). Habilation of the severely and profoundly retarded. *Education and Training in Mental Retardation, 10,* 174–186.

Bellamy, G.T., Rhodes, L., Bourbeau, P., & Mank, D. (1986). Mental retardation services in sheltered workshops and day activities programs: Consumer benefits and policy alternatives. In F. Rusch (Ed.), *Competitive employment issues and strategies* (pp. 257–271). Baltimore: Paul H. Brookes Publishing Co.

Bellamy, G.T., Rhodes, L., Mank, D., & Albin, J. (1988). *Supported employment: A community implementation guide.* Baltimore: Paul H. Brookes Publishing Co.

Bellamy, G.T., Sheehan, M., Horner, R., & Boles, S. (1980). Community programs for severely handicapped adults: An analysis of vocational opportunities. *Journal of The Association for Persons with Severe Handicaps, 5,* 307–324.

Bennett, T. (1962). *The leader and the process of change.* New York: Association Press.

Bernstein, G., & Karan, O. (1979). Obstacles to vocational normalization for the developmentally disabled. *Rehabilitation Literature, 40,* 66–71.

Best, H. (1934). *Blindness and the blind in the United States.* New York: Macmillan.

Bolton, B. (Ed.). (1982). *Vocational adjustment of disabled persons.* Baltimore: University Park Press.

Brickey, M. (1974). Normalization and behavior modification in the workshop. *Journal of Rehabilitation, 15*(41), 44–45.

Brown, L. (1973). Instructional programs for trainable-level retarded students. In L. Mann & L. Sabatino (Eds.), *The first review of special education: Vol. 2* (pp. 84–96). Philadelphia: Journal of Special Education Press.

Brown, L., Shiraga, B., York, J., Kessler, K., Strohm, B., Rogan, P., Sweet, M., Zanella, K., VanDeventer, P., & Loomis, R. (1984). Integrated work opportunities for adults with severe handicaps: The extended training option. *Journal of The Association for Persons with Severe Handicaps, 9,* 262–269.

Brown, L., Udvari-Solner, A., Frattura-Kampschroer, E., Davis, L., Ahlgren, C., VanDeventer, P., & Jorgensen, J. (1991). Integrated work: A rejection of segregated enclaves and mobile work crews. In L. Meyer, C. Peck, & L. Brown (Eds.), *Critical issues in the lives of people with severe disabilities* (pp. 219–228). Baltimore: Paul H. Brookes Publishing Co.

Brunsson, N. (1985). Organizations and change: The irrationality of action and action irrationality. In J.S. Ott, A.C. Hyde, & J.M. Shafritz (Eds.), *Public management: The essential readings* (pp. 207–216). Chicago: Nelson-Hall Publishers.

Bushe, G., & Shani, A. (1991). *Parallel learning structures.* Reading, MA: Addison-Wesley.

Callahan, M. (1992). Job site training and natural supports. In J. Nisbet (Ed.), *Natural supports in school, at work, and in the community for people with severe disabilities* (pp. 257–276). Baltimore: Paul H. Brookes Publishing Co.

Caplan, N., & Nelson, S. (1973). On being useful. The nature and consequences of psychological research on social problems. *American Psychologist, 28,* 199–211.

Chouinard, E. (1957). *Sheltered workshops—past and present.* Paper presented at the Fifth Atlantic City Conference, Atlantic City, NJ.

Conte, L. (1983). *Sheltered employment services and programs.* Washington, DC: National Rehabilitation Information Center.

Conte, L., Murphy, S., & Nisbet, J. (1989). A qualitative study of work stations in industry. *Journal of Rehabilitation, 55,* 53–61.

Developmental Disabilities Assistance and Bill of Rights Act of 1984, PL 98-527. (October 19, 1984). Title 42, U.S.C. 6000 et seq: *U.S. Statutes at Large, 98,* 2662–2685.

Developmental Disabilities Assistance and Bill of Rights Act Amendments of 1987, PL 100-146. (October 29, 1987). Title 42, U.S.C. 6000 et seq: *U.S. Statutes at Large, 101,* 840–859.

Dufresne, D., & Laux, B. (1994). From facilities to supports: The changing organization. In V.J. Bradley, J.W. Ashbaugh, & B.C. Blaney (Eds.), *Creating individual supports for people with developmental disabilities: A mandate for change at many levels* (pp. 271–280). Baltimore: Paul H. Brookes Publishing Co.

Durand, J., & Durand, J. (1978). *Affirmative industries.* St. Paul, MN: Diversified Industries, Inc.

Durand, J., & Neufelt, A. (1980). Comprehensive vocational rehabilitation. In R. Flynn & K. Nitsch (Eds.), *Normalization, social integration, and community services* (pp. 283–298). Baltimore: University Park Press.

Ellis, W., Rusch, F., Tu, J., & McCaughrin, W. (1990). Supported employment in Illinois. In F. Rusch (Ed.), *Supported employment: Methods, models, and issues* (pp. 31–44). Sycamore, IL: Sycamore Publishing Co.

Fabian, E.S., Luecking, R.G., & Tilson, G.P. (1994). *A working relationship: The job development specialist's guide to successful partnerships with business.* Baltimore: Paul H. Brookes Publishing Co.

Ferguson, D., & Ferguson, P. (1987). Parents and professionals. In P. Knoblock (Ed.), *Understanding exceptional children and youth* (pp. 346–391). Boston: Little, Brown.

Flexer, R., & Martin, A. (1978). Sheltered workshops and vocational training settings. In M. Snell (Ed.), *Systematic instruction of the moderately and severely handicapped* (pp. 414–430). Columbus, OH: Charles E. Merrill.

Frank, G. (1988). Beyond stigma: Visibility and self-empowerment of persons with congenital limb deficiencies. *Journal of Social Issues, 44,* 95–115.

Gellman, W., & Friedman, S. (1965). The workshop as a clinical tool. *Rehabilitation Literature, 26,* 34–38.

Glasser, I. (1978). Prisoners of benevolence. In W. Gaylin, I. Glasser, S. Marcus, & D. Rothman (Eds.), *Doing good: The limits of benevolence* (pp. 97–170). New York: Pantheon Books.

Gold, M. (1972). Stimulus factors in skill training of the retarded on a complex assembly task: Training, acquisition, and retention. *American Journal of Mental Deficiency, 76,* 517–526.

Gold, M. (1976). Task analysis of a complex assembly task by the retarded blind. *Exceptional Children, 43,* 78–84.

Gold, M. (1980). *Did I say that?: Articles and commentary on the try another way system.* Champaign, IL: Research Press.

Green, J. (1993). Where are the incentives for supported employment? *Info-Lines,4*(8), 1–3.

Greenleigh Associates, Inc. (1975). *The role of the sheltered workshop in the rehabilitation of the severely handicapped.* New York: Rehabilitation Services Administration, Department of Health, Education, and Welfare.

Grossman, H.J. (Ed.). (1983). *Classification in mental retardation.* Washington, DC: American Association of Mental Deficiency.

Hagner, D. (1992). The social interactions and job supports of supported employees. In J. Nisbet (Ed.), *Natural supports in school, at work, and in the community for people with severe disabilities* (pp. 217–239). Baltimore: Paul H. Brookes Publishing Co.

Hagner, D., & Murphy, S. (1989). Closing the shop on sheltered work: Case studies of organizational change. *Journal of Rehabilitation, 55,* 68–74.

Hagner, D., Murphy, S., & Rogan, P. (1992). Facilitating natural supports in the workplace: Strategies for support consultants. *Journal of Rehabilitation, 57,* 29–34.

Hahn, H. (1991). Alternative views of empowerment: Social services and civil rights. *Journal of Rehabilitation, 57,* 17–19.

Harris & Associates. (1986). *The ICD survey of disabled Americans: Bringing disabled Americans into the mainstream.* New York: International Center for the Disabled.

Harris & Associates. (1994). *Survey of Americans with disabilities.* New York: International Center for the Disabled.

Harvey, T. (1990). Checklist for change: A pragmatic approach to creating and controlling change. Newton, MA: Allyn & Bacon.

Hobson, B. (1981). Community Workshops, Inc.: One hundred years of service. Boston: Community Workshops, Inc.

Indiana Employment Initiative. (1995). [National survey of vocational agencies in conversion]. Unpublished study.

Individuals with Disabilities Education Act of 1990 (IDEA), PL 101-476. (October 30, 1990). Title 20, U.S.C. 1400 et seq: U.S. Statutes at Large, 104, 1103-1151.

Kaufman, H. (1971). The limits of organizational change. Tuscaloosa: University of Alabama Press.

Kiernan, W., & Cibrowski, J. (1985). Employment survey for adults with developmental disabilities. Washington, DC: U.S. Department of Health and Human Services, Administration on Developmental Disabilities.

Kiracofe, J. (1994). Strategies to help agencies shift from services to supports. In V.J. Bradley, J.W. Ashbaugh, & B.C. Blaney (Eds.), Creating individual supports for people with developmental disabilities: A mandate for change at many levels (pp. 281-298). Baltimore: Paul H. Brookes Publishing Co.

Kregel, J., & Wehman, P. (1989). Supported employment for persons with severe handicaps: Promises deferred. Journal of The Association for Persons with Severe Handicaps, 14, 293-303.

Kregel, J., Wehman, P., Revell, G., & Hill, M. (1990). Supported employment in Virginia. In F. Rusch (Ed.), Supported employment: Models, methods, and issues (pp. 15-29). Sycamore, IL: Sycamore Publishing Co.

Luckasson, R., Coulter, D.L., Polloway, E.A., Reiss, S., Schalock, R.L., Snell, M.E., Spitalnik, D.M., & Stark, J.A. (1992). Mental retardation: Definition, classification, and systems of supports. Washington, DC: American Association on Mental Retardation.

Lam, C. (1986). Comparison of sheltered and supported work programs: A pilot study. Rehabilitation Counseling Bulletin, 30, 66-82.

Lam, C., & Chan, F. (1988). Job satisfaction of sheltered workshop clients. Journal of Rehabilitation, 54, 51-54.

Magis-Agosta, K. (1994). From facilities to inclusive employment. In V.J. Bradley, J.W. Ashbaugh, & B.C. Blaney (Eds.), Creating individual supports for people with developmental disabilities: A mandate for change at many levels (pp. 255-270). Baltimore: Paul H. Brookes Publishing Co.

Mank, D. (1994). The underachievement of supported employment: A call for reinvestment. Journal of Disability Policy Studies, 5(2), 1-24.

Mank, D., Rhodes, L., & Bellamy, G. (1986). Four supported employment alternatives. In W. Kiernan & J. Stark (Eds.), Pathways to employment for adults with developmental disabilities (pp. 139-153). Baltimore: Paul H. Brookes Publishing Co.

McAllister, M., & Mank, D. (1992). Rehabilitation facility implementation of supported employment: A survey of five states in the Pacific Northwest. Eugene: University of Oregon.

McGaughey, M., Kiernan, W., McNally, L., & Gilmore, D. (1993). National perspectives on integrated employment: State MR/DD agency trends. Boston: Training and Research Institute on Developmental Disabilities.

McGaughey, M., Kiernan, W., McNally, L., Gilmore, D., & Keith, G. (1994). Beyond the workshop: National perspectives on integrated employment. Boston: Training and Research Institute on Developmental Disabilities.

Mcloughlin, C., Garner, J., & Callahan, M. (1987). *Getting employed, staying employed.* Baltimore: Paul H. Brookes Publishing Co.

Menz, F. (1987). An appraisal of trends in rehabilitation facilities: 1980 to 1984. *Vocational Evaluation and Work Adjustment Bulletin, 20,* 67–74.

Moseley, C. (1988). Job satisfaction research: Implications for supported employment. *Journal of The Association for Persons with Severe Handicaps, 13,* 211–213.

Moss-Kanter, R. (1983). *The change masters.* New York: Simon & Schuster.

Mount, B., Beeman, P., & Ducharme, G. (1988). *What are we learning about bridgebuilding?* Manchester, CT: Communitas, Inc.

Murphy, S., & Hagner, D. (1988). Evaluation assessment settings: Ecological influences on vocational evaluation. *Journal of Rehabilitation, 53,* 53–59.

Murphy, S., & Rogan, P. (1992). Closing the sheltered workshop: A case study of agency change. *OSERS News in Print,* 18–21.

Murphy, S., & Rogan, P. (1994). Involving co-workers to support training employees with disabilities. *Supported Employment InfoLines,* July–August, 4–5.

Murphy, S., Rogan, P., Olney, M., Sures, M., Dague, B., & Kalina, N. (1994). *Developing natural supports in the workplace: A practitioner's guide.* St. Augustine, FL: TRN.

Murphy, S., & Ursprung, A. (1983). The politics of vocational evaluation: A qualitative study. *Rehabilitation Literature, 44,* 2–12.

National Association of Sheltered Workshops and Homebound Programs. (1968, December). Resolution passed at the annual meeting of the National Association of Sheltered Workshops and Homebound Programs, San Francisco, CA.

National Institute on Disability and Rehabilitation Research. (1993). *Consensus statement on supported employment for people with severe mental retardation: Vol 1.* Washington, DC: Author.

Nelson, N. (1971). *Workshops for the handicapped in the United States.* Springfield, IL: Charles C Thomas.

Nisbet, J. (Ed.). (1992). *Natural supports in school, at work, and in the community for people with severe disabilities.* Baltimore: Paul H. Brookes Publishing Co.

Nisbet, J., & Hagner, D. (1988). Natural supports in the workplace: A reexamination of supported employment. *Journal of The Association for Persons with Severe Disabilities, 13,* 260–267.

Nisbet, J., & Vincent, L. (1985). The differences in inappropriate behavior and instructional interactions in sheltered and unsheltered work environments. *Journal of The Association for Persons with Severe Handicaps, 11,* 19–27.

Nitzberg, J. (1989). *Ode to the sheltered workshop as a career for retarded workers.* Paper presented at the meeting of the New York State Association for Retarded Citizens, Monticello, NY.

Olshansky, S. (1972). Changing vocational behavior through normalization. In W. Wolfensberger (Ed.), *Normalization: The principle of normalization in human services* (pp. 150–163). Toronto, Ontario, Canada: National Institute on Mental Retardation.

Paine, S., Bellamy, G., & Wilcox, B. (Eds.). (1984). *Human services that work: From innovation to standard practice.* Baltimore: Paul H. Brookes Publishing Co.

Parent, W., & Hill, M. (1990). Converting from segregated sheltered employment to supported employment. In F. Rusch (Ed.), *Supported employment: Models, methods, and issues.* Baltimore: Paul H. Brookes Publishing Co.

Parent, W., Hill, M., & Wehman, P. (1989). From sheltered to supported employment outcomes: Challenges for rehabilitation facilities. *Journal of Rehabilitation, 55,* 51–57.

Peters, T., & Waterman, R. (1982). *In search of excellence: Lessons from America's best-run companies.* New York: Warner Books, Inc.

Pomerantz, D., & Marholin, D. (1977). Vocational habilitation: A time for a change. In E. Sontag, N. Certo, & J. Smith (Eds.), *Educational programming for the severely and profoundly handicapped* (pp. 129–141). Reston, VA: Council for Exceptional Children.

Power, P., & Marinelli, R. (1974). Normalization and the sheltered workshop: A review and proposals. *Rehabilitation Literature, 35,* 66–72.

Provencal, G. (1987). Culturing commitment. In S. Taylor, D. Biklen, & J. Knoll (Eds.), *Community integration for people with severe disabilities* (pp. 67–84). New York: Teachers College Press.

Racino, J. (1994). Creating change in states, agencies, and communities. In V.J. Bradley, J.W. Ashbaugh, & B.C. Blaney (Eds.), *Creating individual supports for people with developmental disabilities: A mandate for change at many levels* (pp. 171–196). Baltimore: Paul H. Brookes Publishing Co.

Rehabilitation Act Amendments of 1986, PL 99-506. Title 29, U.S.C. 701 et seq: *U.S. Statutes at Large, 100,* 1807–1846.

Rehabilitation Act Amendments of 1992, PL 102-569. (October 29, 1992). Title 29, U.S.C. 701 et seq: *U.S. Statutes at Large, 100,* 4344–4488.

Revell, G., Wehman, P., Kregel, J., West, M., & Rayfield, R. (1994). Supported employment for persons with severe disabilities: Positive trends in wages, models, and funding. *Education and Training in Mental Retardation, 29,* 256–264.

Revell, W., West, M., Wehman, P., & Kregel, J. (1994). Programmatic and administrative trends affecting the future of supported employment: A fifty state analysis. In P. Wehman & J. Kregel (Eds.), *Supported employment: Challenges for the 1990's.* Richmond: Virginia Commonwealth University, Rehabilitation Research and Training Center.

Rhodes, L., & Valenta, L. (1985). Industry-based supported employment: An enclave approach. *Journal of The Association for Persons with Severe Handicaps, 10,* 12–20.

Riscalla, L. (1974). Could workshops be obsolete? *Journal of Rehabilitation, 40,* 17–19, 36–37.

Rogan, P., & Hagner, D. (1990). Vocational evaluation in supported employment. *Journal of Rehabilitation, 56*(1), 45–51.

Rogan, P., Hagner, D., & Murphy, S. (1993). Natural supports: Reconceptualizing job coach roles. *Journal of The Association for Persons with Severe Handicaps, 18,* 275–281.

Rogan, P., & Murphy, S. (1991). Supported employment and vocational rehabilitation: Merger or misadventure? *Journal of Rehabilitation, 57*(1), 39–47.

Rosen, M., Bussone, A., Dakunchak, P., & Cramp, J. (1993). Sheltered employment and the second generation workshop. *Journal of Rehabilitation, 59,* 30–34.

Rothman, D. (1971). *The discovery of the asylum: Social order and disorder in the new republic.* Boston: Little, Brown.

Rothman, D. (1978). The state as parent. In W. Gaylin, I. Glasser, S. Marcus, & D. Rothman (Eds.), *Doing good: The limits of benevolence* (pp. 69–95). New York: Pantheon Books.

Rucker, R., & Browder, D. (1994). Conversion to integrated employment: Ten recommendations for change. *InfoLines, 5*(5), 1–3.

Rudrud, E., Ziarnik, J., Bernstein, G., & Ferrara, J. (1984). *Proactive vocational habilitation.* Baltimore: Paul H. Brookes Publishing Co.

Rusch, F. (Ed.). (1990). *Supported employment: Models, methods, and issues.* Sycamore, IL: Sycamore Publishing Co.

Rusch, F., Johnson, J., & Hughes, C. (1990). Analysis of coworker involvement in relation to level of disability versus placement approach among supported employees. *Journal of The Association for Persons with Severe Handicaps, 15,* 32–39.

Rusch, F., & Mithaug, D. (1980). *Vocational training for mentally retarded adults: A behavior analytic approach.* Champaign, IL: Research Press.

Schalock, R., & Karan, O. (1979). Relevant assessment. The interaction between evaluation and training. In G.T. Bellamy, G. O'Connor, & O. Karan (Eds.), *Vocational rehabilitation of severely handicapped persons* (pp. 33–54). Baltimore: University Park Press.

Scheer, J., & Groce, N. (1988). Impairment as a human constant: Cross cultural and historical perspectives on variation. *Journal of Social Issues, 44,* 23–37.

Scott, R. (1967). The factory as social service organization. *Social Problems, 15,* 160–175.

Stone, D. (1984). *The disabled state.* Philadelphia: Temple University Press.

Taylor, S. (1988). Caught in the continuum: A critical analysis of the principle of the least restrictive environment. *Journal of The Association for Persons with Severe Handicaps, 13,* 41–53.

Taylor, S., Racino, J., & Rothenberg, K. (1988). *A policy analysis of private community living arrangements in Connecticut.* Syracuse, NY: Center on Human Policy.

TenBroek, J., & Matson, F. (1959). *Hope deferred: Public welfare and the blind.* Berkeley: University of California Press.

The Association for Persons with Severe Handicaps. (1989). [Resolution on integrated employment]. Unpublished TASH employment committee resolution.

The Association for Persons with Severe Handicaps. (1993). Issue watch: Choice and the Rehabilitation Act. *TASH Newsletter, 19,* 8.

Tichey, N., Fombrun, C., & Devanna, M.A. (1982). Strategic human resource management. *The Sloan Management Review, 23*(2), 48.

Turner, M. (1983). Workshop society: Ethnographic observations in a work setting for retarded adults. In K. Kernan, M. Begab, & R. Edgerton (Eds.), *Environments and behavior: The adaptation of mentally retarded persons* (pp. 147–172). Baltimore: University Park Press.

U.S. Department of Education. (1993). *Vocational rehabilitation service projects for individuals with disabilities: Supported employment statewide demonstration projects—Absolute priority* (CFDA No. 84.128B). Washington, DC: Author.

U.S. Department of Labor. (1977). *A nationwide report on sheltered workshops and their employment of handicapped people: Vol. II. Workshop survey.* Washington, DC: U.S. Department of Labor, Employment Standards Administration.

U.S. Department of Labor. (1979). *Study of handicapped clients in sheltered workshops and recommendations of the Secretary: Vol. II.* Washington, DC: U.S. Department of Labor, Employment Standards Administration.

Vash, C. (1980). Sheltered industrial employment. In E. Pan, T. Backer, & C. Vash (Eds.), *Annual review of rehabilitation, Vol. 1.* New York: Springer-Verlag.

Vogelsberg, R.T. (1990). Supported employment in Pennsylvania. In F. Rusch (Ed.), *Supported employment: Models, methods, and issues* (pp. 45–63). Sycamore, IL: Sycamore Publishing Co.

Warner, G. (1986, February 9). Closing to impose barrier on disabled. *Buffalo Evening News.*

Wehman, P. (1994). Toward a national agenda for supported employment. *The Advance, 5*(2), 1–3.

Wehman, P., & Kregel, J. (1985). A supported work approach to competitive employment for people with moderate and severe handicaps. *Journal of The Association for Persons with Severe Handicaps, 10,* 3–11.

Wehman, P., & Kregel, J. (1994). *At the crossroads: Supported employment ten years later.* Richmond: Virginia Commonwealth University.

Wehman, P., Sale, M., & Parent, W. (1992). *Supported employment for persons with severe disabilities: From research to practice.* Andover, MA: Andover Medical Publishers.

West, M., & Parent, W. (1992). Consumer choice and empowerment in supported employment services: Issues and strategies. *Journal of The Association for Persons with Severe Handicaps, 17,* 47–52.

West, M., Revell, W.G., & Wehman, P. (1992). Achievements and challenges I: A five-year report on consumer and system outcomes from the supported employment initiative. *Journal of The Association for Persons with Severe Handicaps, 17*(4), 227–235.

Whitehead, C. (1979). Sheltered workshops in the decade ahead: Work and wages or welfare. In G. Bellamy, G. O'Connor, & O. Karan (Eds.), *Vocational rehabilitation of severely handicapped individuals.* Baltimore: University Park Press.

Whitehead, C. (1987). Integrated employment and rehabilitation facilities: Responding to change. *Journal of Job Placement, 6,* 16–20.

Wolfensberger, W. (1967). Vocational preparation and occupation. In A. Baumeister (Ed.), *Mental retardation: Appraisal, education, and rehabilitation* (pp. 232–273). Chicago: Aldine.

Wolfensberger, W. (1975). *The nature and origins of our institutional models.* New York: Human Sciences Press.

Index

Citations followed by "t," "f," or "n" indicate tables, figures, or notes, respectively.